ACHIEVEMENT

ACHIEVEMENT
The Righting of a Great Wrong
1914-1918

A Commentary in Too Many Words

Ian W. Hall

Matador
9 Priory Business Park
Kibworth Beauchamp
Leicestershire LE8 0RX, UK
Tel: (+44) 116 279 2299
Fax: (+44) 116 279 2277
Email: books@troubador.co.uk
Web: www.troubador.co.uk/matador

ISBN 978 1783060 948

British Library Cataloguing in Publication Data.
A catalogue record for this book is available from the British Library.

Typeset by Troubador Publishing Ltd, Leicester, UK

Matador is an imprint of Troubador Publishing Ltd

Printed and bound in the UK by TJ International, Padstow, Cornwall

COVER

The photograph of medals on the cover was taken by Ellen Hall and subsequently enhanced professionally. They are the miniature (replica) medals of her great grandfather, Albert Lucas, showing the Military Medal, gazetted, February 1918, 1914-1915 Star, British War Medal, Victory Medal and Territorial Efficiency Medal. The originals of these awards are in the care of the Regimental Museum, The Royal Warwickshire Regiment, St. John's House, Warwick.

Dedication

This commentary is added to the wealth of words already available as my recognition of a generation of Britons worldwide, who, realising the monstrous danger faced by their community, committed themselves with their Allies to right a great wrong and in so doing defeated over mighty ambitions with ferocious determination and a dignity of spirit that is their everlasting memorial.

Ian W. Hall.
Verwood,
Dorset.

CONTENTS.

Dedication		vii
Preface		xi
1.	Introduction; Approach March	1
2.	The People of Britain and their Army	31
3.	The Military; Industry, Supplies and Manufacturing	50
4.	Technology and Military Operations	63
5.	Military Considerations; Reconnaissance	76
6.	Soldiers, Officers, Leadership and Discipline	88
7.	Army Organisation and Operations; Advance to Contact	115
8.	The Business of Battle; Engagement	138
9.	Casualties; Cause and Effect	164
	Table of losses	177-178
	Casualty Statistics; Commentary	179
10.	The Royal Navy	188
11.	The Royal Flying Corps; (Royal Air Force)	205
12.	America; The United States	212
13.	German Perspectives	217
14.	Generals, Historians and Critics.	230
15.	Conclusions; Fighting Through	244
Appendix I, Army ranks and formations.		251
Acknowledgements, Bibliography and Reading list.		258-264
Index		265

PREFACE

The reader deserves some explanation to appreciate the reasons for this amateur expedition into the commitment of Britain and its Empire to the Great European War of 1914 to 1918, surely one of the most overwritten events of recent history. This account was not originally prepared with any ambition for commercial publication. For better or for worse it was prepared as an adjunct to the family history, often written in parallel with the affairs of the 700 or so relatives it has been possible to trace. This war touched the family only lightly but as their lives became more of a reality through the research, the consequences of the conflict for individuals and society were recognised. The trite observation that 'this could be the end of civilization as we know it', is both precise and, in its phrasing, a reflection of the Edwardian era; the world and society changed forever in a period of four years. From that appreciation came eventually the decision to offer this link in the continuum of history to a wider readership. This war though was only Act I of the epic 'Great European Tragedy'.

I used my own life time experiences to explain lessons from the events of the Great War. Children born during the 1930s are now uniquely placed to offer a link with events of the way things were for subsequent generations who will only see a two dimensional image of events. Amongst those with whom we are familiar were: parents, grandparents, uncles, cousins of various degrees, who in numerous roles, experienced, fought and survived the Great War. We lived our childhood alongside those with experience of the previous war and matched their advice to our actions. We lived through Act II of the 'Great European Tragedy', the dark and dreadful events of the World War of 1939–45, accepting the requirements and constraints placed upon families, there was no alternative. As time moved on a curious change took place in the general perception of the two events. The second act of the tragedy from 1939–45 was seen to have a good purpose, the first from 1914–18 was a waste, bungled. Yet neither war was sought by Britain. And, Britain in concert with Allies defeated the enemy on both occasions. This is a contradiction not easy to reconcile with the judgments made by the nation and the governments both in 1914 and 1939. Each time the government of the day and the population at large was satisfied that war was the only just option. Each time the outcome was welcomed and counted as a job well done. Now there is a sharp divide; 14/18 bad war, 39/45 good war.

On the basis of the paragraphs above I am offering readers a plain man's guide to the 'Great War', on the Western Front, an opportunity for those new to the subject to focus their attention on critical aspects of events prior to and during the course of the war. It is not original research; the information draws on published sources for the main part of the text, there are a few very minor diversions into fiction to illustrate the character of 'Tommy Atkins' which you will need to accept as written, plus an occasional quotation to reinforce my case.

The 'Great War' did not appear in 1914 out of clear, blue, August sky; it was the first act of this two part drama that had been a couple of hundred years in the making. This is an invitation to take a journey, a package tour, with a guide for the excursions, each section and chapter dealing with separate aspects of events. The traveller will visit the nations of Britain and Continental Europe, wonder at the empty splendour of European Monarchies, have the pleasure of making a comparison with the comparable British systems, explore the foothills of the Industrial Revolution, look briefly on the United States of America and eventually Germany. The political, social, industrial and military context of events and organisation will be described as a way of introducing the tourist to a subject of enormous complexity in sufficient detail for anyone who wishes to take their studies further to recognise familiar landmarks of information in more detailed and academic accounts of events. We shall also make one or two diversions into the by ways of history to remind readers of events that shaped Britain in particular and its place in the world.

The title of this work betrays the sentiments of the author and I accept that I have made a case to substantiate the argument that, despite the casualty figures and the received wisdom of some pundits and portions of the media, Britain and her armed forces made the best of the difficult circumstances foisted on Europe by Germany in 1914 and the outcome deserves more credit than it receives. The British armed forces, the army in particular, receive some detailed attention in this account, the role and historical origins are described in brief, significant events and leading personalities that determined the outcome are reviewed and an attempt made to place them in the context of the time. There is though no detailed consideration of individual battles or actions. It was not the intention of this account to consider in exhaustive detail the innumerable events that contributed to the final result, others more competent and better informed than I have provided such material in numerous weighty volumes.

The Royal Navy and the Royal Flying Corps (subsequently the Royal Air Force) receive only limited attention, the navy because it did not participate in the war on the ground with the exception of one division of sailors (63rd Royal Naval), the account of the contribution of the Royal Flying Corps is limited because it deserves and has received detailed accounts of its own from other writers.

For any consideration of this subject to have credibility the issue of casualties has to be addressed, providing a guide for the traveller on this topic was the most awkward of all the commentaries. There are two reasons, first there is no easily available source material on which the numbers of killed, wounded and prisoners agree and then there is the issue of interpretation as you will find when you reach this part of your travels, second there is the problem of emotion. For those whose families were devastated by the loss or injury of their kin there must be understanding and sympathy. For communities, who mourned the death of their young men, in particular when it was the outcome of the events of one day, the grief was real; no one should gainsay the despair experienced. The war memorials of the cities, towns and villages of Britain are not just public monuments, each one is the repository of personal grief and public respect.

This excursion is in the first place a guide, a journeyman writer's personal analysis done in the context of the family history, not a study of substance in the mould of John Keegan, Richard Holmes and numerous other writers and historians. Hopefully this journey will encourage further enquiry by some readers. There are numerous aspects that can be studied in more detail, my efforts have been concentrated on putting all these starting points for further study into an historical context, not the isolation of sensational aspects of the conduct of events, it is the 'continuum of history' which is essential to understanding these events.

I believe that each generation has a responsibility to leave as a legacy some account of the society and experience of their times, this is mine. I have also completed the account because I wanted to understand why once again, my evaluation of circumstances was contrary to much received wisdom. I now have the advantage of knowing that I am one of an informed minority. Perhaps one day the defects of the arguments critical of the achievements of Britain's armies during the Great War will lose their fashionable attraction. I hope so.

Ian W. Hall.
Verwood,
Dorset.

CHAPTER 1

Introduction; Approach March

The extent to which the events leading to the Great War have been reviewed, examined, analysed and described are exceeded by only one other event of the last hundred years, the war of 1939–45. It seems therefore excessive to add this footnote of comment to all the weighty considerations and analyses that have explained, *'ad nauseam'*, to readerships of all persuasions how very badly things were done and how the author(s) or their favoured military or political leaders would have done things so much better. The journalists who have added to the many volumes devoted to the subject have generally been following up a good story and in most cases are honest enough to admit that their motives are those of people doing their job. Others have been less explicit of their motives.

Having read numerous accounts of the events in Western Europe for the fifty-one months period of the conflict from August 1914 to November 1918, as well as the period immediately prior to the fighting, there remains an overwhelming impression in my mind of preconceptions by writers already decided on their conclusions then using the most suitable available information, of which there is an abundance, to support their contentions. There are exceptions of course, Gen. Sir A. Farrar Hockley makes no attempt to conceal that he writes from the standpoint of a trained soldier and former senior commander and comments accordingly. Richard Holmes and John Terraine also come clean as to their approach and beliefs.

There are additionally other written accounts so constrained by time and location, such as that of Mr. Terraine's account of the last weeks of the war leading to the Allied victory, that exclude themselves from criticism by reason of their limited time scale. Also there are those dealing with a specialist aspect of events, such as the work of the mining companies. One publication needs high praise for telling things as they were, *The War the Infantry Knew*, by Capt.J.C.Dunn, DSO, MC and bar, DCM, MB, BS, RAMC, Medical Officer (MO) to 2nd Bn. Royal Welch Fusiliers, (23rd Foot). A wholly exceptional account that should be required reading immediately after Siegfried Sassoon's, *Memoirs of an Infantry Officer*. The output of the War Poets is probably the most suspect, great communicators, enthusiastic soldiers of the moment, borne on the high tide of national emotion to enlist, but not by training or inclination sympathetic to military realities. They found great difficulty reconciling their emotions to the practical way in which modern warfare is waged.

The problem faced by anyone who disagrees with the received wisdom of the *guardianista* junta, who act as the conscience of the day and thought police, is that questioners have no credibility. The culture of shock and horror that masquerades as informed opinion has so infected the general appreciation of the subject that commentators who advance differing views are condemned out of hand. That standpoint amounts to academic treason, if you can only sustain your point of view by denying your opposition free and respectable expressions of their views then you deny the very purpose for which the war was fought, condemned out of your own prejudices.

This commentary on to which I venture with some trepidation is offered only as a personal view, not justification of particular policies, battle success or defeat, tactics, faulty or otherwise. This is no more than a citizen's summary suggesting that an essential prerequisite of any judgement needs to find an answer to the question; what was the alternative? That, it seems to me, is the issue the professional commentators avoid with their freely offered criticism, lest it spoil both their own preconceptions and those whose prejudices they wish to reinforce. There is also the trap into which some fall of substituting the values of the later portion of the twentieth century on the judgements of those faced with the need to make decisions in a different era. Finally, to my amateur eye, too frequently events are vilified for poor results as a consequence of the enemy's ability to defy one's efforts. There is an almost total lack of acceptance that in an armed conflict any worthwhile opposition's aim is to defeat your intentions, *Quelle Horreur*.

In this text I have generally confined myself to the events in Western Europe with mention only of events in Asia Minor. The Middle Eastern and African campaigns are not featured for the good practical reason that other commentators have also avoided paying too much attention to these events, all that is except the late LAC Ross, aka Lawrence of Arabia (Col. T. E. Lawrence, DSO.)

There is an atmosphere of reluctance amounting to distaste when it comes to discussions on the achievements and merits of the Great War. There is a sense in the way that some writers approach the subject that the politicians of Great Britain engineered the outbreak of war on their own, as if the cohorts of politicians and military talking heads in Germany, Austria, Russia and France were on a separate planet. No, it must have been the political nexus of Britain that betrayed a generation with an easy promise of completion by Christmas only matched by the crass failure of the generals to save the lives of the forces at their disposal: in particular the professional soldiers who were responsible for the British contribution to the Allied cause rank for harsh criticism. It is notable though that those taking this position never stay around to argue their case when asked, "and what would your alternative have been?"

A further impediment to reasoned discussion of the conflict is the almost total denial that there was a competent enemy army as the opposition. The German Army had trained, rehearsed, planned, organised every soldier, NCO, officer and general for at least twenty years to a degree of military skill that quite simply made it the best of its type in Europe. This was the army faced by France and Britain, professional, motivated and supremely self confident, but they came second, fifty-one months after they marched into Belgium and France.

N.B. In this appreciation I have used the term Great War as the preferred term to describe the whole conflict. This was the term used by those who lived through the events; it seems reasonable to me to accept their judgement that it was 'The Great War', later generations must find terms for the events of their times without revising the opinions of those whose lives were affected by past activities.

Political Perspective

It is feasible to take almost any date in the 900 years preceding the outbreak of war in 1914 and argue a connection through a series of events and coincidences allowing an arguable *'causus belli'* for the war to be sustained. In reality Europe, within a recognisable political framework, developed following the Treaty of Westphalia that brought the Thirty Years War to a welcome conclusion in 1648. Progress towards the conflict to settle the grievances and ambitions, real or imagined that were inherent in the event of 1914, became increasingly rapid following the Revolutionary/Napoleonic Wars that culminated with Waterloo in 1815. Events that welcomed the beginning of the nineteenth century in a way that echoed down the years. This was the point when politicians recognised the opportunities available to exploit military advantage by the mobilisation of a complete nation for war like purposes. The end of war as an engagement between paid professionals had arrived. Of the major European military powers, only one, Britain, decided to live with her professional army and also applied the volunteer principle to the Royal Navy in peacetime service.

In the years that followed the defeat of the *Grande Armee* of France under Napoleon at Waterloo in 1815, the politicians of Europe faced requirements for which past experience provided few examples. The effect on countries of demands for democratic political government(Britain and France), unification (Germany and Italy), and independence (Poland, Belgium and Greece) were in themselves a disturbance to society, albeit essential. The Industrial Revolution and the consequential changes to technology including armaments, transport (railways) and information systems (newspapers and postal services), changed pace several times to meet the commercial demands of the newly affluent society and competitive businesses. The joint stock (limited) Company, Stock Exchange, International Banking and private wealth outside the control of ruling political systems within previously stable nation states, all presented unique political challenges.

The geographical fringe states of mainland Europe added to the uncertainty, Greece fought the derelict Ottoman Empire for independence in the third decade of the century, assisted by British sea power. Italy was reunified by the political firebrand Garibaldi in 1851. The power of the Vatican as a secular government was eliminated. Spain maintained her determined decline into obscurity, Portugal struggled with poverty. Poland seethed as a Russian province and the Balkans were murderously unstable. The Balkan nations were predisposed to violent internecine warfare as a way of life even after the conflict of 1914/18 was concluded. A mixture of Orthodox and Roman Christian with Muslims added for good measure, all in a melting pot of territories lacking the essentials of social cohesion, maintaining whatever passed as an identity by reason of fear of the warring tribe next door, determined to defend what they each held and take any advantage that came available, short or long term. Of the remainder perhaps mention of Belgium's situation should be included. This was a country carved out of the Netherlands previously under the tutelage of Spain, Austria and France. The 1815 Congress of Vienna attached the area now recognised as Belgium to the government of the Netherlands, this was not a successful arrangement and following local unrest and the Treaty of London in 1835, Belgium was established as a nation state, neutrality was underwritten in the treat by Britain, France and Prussia and renewed in 1872, by which time the modern Germany had almost completed the process of unification.

These were the conditions at the edges, the bit part players, hoping for favourable notice from one of the leading actors on the European stage. To which confusion must be added the new political theories developing under the guise of anarchism, syndicalism, socialism and Marxist communism. Each of the alternative systems had their protagonists and followers, all suffering the same defect, none of the proposals had been used to run anything at all, let alone a nation state.

The major powers of continental Europe in 1914 were; the dual monarchy of Austria/Hungary, France, the newly unified Germany and Russia; the latter having two thirds of its landmass in Asia. Additionally a few miles from the coast of France lay Great Britain, keeping a wary eye on events from the back garden of European politics but devoting the attention and efforts of governments to running the rest of the world. With the exception that is of the United States, who since 1776 had to be regarded as rebellious colonists in secession from the government of the Crown.

Austria/Hungary appears to have been locked in a time warp by some historical accident. The Emperor Franz Joseph, of the House of Habsburg, succeeded to the Imperial throne in 1848. When the Great War began in 1914 he had defined the policies of his nation and the associated Hungarian Monarchy for sixty-six years. Of the opinions and comments made of his influence on affairs the one word never found is, moderniser. Known for his pedantic attention to the detail of state administration, and wearing too many medals, he took his responsibilities seriously without the ingredient of inspiration to move his nation out of the eighteenth century. Austria preserved an Imperial Court of ferocious formality; a formality that spilt over into all levels of society and the armed forces. Notwithstanding these handicaps the Imperial government had territorial ambitions in the Balkans, eventually succeeding in 1911 in absorbing Bosnia Herzegovina, whose capital was Sarajevo.

The Emperor was estranged from his wife the Empress Elizabeth for many years. She was assassinated in 1898. Elizabeth left only a stunning portrait by Winterhalter as evidence of her place in history. The Empress moved through European society for several years and during visits to England rode out with the Cheshire hunt. There is a real possibility that whilst in the hunting field she was in the company of Friedrich Engels, a junior partner in a textile business in Salford, adjacent to the City of Manchester. This was the Engels who at the same time was cooperating with Karl Marx, working in Chetham's Library, Manchester, writing the manifesto of the Communist Party. Should such an encounter have taken place it would be a delicious example of historical irony.

The Imperial Heir, Crown Prince Rudolph, only son of the marriage, died by his own hand in unusual circumstances. This meant that Franz Ferdinand, Great Nephew of the Emperor, became heir to the dual monarchy. Franz Ferdinand as a young man clearly did not rate his chances of becoming Emperor. He went and married a young lady who was not of appropriate quality. This marriage was 'morganatic' when Franz did become heir, the effect of this was that his wife would not be able to assume the rank and title of Empress. Presumably then Austria could have faced the situation, if Franz had become Emperor, of an announcement at some very grand state function on the lines of; 'His Imperial Majesty and Highness, Franz Ferdinand the First, Emperor of Austria, King of Hungary etc.unt Frau Habsburg. The mind boggles at this example of the tyranny of etiquette. In practice when there was a formal court event in which Franz Ferdinand had an official role to play as heir, his wife was least in the order of precedence, entering the room last and unescorted.

There in the personalities and preferences of a small group of favoured aristocrats, the ingredients of a four year war began to gather in an untidy pile, combining nationalism, ambition, greed and a dose of megalomania for good measure.

The second and dominant nation of the European Central Powers was, post Bismarck Germany, a nation formed during the nineteenth century from the numerous autonomous kingdoms, electorates, principalities, palatinates, cities and assorted territories amounting in all to about 160 self-governing states occupying the strategically vital land from the Baltic to the Danube and the Low Countries, Belgium and Holland, to the Russian border; wherever that border happened to be in the year in question.

The history of Germany prior to the defeat of Napoleon was largely one of alliances and coalitions. The religious wars that were brought to an end by the 1648 treaty had a lasting effect, separating Protestant and Catholic to their mutual detriment. The states with the largest landmass such as Saxony, Bavaria and Prussia were all politically significant and economically well placed; others had to make the best of their situation and any odd scraps that fell from the rich man's table. Prussia was the dominant power militarily, economically and in population terms. Frederick II (reigned 1740–1786), took on a well organised military establishment, he turned his energy to his inheritance and organised an advanced standing army, without a mission. Until that is, you start counting the conflicts of the eighteenth century. The wars of the Spanish Succession, the Austrian Succession, the Seven Years War and so on. Name a European war and Prussia always seemed to find she had an interest to defend, or exploit.

The legacy of Frederick was a state with a modern army, not a modern government, the means of defence and state control, without the mechanism to regulate the ambition of the oligarchs; a dangerous state of affairs.

Following the Vienna Congress in 1815 that finally put an end to the Napoleonic wars, Europe had to set itself to rights. By the 1830's realisation had dawned on the major German states that the numerous states and administrations was more than just inefficient, it was a major disadvantage to trade and economic development. The eventual outcome of the contact between the states was the establishment of a customs union, the Zollverein, allowing free passage of goods and materials within the territory that was, to all intents and purposes, eventually to lead to the formation of the unified Germany in 1871. The Germany whose armies took the field in 1914 with the resources and benefits acquired by the introduction of a homogeneous economic system were part of the Prussian dowry to the unification wedding.

From the time that the customs union became an effective economic influence in the nascent German state, unification proceeded apace; driven by the ambition and vision of Bismarck and the acquiescence of the King of Prussia and his fellow rulers, a new force took its place centre stage in the complicated politics of Europe. Two quick wars against Austria/Hungary (1866) and France (1871–72), the annexation of Alsace, Lorraine, Schleswig and Holstein and the deed was accomplished. A new nation state imperial, autocratic, ambitious with the added disadvantage of a military establishment that acted as an independent estate within the body politic, and without a decent 'Bagehot*' democratic check or balance in sight.

There was one further change that somehow escapes the notice of commentators, yet it contains significance for future events that should be taken into account. From 1715 the King of England was also the Elector (King) of Hanover, until 1803 and the dissolution of the electorate by Napoleon. The wars of the eighteenth century fought by European coalitions financed by British money must have been advanced by this

---

* Walter Baghout (1826–77), Lawyer and author of *The English Constitution*.

duality of influence. Parliament and the government of the day in Westminster advised the King. The King, knowing the view of his ministers, would, it seems as the need arose, find it a not inconsiderable advantage to be able to approach his neighbours as Elector of Hanover. This situation changed in 1837 with the accession of the young Queen Victoria; women were unable to ascend the throne of Hanover if an heir male, however remote, was available. Victoria's replacement was the Duke of Cumberland, this was very fortunate for the British Monarchy; the Duke was disreputable and it is alleged, had various unpleasant habits of a personal nature.

Britain thus lost her means of immediate access to the Courts of Europe; diplomacy remained the only means of entry from now on. It also opened the way to the charge of 'isolationism' allowing the imperialist to gain the advantage and turn the emphasis of government to the imperial and colonial responsibilities that paid such attractive dividends. Europe, and in particular the German states, lost the opportunity to benefit from the example of British government that, whatever its imperfections, separated the powers, curbed the executive, controlled the armed forces and above all, despite disturbances, avoided bloody revolution during the unsettled years of the nineteenth century.

The development of a unified system of government for the new Germany was dominated by the landowning Junkers of Prussia, who had in the past provided the officer class for the Prussian Army. They saw no good reason at all why they should relinquish either sphere of influence. The Franco Prussian war of 1871/2 was the final scene of the prelude to the drama of European history. Prussia had been the military colossus between France and Russia during the eighteenth century and the first two decades of the nineteenth century. Frederick the Great had created a formidable military organisation. The state of Prussia was a powerful political force in continental Europe and frequently an ally of Britain. Britain made common cause with the Prussians as a matter of expediency as much as any other reason. Prussia was not a naval power, what sea board was available was in the Baltic, easily blockaded in the narrow seaways between Sweden and Denmark, even better Prussia was not concerned with imperial adventures. The victory over France and the treaty finalised at Versailles also marked the announcement of the creation of the united Germany with William, Prussian King of the House of Hohenzollern taking the imperial title of Kaiser. With an adept piece of sleight of hand, Bismarck rubbed Prussia, Bavaria, Saxony *et al* off the map of Europe and at the same time, with a superb use of smoke and mirrors, foisted Prussian domination of affairs on to the remainder of the Germany states, grand duchies, principalities and kingdoms.

Time and the ambitions of the Kaiser and politicians of the German ruling oligarchy created an atmosphere of rivalry and antagonism against Britain that was continually frustrated by the offshore position of Britain. It was very difficult to sustain a grievance against Britain when there were no common borders or disputed resources of minerals or population over which a squabble could be engineered.

As an aside in this account, one's imagination can be allowed to run riot for a moment to imagine the possibilities of discussions that could have followed, circumstances being different, if Otto, Count von Bismarck, short suited on humour as a personality trait, granted an Audience of Victoria, Queen of Hanover and Britain, explained some of his more ambitious schemes and plans. The Queen would have had proper grounds for complaint that "she was not amused". The Count for his part might just have been discomforted by examples of regal displeasure. It has to be acknowledged however that when they did meet informally they found common ground and mutual interests.

There was in the new state a neat bit of camouflage, The Reichstag was Germany's parliament, elected by universal male suffrage with a substantial representation from newly emergent left wing parties, but seriously short of power. When push came to shove the assembly could only huff and puff. Policy was made by the Chancellor who took his lead from the King, subsequently Kaiser (Emperor) after 1871.

The wars of 1866 and 1871 differed; the foray against Austria/Hungary in 1866 was carried out in the spirit of bringing an errant child into line, as well as banishing Austria from a role in the affairs of Germany. Bruised pride for the one part and a generous treaty on conclusion of the hostilities prevented lasting ill will but ensured the dual kingdom did as it was told in the future. The war against France was a different matter, lasting eight months it was hard fought by a French

Army disadvantaged by an inefficient supply system and unprepared for the quality of the reformed Prussian Army equipped with the new breech loading Mauser rifle.

The outcome included annexation of Alsace and Lorraine, the end of the second Empire, the abdication of Napoleon III and the formation of the third republic. The legacy France carried forward for two generations was suspicion, resentment and an ambition for revenge against Germany.

From this time onwards both France and Germany maintained substantial standing armies, developed new weaponry, trained their officers and brought defence policies to the front of the national political agenda. As the uniforms of the day were rather extravagant and colourful the old English comment, "all dressed up and nowhere to go", seems rather apposite; a state of affairs that usually leads children to get bored and look for trouble. And that is exactly what happened.

Bismarck really had been able to forge a new nation out of the untidy arrangement of semi autonomous states that had gone before. The new Germany suffered a major disadvantage in military terms; it was between two other major powers, France and Russia. Realising the inherent dangers of this situation Bismarck promoted and negotiated a treaty of mutual cooperation between Germany, Russia and Austria/Hungary, with a secret reinsurance clause providing for mutual assistance in the event that one of the nations party to the treaty came under attack. This arrangement had the essential objective for Germany of preventing the strategic and tactical nightmare of war on two fronts. Otto, Count Bismarck; advanced in the Prussian nobility to the rank of Prince, architect of the new Germany, confidant of Kings, Emperors and Heads of State; except Britain, who as a nation was more than a bit cautious about all this building of a new political empire by someone else, but Otto was the man of the moment.

Then the old Kaiser died at the age of ninety, succeeded by his son, Frederick III, who died himself, after a reign of ninety days, from throat cancer, leaving a grieving widow; the Dowager Empress Victoria, daughter of H.M. Queen Victoria. The vacancy for Emperor was taken up with enthusiasm by Kaiser Wilhelm's grandson, Wilhelm II, known to all and sundry, but not to his face, as Willie: vain, erratic, greedy, ambitious, envious and if other information is credible, unable to put his mind on anything for more than a few minutes at a time. He aspired to a military image without undertaking the rigorous training through which an officer of the German Army achieved a senior command appointment. Not insane in the manner of Ludwig of Bavaria, he was nevertheless intellectually several pfennigs short of a mark. He was an outstanding argument against the virtues of hereditary monarchy.

Within no time at all Bismarck had been retired to his estates, the mutual cooperation treaty and its reinsurance clause, repudiated, followed promptly by a treaty of cooperation between Russia and France. Then just when things couldn't get worse, Willie was sold a naval rearmament scheme by a snake oil salesman, who happened to be an Admiral, Tirpitz. The scheme was based on the hopeful premise that the British government and the Royal Navy would do nothing to catch up or keep pace with the expansion of German naval influence; a proposition of dubious quality at the very least.

That was not all, a secret plan for the invasion of France by way of Belgium was put forward by another huckster, Schifflein (Field Marshal, Alfred von) and guess what, Willie bought a copy, gave it to the German (Prussian) General Staff and exclaimed "I have a dream"; well perhaps he did say it first Rev'd. Mr King, sorry about that. The problem with buying copies is that you don't acquire the intellect that understands all the implications of the scheme. So it was to prove.

Last, but by no means least, in the catalogue of German indulgence was the persuasive self developed argument that Germany deserved additional living space both in Europe and as colonial territory. Envious eyes were cast towards Eastern Europe, provinces such as the Ukraine, to which Germany had no sustainable claim, as well as areas elsewhere in the world under the administration of other European states.

The untidy pile of grievances, real and imagined that Austria/Hungary accumulated prior to 1914, was enthusiastically supplemented by the new Germany. The pile was taking on a perilous appearance of near collapse for anyone who cared to look; few cared, fewer looked.

Leaving the Central Powers in their land of make believe, the situation of the Allied powers, Russia, France and Britain needs to be reviewed with the same degree of healthy scepticism. First Russia, essentially of this nation, either much needs to be said or very little. That great wordsmith Winston Churchill was to say of this ally in two wars that as a nation it was "an enigma wrapped in a mystery"; the most eloquent of explanations in six words.

Prior to the events of 1914 Russia had maintained the 300 year rule of the autocratic and authoritarian Tsars, the Romanoffs, propped up by an aristocratic establishment expanding with each generation to a totally unmanageable overload of privilege and complicated interrelationships. And that was before the Tsars' government attempted to administer the affairs of the largest of Europe's nations, straddling two continents, reaching from the Pacific Ocean to the Baltic and from the Arctic Circle to the border with Persia (now termed Iran) on the Indian Ocean. The sheer scale of the task was beyond the imagination of most competent politicians and bureaucrats; of these Russia and her Tsars had none anyway. On top of the startling physical extent of the nation it carried the baggage of the all pervasive Russian Orthodox Church and the status of the Tsars as demi-gods to a peasant population. The whole nation was administered on the fiat of the Tsar and his ministers of the day, enthusiastically supported by a secret police establishment that preserved its position by finding a plot behind every peasant kulak.

There was also the military establishment based on a conscript army and an aristocratic officer class that compared with the British system which gave the latter the substance of democratic respectability. The Russians had engaged in an unpleasant local war against Japan in 1899–1905, and lost. Not just the land war but the war at sea as well, two fleets destroyed in separate encounters. From this debacle an ineffective and corrupt administration had to rebuild the *material* and morale of the largest European Army.

This deplorable state of affairs did not prevent Russia making an alliance of mutual support with France following Willie's repudiation of Bismarck's tripartite reinsurance provision that included Austria/Hungary. With all the benefit of hindsight the comment has to be made that the French government of the third republic must have had motives and reasons for concluding such an agreement that are now hidden by time, events or misunderstanding and modern perceptions of international affairs. Russia was a basket case nation in terminal decline; as an ally no more use than a busted flush to a blind poker player.

War against Russia in Europe was, and remains to this day, fraught with difficulty. The scale of operations is now, and certainly was at the beginning of the twentieth century, too enormous to contemplate. There is just too much space. An essential maxim of military strategy is that land captured must yield a worthwhile military objective such as a key communications point for road and rail movements. Territory, by itself, is just a liability to be held and controlled; that requires troops in abundance, who all have to be accommodated and fed. The geography of Russia was long on land, short on key tactical objectives. Recognisably the problems of the original Russian campaign and the retreat from Moscow in 1812; not one of the Emperor Napoleon's number one hits with the *Grande Armee*.

The feature of Russian resources that seemed to loom large in the perceptions of other European powers and their military planners was the manpower available to the Russian Army. It has to be allowed that Russia had a population that dwarfed that of other countries and even the combined population of the Central Powers was less than half that of Russia. In the cold light of hindsight though, questions must be asked about the dispersion and quality of the available recruits. To bring recruits from central Asia who are functionally illiterate, have never heard of Germany, France or Britain and turning them into effective soldiers at short notice is a task of the magnitude of one of the labours of Hercules; not impossible but needing high quality organisational skills. Not the Russian's strong suit.

One certainty of any campaign fought in European Russia is that, eventually, the invader has to fight actions against 'General' Winter, few if any have ever won.

The mystery has to be, why the politicians of Europe did not recognise the fault lines of any military expedition in which Russia was engaged, either as ally or opposition. For the Allied powers of 1914–18 this was the weakness of the coalition.

Weakness or not, France as the second of the Allied powers with an army based on conscription had made her alliance with the Tsar's government in the hope that the possibility of war on two fronts, against two armies of significant size, would deter the Central Powers of Germany and Austria/Hungary from aggressive war like action. The ubiquitous philosopher of ordinary life, Murphy, was to observe, succinctly, "If something can go wrong, it will". Right again Murphy, as events in 1914 emphatically demonstrated.

France arrived at the opening years of the twentieth century after more than a hundred years of effort. The disturbances started in 1789 with the now famous revolution; storming the Bastille, the terror, the guillotine and so on, closely followed by the rise to power of Napoleon, and the equally rapid removal within a few short years, of a competent administrator, great soldier and effective diplomat whose Achilles heel was to overplay his hand. He went for the grand slam, when perfidious Albion still had some cards in her hand. These included, sea power, the Kingdom of Hanover, an army that prospered on a good scrap against long odds, plus a fistful of money. Not a bad hand for the no hoper of the European political spectrum.

France had another look at monarchy under the restored Bourbons, decided the price was wrong and voted for the second republic, whereupon look who turns up centre stage, the nephew of Bonaparte, original version, and before you can say coronation in French we get the second empire and Napoleon III. This was the government that Bismarck decided needed to be given a lesson in German culture in 1871/72. Eight months of conflict, defeat, the loss of Alsace and Lorraine and the end of the second empire. This was followed by a nasty bit of revolutionary misbehaviour before the third republic got on its unsteady feet. Small wonder the French had a jaundiced view of their neighbour next door to the east; to add to the already dim view she held of Britain; perfidious Albion, a nation of shopkeepers.

From this long and uncertain design stage however, came a government of a popular democracy, representation of the people and separation of the powers with the military and the officer corps answerable to the political leadership of the day.

The conscious perception of the French for the quality of their military inheritance was, by the time the twentieth century arrived, at best optimistic. No great depth of historical knowledge is needed to recall that in the wars and campaigns of the eighteenth century, the French Army lost more often than it won in the wars against Britain. From the Sun King's (Louis XIV) tussle at Blenheim and onwards, France was on the losing side in wars against England in Europe, until the advent of Napoleon. The French were also outfought by the British Army in Canada and India: events which followed historically significant encounters at Crecy and Agincourt. The campaigns of Henry VI in France were badly conducted and saw the English expelled from France except for Calais.

Napoleon was the star who made the reputation of the French military image. Even then however, when the French faced the British under Wellington with Spanish and Portuguese as allies in the Peninsular War, they were defeated. Waterloo was a military catastrophe for the French but not recognised as such. The French were British Allies in the sorry campaign in the Crimea, learning little it seems and arriving less than twenty years later at the Franco Prussian war (1870/1), and being soundly beaten.

There remained, however, for the nation a belief in the essential superiority of its army. To some extent this could have arisen from the quality of the soldiers who fought for France in its colonies as the Foreign Legion. This independent army never set foot in metropolitan France as a formed unit, its utility and ferocious fighting ability was reserved for overseas encounters.

The second, and tongue in cheek opinion, is to lay the blame on the French language itself. After all, the French officer who attends, 'L'Ecole Superieur de la Guerre'; has got to think of himself as the bee's knees after graduation from an establishment with such a grand title. So much more impressive than the British equivalent, 'Staff College', with only the modest initial letters, 'psc', after your name in the army list, the letters of course being in lower case. The British Army always did understatement very well.

It really would be more apposite for a French wit to have remarked, when told, 'that the sun never set on the British Empire' to have offered the opinion that, "the reason for this state of affairs was quite simply that God didn't trust the British in the dark". Instead of which it was Oscar Wilde, an Irishman.

The uncomfortable fact is, however, that in 1914, this nation believing itself a paragon of military virtue committed its army to a high intensity conflict with some of the infantry wearing the uniform of horizon blue overcoat and red pantaloons of the nineteenth century and carrying a rifle that was inadequate for the job, until hastily modified. Infantry officers of the French Army stepped out onto the battlefield of 1914 wearing white gloves The mounted formations were no better served, some units rode into battle their chests covered by super shiny breast plates and attractive helmets with horsehair plumes. No surprise therefore that more than sixty French general officers had to be relieved of their commands before the end of September and banished to the city of Limoges to await their fate. The rank and file of the French Army were even more poorly paid then their British contemporaries and had leave provisions that were a source of real grievance to the front line soldier. The German Army must have wondered if they were seeing things as they settled behind their Mauser rifles and Maxim machine guns, eight per regiment of four battalions, and opened fire.

As if this was not enough the vaunted French Plan XVII was fatally flawed, the advance into Alsace and Lorraine was committing the army to undertake an aspect of the 'swinging door' ploy that Schifflein had built into his infamous plan of attack.

Then there was the army of the unified Germany, the ultimate legacy of Frederick the Great. The German Army was perceived as everything that was perfect in military terms, based on an officer caste of the Junkers, with military academies to school aspirant officers to undertake their military responsibilities, their destiny, universal conscription of most healthy young men for army service, followed by obligations to undertake annual training for the reserve forces, almost unchecked investment and, to crown this list of advantages, the Germans had a 'General Staff' to plan their activities to the last horseshoe nail.

The German Army took everything very seriously, to the extent that one Chief of Staff set his subordinates a study exercise of significant complexity, to be completed in seventy-two hours and available for discussion at a specified time on the morning of December 26th. A senior British Officer learning of this event took the view that the staff should have considered their Chief to be temporarily insane, thrown the study paper in the bin and taken themselves off to the races.

The German Army was a wonderful machine, planned, equipped and trained to perfection. Nevertheless there was one awful flaw, it had never fought a war, and never been on campaign. The Prussians had fought the Austrians and the French but this new, shiny, all purpose paragon of virtue had never experienced enemy fire, never found itself faced with professional soldiers whose orders were: kill the enemy, no retreat in the face of great odds and win the day. The new German Army had never had to face about and form the equivalent of the 'Thin Red Line', as did the BEF's II Corps at Le Cateau on 26th August 1914. The Germans' experiences between 1914 and 1918 were the penalty for their hubris

As the years drew nearer to Armageddon a glimpse of realism broke across the English Channel. That affable Prince Edward from England who loved the sea air at Biarritz, thought his German cousins to be somewhat dull, and made friends with so many pretty girls in France, succeeded Queen Victoria, his elderly mother, as King Edward VII. A change of mood slipped into the political, military and diplomatic scene almost unnoticed and very nearly too late to be effective. For France delusion and illusion with were, 'too much with the nation late and soon'.

With the exception of Great Britain these were the nations comprising the '*Dramatis Persona*' as the end of civilisation, as the old order knew it, approached.

Britain is frequently accused of ignoring Europe, and developing an imperial trading empire to the detriment of relations with continental Europe. Is this an example of thinking of the answer and arranging the facts to support your contention? To which we can reasonably reply, following the demise of the Stuart monarchy in 1688, it was William of Orange and his wife Mary, daughter of James II, who took the throne of England. In due course of the death of William III, Parliament offered the throne to the Elector (King) of Hanover, five kings followed of the House of Hanover, Queen Victoria married a German princeling, Albert of Saxe Coburg Gotha. Then go and read the Battle Honours of the British Regiments of the line. Most of the countries of Europe have been on the receiving end of a visit of some description from British forces. It may not have been that the action and policies were the preferred course of action for the government of the locality, but for certain Europe was not ignored.

Democracy and the Armed Forces

Britain itself had found a way to stable, economically sound government and a just system of administration for the people, not without trials and tribulation but the amount of blood on the street was very limited. By comparison with many nations Britain had a head start. The state, judiciary and church were separated, the monarchy was constitutional, the armed forces under parliamentary control. The national economy was commercially and industrially sound, with competent public and private administration of affairs and by the norms of the times a democracy with an enviable amount of individual and corporate freedom.

Industrially the achievements are difficult to understate, the motto could well have been, 'you want it we make it'. Almost any manufactured item could be found somewhere in Britain. Additionally there was enormous experience of civil, railway and structural engineering, and a merchant fleet that sailed to every port in the world.

The weaknesses were from the viewpoint of the forthcoming conflict in two aspects of life. Britain could not feed itself from its own resources, imported food was essential to maintain the way of life of the population. Even the national beverage, tea, came from India or perhaps China, according to taste. The second deficiency was in the manufacture of organic chemicals, Germany lead the field in this product group. In particular Britain did not have the capacity to manufacture sufficient explosives to sustain a high intensity conflict of any significant scale or time. These were dangerous deficiencies.

The army occupied a curious position in the national organisation and political thinking during the eighteenth and nineteenth century and until the appalling campaign in the Crimea between 1853 and 1856. As a general principle Britain has disliked large standing armies. Only in times of war has the call gone out for volunteers from the population at large to join the ranks. With some notable exceptions such as The Tower of London, London barracks such as Chelsea, and other major cities such as Carlisle, Colchester, Windsor and Edinburgh, there were few garrison barracks; soldiers were billeted on the local population, publicans and in tented camps.

It was a policy of dispersion, the body politic wanted to avoid the threat of any sort of coordinated military insurrection. The other ranks as soldiers were not well regarded, well paid or well fed. The discipline was draconian and the average recruit only found his way into the Recruiting Sergeant's company as a consequence of the unattractive conditions of labouring work in agriculture or to escape the consequences of his own, sometimes criminal, actions. There were just a few who joined who were from the families of regular NCO's, there was a tradition of service on which the army relied to provide experience in the ranks when expansion was needed. There was also available, The King's German Legion (KGL) mercenaries, almost to a man, who supplemented the British force when the Hanovarians ruled the dual monarchy.

The officers have been generally badly represented in history. The purchase system for an officer's commission was originally introduced as a means for them to make an investment in the national system, providing a financial interest in the 'status quo' and a safeguard of sorts against an army sponsored or supported revolution. This system applied to the regiments of cavalry and infantry of the line including the Guards. Not all officers in these regiments purchased their commissions, there were officers commissioned from the ranks, though these could not be sold. (That which is awarded cannot be sold, was the precept.) Commissions in the formations now recognised as Engineers, Artillery and Ordnance were army commissions, not bought or sold. Commissions to the rank of Colonel or above could not be acquired by purchase; again, they were army commissions. The criticisms tend to look a bit frail when the questions is posed, who won? Armies need to be judged on their win rate and despite the hostility of some commentators the facts of the situation put the achievements of the British Army in the winner's enclosure too many times for the system not to have suited the needs of the day.

To continue the policy of dispersion the governments of the day did two things. Regiments were raised and disbanded on an '*ad hoc*' basis, as they were needed for campaigns and emergencies. An inspection of the history of the infantry of the regiments of the line is needed to confirm this practice. The regiments of foot with seniority numbers above fifty could face disbandment to be re-raised as the need arose. Only the first twenty-four in the precedence order were reasonably assured of continuous establishment. Secondly the colonial expansion needed some visible symbol of authority, what better than a battalion or two whose cost could be charged to the local administration. You can see the Whitehall mandarins dreaming up the scheme. The British Army became adept at making the best of what was available.

The foreign and defence policy of successive British governments was based on ensuring divided national power coalitions in Europe and in particular the independence of the low countries, a navy of sufficient strength to deter any invasion and an army with sufficient experience to expand with volunteers, when needed to meet an emergency. Always providing there was sufficient time. Time to put all the pieces in place, Wellington needed three years in the Iberian Peninsula before he could be confident of the outcome of his campaign against the French.

The only place where there was a serious concentration of the British Army was India. Here the units of the Sovereign's Army were supplementary to the Indian Army. The Indian Army replaced the armies of the Honourable East India Company (HEIC), following the Indian Mutiny of 1857. Even that simple statement needs qualification for the Company's Indian Army was divided. The three presidencies, Bengal, Bombay and Madras each had an organised military component. It was the army of the Bengal Presidency which was the centre of the 1857 mutiny. Each of these Company armies soldiered to some extent with the retained armies of the Princely States who remained within the command of their titular prince. (And you wonder why there was a mutiny.)

The two components of the garrison of India, following the demise of the army of the HEIC, were closely associated, although each with its own command structure. The Sovereign's Army, following the unpleasant events of the Indian Mutiny, provided the artillery. The Indian Army providing the largest portion of the infantry of the line, as well as the cavalry units. Many of the regiments of the Indian Army originated with irregular formations of the HEIC armies. Some of the mounted regiments such as Skinner's, Probyn's and Hodson's were socially exclusive to a degree that exceeded anything found in the British Army. Then just to add to the complications the Gurkha Regiments were tacked onto the organisation of the army of the HEIC from 1818.

The Indian experience was vital for aspirant senior officers. This was the only opportunity for the higher formation headquarters and their commanders to gain experience of managing and deploying a division in the field with all its components, including support troops such as Engineers and supply train. Despite the opinion of numerous non military commentators, you do not glue the required number of units of a formation together overnight and expect them to achieve effective fighting efficiency with immediate effect. There is a substantial learning period whilst the commander introduces and defines the standards by which the subordinate units must operate. In particular the commanding general and his subordinate commanders must, in war conditions, learn to read the mind of the opposing commanders. You don't think so? Why do you think Wellington said immediately prior to deploying his forces at Waterloo "He's humbugged me."? Napoleon had achieved the unexpected; surprise, a key element of war?

Commanders of the time, prior to 1914, were not allowed this essential preparation period. Not until the later days of the 1939–45 war were generals such as Slim and Montgomery allowed the opportunity of preparation. It was one of the essential lessons of the Great War, but the body politic pushed it aside because of the inconvenience and cost of maintaining large troop formations and headquarters.

The cost of this inadequate preparation prior to 1914 was to lay an account for casualties at the door of the nation. Here perhaps we begin to see the glimmer of light as the guilt for this failing is shifted onto those whose decisions are not so easily seen and blame apportioned.

The organisation of the army had been reformed well, on two occasions prior to the 1914 conflict. In 1881 the Cardwell reforms provided a sensible distribution for county based recruiting and depots for the regiments using a two battalion structure, one overseas and one for training and reinforcement at the depot. There was more but these changes together with the improvement of the command structure provided the basis of an organisation competent to deal with the demands of the government of the day. The Haldane reforms of 1908 were to provide a realistic and straightforward arrangement for a home defence army of part time soldiers under the terms of their enlistment. It was not intended that these units of territorial forces should incur a liability for overseas service. That was not to say that individuals could not volunteer for the regular service. If this took place the territorial soldier concerned transferred to the regular service on new terms of engagement.

There was the army prior to 1914, small, professional, dispersed, the necessary adjunct to civilian colonial administration. Self-sufficient in adverse conditions, drawing a significant proportion of its officers from a clique of families and following the same process for many of the men who served as warrant officers and NCOs. Dispersion though is contrary to established military doctrine that emphasises the importance of concentration of resources and firepower. This was not a military caste system to be compared with the Prussian Officer Class. It was one of those informal systems at which the British and in particular the English excelled. An arrangement of responsibilities within the nation to provide professionals for the establishment; not just the armed services the but Civil Service, the law, medicine, the Church and other sections of national life. They all needed a continuing supply of young men to undertake the needs of the state, as it was at that time.

The control of the armed forces in a democracy was a complex issue to resolve following the Cromwellian civil war. The new Model Army had given England and Wales a taste of rule by a military command, it was not an experience appreciated by the population at large or those opposed to the Lord Protector.

Restoration of the monarchy seemed at first sight to provide the opportunity to dispense with an army as a permanent feature of the state's organisation; and that's what happened. All did not go according to plan; there were some dangerous moments as the restored monarch wobbled on the throne from which his father had been evicted. Then in the nick of time Colonel George Monck, later the Duke of Albemarle, arrived from an outpost at Coldstream in the border country of England and Scotland with his Regiment of Foot, subsequently His Majesty's Second Regiment of Foot Guards (Coldstream Guards). The good Colonel Monck was not one to see unrest without doing something about it, and that's what he did. Charles II, of the House of Stuart, stayed put as the restored King.

The events created a dilemma, who ruled the nation? How were the forces of the Crown to be controlled? Being English you don't solve problems, you compromise in a stylish manner and leave all parties with a share of satisfaction. The outcome of this particular compromise must be one of the neatest ever devised. The monarch remained head of the armed forces. Officers and men swear allegiance to the sovereign of the day. The sovereign's command authority became more limited as time went by. It was at the Battle of Dettingen in 1743 that for the last time a British sovereign, George II, commanded his troops in the field.

Parliament and the government of the day assumed control of the actions and policies of the armed forces. This arrangement is not replicated for example in the USA. The President of the United States is the Commander in Chief. This American arrangement places the armed forces under the jurisdiction of an elected politician; at the same time it allocates ultimate military authority to someone to whom the culture of command and discipline of military strategy are unappreciated arts, at the very best.

The solution reached by the government and armed forces of Britain provided a comfortable way of resolving the possible conflicts arising from an over mighty army assuming the role of government. Experience shows with all the benefits of hindsight that it contains in the terms of 1914 a near fatal defect. The armed forces of the Crown have to assume the profile and arrange their deployment, equipment, organisation and planning to meet the policies and tasks set out and defined by parliament. This arrangement assumes that the government's policies and its ideas for the defence of the nation are right. If past decisions are wrong the soldiers take the blame.

In the context of the British political system the army therefore occupied an anomalous position. Under peacetime conditions it was required to conduct its affairs under the direction of the government of the day. Deal with the occasional emergency or insurrection and plan for the future within the objectives and time scales set by political masters. This is a system that has a lot of advantages for the politician, but few for the army.

Even in circumstances when the professional opinion of the army's command structure is that the government has got things wrong, the generals can exercise little power. The Chief of the Imperial General Staff (CIGS and head honcho) could not, on his own initiative, send the Quartermaster General (QMG) to see that nice man at Vickers and order up an extra 2,000 artillery pieces (calibres various) with a couple of million rounds of ammunition as back up, for the simple reason that without parliamentary approval, they had no money with which to make payment for the goods. Put in starkest terms if the politicians get their assessments wrong, the army and/or the navy goes to war wrongly organised, incorrectly equipped and always, as a matter of course in Britain, short of essential supplies. It is the continuing story of military matters, the assessments were wrong in 1914, 1939, 1951 (Korea), 1953 (Malaya), 1968 (Borneo), 1981 (Falklands), 2004 (Iraq) and 2006 (Afghanistan). This means soldiers and their officers get killed and injured, politicians stay at home, with one or two honourable exceptions.

Britain's system meant that only when the sovereign by and with the consent of Parliament declares war, are the commanders in a position to require the state to provide for the practical needs of the army to carry out the decision to meet and defeat the enemy in battle. There is no room for an accommodation or conciliated outcome. Like it or not that is what is meant by war, the defeat of the enemy, to send him packing bag and baggage from the battlefield. There is no alternative available to the soldier that is his task. Governments may allow military surrenders when further resistance in the field is futile. As in Holland and Norway in 1940, the '*de jure*' governments, in exile, of the nations concerned reconstituted their forces and continued the war with their allies until the enemy was defeated.

Who, we have to ask, would consider an action such as the invasion of

France? For sure the Belgians, Italian, Swiss and Spanish neighbours could be relied on to mind their own business. Only German ambitions were sufficiently distorted to envisage such a dangerous plan; only Willie and his coterie of sycophants were sufficiently misguided to think they could get away with such a scheme.

As a recapitulation we should remember that in the decades prior to 1914 the British Army had been limited in size, dispersed over numerous overseas stations and lightly armed: essentially a field force for colonial operations. Not until 1908 did any consultations take place with the French government and the French General Staff to consider what contribution Britain could make in the event of a major European war. The outcome of these discussions provided a scheme to mobilise a force of six divisions to supplement the army of France if there was an invasion. This small army, by continental standards, deployed by one of the world's leading economies could not be interpreted as a real and present threat to the security of nations in continental Europe, neither apparently was it a deterrent to Willie and the German General Staff.

The Commanders of British Armed Forces have a duty to deliver to Parliament the defeat of the enemy. This task is not some optional extra to add to the task of the defence of the realm. Commanders are subject to military law, in exactly the same way as Tommy Atkins. Those unable or unwilling to set about the task with sufficient commitment will be dismissed. Suddenly Parliament turns the tables and when the going gets rough, hands the responsibility for success to those who previously have been kept firmly in their place.

DUTY, that four letter word, it marks out the difference in perceptions between the soldier and those who choose the expedient of politics or pontificate through the media. There it is, four letters, the price for each letter is always to be reckoned by the lives of Tommy Atkins and his leaders, commissioned and otherwise. The soldiers and their commanders are under no illusions in respect of the inherent responsibilities that are incurred by their political masters when the war card is played.

Note. There is one of those unusual anomalies at which the British excel in respect of its unwritten constitution. The navy is the sovereign's and does not have to be authorised by Parliament. The defence of an Island state from Anglo Saxon times depended on the quality of its navy. Even during the years immediately prior to the 1914 war, Admiral Fisher saw the army only as a projectile to be fired where needed by the navy. The army though belongs to Parliament, until the later years of the twentieth century, legislation was required annually to authorise the continued existence of this useful organisation. More conveniently now the appropriate legislation is included in the revisions of the Army Act that out of necessity are needed periodically. Odd don't you think?

Retrospect for the Approach March

There then was the condition of Europe, oligarchy, autocracy and democracy allied and opposed by circumstance or habit. Ambition and attitude balancing resentment and fear, armed forces of some significance and none; too many generals on the lookout for their opportunity for glory and a place in history, without the least understanding of the power for destruction modern warfare would create, all waiting for Willie's next tantrum.

All that was required was a detonator to set off the reaction from which Europe would never recover. Enter Gavrilo Princip in the Serbian capital Sarajevo equipped with a pistol, whose few rounds would cost twenty million lives.

Whatever the circumstances of other armies, the British Army found itself committed to a war for which it had not; been financed in the years before contact, not planned, equipped, officered or been of an adequate size for a major European war. As on previous occasions; the army mustered, marched to the sound of the guns, formed the thin red line, dressed by the right, kept the line straight, presented arms aimed and, held its fire until the word of command. For Willie this was 'a contemptible little army', used as he was to armies in the mass. He forgot the lessons of history, if he ever knew them. Remember also Napoleon referred to Wellington as 'The Sepoy General', do they ever learn?

This was the first point in the procession of events where there were make or break alternatives for consideration by the British government of the day. Britain had no formal alliance to join wars with continental powers. Britain was not under immediate threat of invasion, no direct military or naval action was apparent that would encroach on her sovereignty. Why then did the nation go to war? On a popular level the defence of 'Gallant Little Belgium' was the sentiment of the people. At government level it seems to have been the implications of not fighting in support of the French that carried the day. A further military defeat of France, the occupation of Belgium, German access to naval facilities a few hours steaming from the East Coast of Britain and the German Navy treating the straits of Dover and the English Channel as an adventure playground for its submarine force, such things were too awful to contemplate. Practically, this meant that if France were unable to sustain a campaign against Germany, the delayed introduction of a British force into the battle would almost certainly be too little too late. A defeated France and Belgium would leave no practical position by which the British could take the German Army to task and launch an opposed sea borne landing on continental Europe.

In the context of the day, the government of Herbert Henry Asquith, Great Britain and her King, were between a rock and a hard place, war against Germany was the only option. The nation went to war, on a tide of enthusiasm to be home for Christmas. The new Minister for War, Earl Kitchener of Khartoum was not deceived, he planned for a long game: three years at least, was his initial view, but fate and a German mine intervened to prevent him seeing matters to a conclusion.

Before leaving this section of the appreciation there is one other comparison that has at least to be noticed and added into the equation of success and failure. The democracies Britain and France separated the responsibilities of political control from the command function of the armed forces, the Central Powers did not. The Tsar of Russia began the war without command responsibility but when things began to go badly in 1916 the Grand Duke Nicholas, who did at least know one side of a map from the other, was dismissed and the Tsar took the top military job. This he did, we are lead to understand, at the insistence of his wife Alexandra whose military accomplishments seem to have escaped the notice of historians for the period.

The essential disadvantage of the combination of responsibilities as head of government and the armed forces is that, if the events go against you, then the 'head honcho' has no one else to blame. He wanted the glory of success and conversely had to accept the bitterness of defeat. Willie was the classic amateur whose ambition and greed was only exceeded by the avarice of his immediate advisers.

Willie and Franz Joseph were the prisoners of the *status quo* of their political systems; Emperor Franz exited the scene in his dotage in 1916 before the account was presented for settlement, leaving his successor to clear things up. Willie stayed to the end then jumped ship at the last minute for lonely exile in Holland, even ignored by the German Army when it occupied Holland in 1940. Nicholas lost his nation, his wife, family, life and the war and as an encore set the scene for the introduction of one of the most vicious political systems experienced by the modern world.

Quite wrongly these men were never called to account, indeed some, such as Hindenburg, were allowed to go bungling on creating even more chaos in the wake of their incompetence.

In Britain, 1916 brought Lloyd George to the position of Prime Minister and the loss by drowning of the Minister of War, Kitchener. The Welsh Wizard (LG) was a dangerous man in the position of Prime Minister for various reasons but most importantly, a passionate belief in his own infallible judgement of military operations and character. He was at odds with Haig, British C in C in France, December 1915 to January 1919, who was by contrast to LG, a dispassionate man not given to too many words. Inevitably LG decided Haig should go; in this he faced one significant problem, he hadn't got an alternative commander of the stature and experience of the incumbent. Haig stayed.

Come the end of the conflict LG took his revenge, the loyal commander was ennobled, awarded a significant pension and never again given military responsibility. The wartime premiership of LG though was the high point of his career; as the air cleared after the war his fortunes and those of the Liberal Party declined. Additionally LG's reputation was seriously compromised by scandals surrounding accusations of the sale of honours through a disreputable middle man, 'Maundy Gregory' and separately the sale by LG of shares in the Marconi company. Sometimes there is some form of justice, for Haig was the better man.

Once again in 1919 the political establishment put the armed forces and in particular the army firmly in their place. Only to find that the so called 'War to end wars', was no more than an interruption, a half time break of twenty years for drinks, then the services of Tommy Atkins were needed yet again, to defeat the rebuilt German Army in Act II of this European tragedy.

CHAPTER 2

The People of Britain and their Army

"The English Infantry is the most formidable in Europe,
but fortunately there is not much of it."
Thomas Robert Bugeaud, 1784–1849, Marshal of France.

Armies are the instrument by which the state defends its territorial integrity, its citizens and its natural resources from armed incursion. The state also exploits the use of force, or the threat of force by their armies to pursue needs for the control of resources and territorial expansion. The arrangement of a population, however small, into a unified force under a single commander to achieve these goals is one of the very earliest ways in which man sought to organise his way of life to a common end.

Armies are machines whose principle components, people, are glued together by a command system, in pursuit of the common goal of war. (Statement of the blindingly obvious.)

And, before we get too hung up on aggression and war, let us recall that there is more than a little evidence that early tribes of the 'hunter gatherer' period of human development combined together to stampede herds of the wild animals, that roamed the territories in which early tribal man was living, into killing grounds where their primitive weapons could be used effectively to slaughter their prey. By this means providing food for the tribe for days or weeks and, as a bonus, some nice new skins to wear. That seems to me just as much the act of an army, as warfare was conducted in the twentieth century. Threats were reduced and resources secured to feed and clothe the population. The difference in the species harassed, hairy quadruped versus bi pedal *'homo erectus'* or some similar ancestor, is a matter of detail not principle.

Localised activity of the type suggested above is not historically the common form or purpose of armies. Since the time nation states had a recognised existence armies have been one of the defining features. China, Babylon, Persia, Egypt, ancient Greece, Rome, the Moghul Empire in the Indian sub continent to name but a few, all had armies sharing organisational features and objectives with modern equivalents. Additionally the roving horsemen of the Steppes organised by Ghengis Khan, although not the product of a nation state, was nevertheless a mercenary army available for hire as well as spending more than a little time on self interested missions of plunder, pillage and rape.

The objectives of these armies were as outlined in the earlier paragraph, with the emphasis in almost all cases on the old fashioned sports of plunder and conquest. Reading of these past events there is a common thread to the objectives of national leaders and their commanders: "Take over the shop next door anyway you like, make sure there is plenty of booty and not too many extra mouths to feed". The common theme of naked aggression is too obvious to miss in all the accounts, including those in a biblical context, such as Judas Maccabaeus.

The reason for restating these fundamentals is to emphasise that armies, when committed to war, are aggressive and have a single objective, winning the military confrontation. This is the bit the 'politicians' are unable to reconcile with their instinct. Wars and battles are about winning, not 'reaching an understanding' or 'compromise'. There is no room for 'political accommodations' and negotiations. The purpose and duty of soldiers and armies is to win battles and wars. One officer with more than a little cynicism commenting on political attitudes to matters military observed, "Dead soldiers don't vote".

In the later part of the nineteenth century Britain liked its army, principally because most of it was out of sight overseas and that part that was based in the United Kingdom (this included at this time the part of Ireland now known as Eire, the Republic of Ireland) was represented by the band usually to be found on a Sunday afternoon in the fine weather playing the well liked tunes by Sir Arthur Sullivan, of G&S fame, to appreciative audiences of respectable citizen tax payers. The idea of Tommy Atkins being needed to straighten out the mistakes of other people in continental Europe was not an idea worth consideration. Sir Edward Grey, Foreign

Secretary and gentleman to boot, would see to that!

The issue then becomes, in this appraisal of the events leading to the Great War, who was Thomas Atkins, his corporals, his sergeants, his sergeant majors and his officers. The professional army decimated in the first six months of the conflict, that nevertheless, picked up the challenge and rescued Europe from the near certainty of German hegemony, eventually leading the advance against the German Army to the defeat and the armistice of 1918.

The eighteenth century had established in the perception of the British public a sense of an island nation with a place in the affairs of the world. 'Britannia Rule the Waves' was a popular song as an expression of national sentiment in much the same way that Shakespeare had appealed to the Elizabethans with the lines from Richard II, "This happy breed of men, this little world/ This precious stone set in a silver sea". Odd that, such a stirring speech was put into the mouth of an unsatisfactory and eventually deposed monarch.

Britain's identity and influence in contemporary affairs was defined for the populations by a history that ensured that separation from neighbouring continental countries by the sea encouraged independence. This identity had become a feature of the nation as internal conflicts disappeared. The Battle at Bosworth Field in 1485, the death of Richard III, the accession of Henry Tudor as Henry VII followed by his son Henry VIII, made what had been an amalgamation of self interested fiefdoms into a governed nation of sufficient authority and wealth to cause resentment amongst other rulers and attract some, less well protected or affluent to join the party. The Crown and Parliament settled their respective spheres of responsibility with the civil and parliamentary wars and the restoration of the monarchy. (The monarch reigns, Parliament rules.) Scotland provided England and Wales with a new King on the death of Elizabeth I; James I of England and Wales, VI of Scotland. In due course Scotland began to run short of money, big country small population, and by the Act of Union of 1707 came the United Kingdom. At the same time there remained tribal, but non violent, rivalries, not just between, for example, Scotland and England but also between the people from neighbouring counties, such as Lancashire and Yorkshire. This was the cement of the nation, the confidence to be different within a nation state.

Now we should take a look at the changes to the nation's population that preceded the Great War in the hundred years or so prior to the events of 1914, to focus on the men and women who went to war. Fortunately Britain began to count and classify its population from 1801 and this means a sound base of information to lend some authority to this rag bag of opinions and historically convenient detail.

Beginning with the population of the nation in the first year a national census was taken. The statistics are for Britain (England, Wales and Scotland). Ireland was not included in the 1801 census and subsequent information has not shown details for occupational groups, although this may be available from a more sophisticated source. The importance of this information is to emphasise the fundamental change the Industrial Revolution wrought on the structure of British society in fifty years, in the first half of the nineteenth century. The population increased by more than four million and the manufacturing businesses of the nation absorbed three quarters of this total, over three million souls found work in the factories of the nation. Meanwhile the numbers in military service remained virtually unchanged.

1801   Numbers employed by selected occupational census groups.

	Agriculture	Trade/Man'f.	Army/Militia.	R'gd ship'g.	Total
Totals	2,078,885	2,136,786	198,351*	144,558	4,558,550
as % of pop'n:	12.7	13.1	1.2	0.9	27.9
Population of Britain (total)					16,345,646

---

* These totals need to be treated with some caution; the numbers for 1801 include the militia, who were not on the permanent establishment of the army. Also the figures include only the military in Britain. The numbers on campaign or stationed overseas on garrison duties have not been found. The argument remains valid though even on these figures. In 1801 at a time of war with Revolutionary France, if the army was double the census figure it would still amount to only 3.6% of the population. The 1851 census would allow the strength of the army to be three times the home establishment at 257,450 and 1.23%. Britain's Army was tiny when account is taken of the political ambitions of the nation and the size of the armies of potential enemies.

Fifty years later the return gave the following figures:

1851	Agriculture	Trade/Man'f.	Army/Militia.	R'gd ship'g.	Total
Totals	2,472,356	5,285,310	85,818	NR	7,757,666
as % of pop'n:	11.9	25.4	0.41		
Population of Britain (total)					20,816,351

(By the time of the 1911 census the population of Britain was 45,370,530, an increase of more than 275% since 1801.)

The military situation for Britain in 1801 as the revolutionary phase of the war with France dawdled its inconclusive way towards the Treaty of Amiens in 1802, remained dangerous. The army was too small, badly organised and poorly lead. The Napoleonic phase of these French wars recommenced in 1804. The army and home service militia amounted to 1.2% of the eligible male population. In 1914 the strength of the regular army and reserves was 525,000, approx 0.15% of the population. Additionally there were 245,800 (Sept 1913 return) of the reformed Territorial Force (TF) (subsequently re-titled Territorial Army) together the total available for service amounted to 770,800. No more than 0.21% of the population, about 0.5% of the nation's men. Times were different but such a disparity in the strengths of land forces available for national defence is outrageous. The price for the misjudgements and prejudices of the previous 250 years were to be called in as a national debt against the men of the nation, 1914 Term. The price for past errors would be laid, in the myths of the 'chattering classes', on the shoulders of the professional soldiers who were, and still are, disliked and resented by the political oligarchy of the nation.

In the years to 1914 the population had increased to 45,750,000 and the emphasis moved even further towards the manufacturing sector of the economy for employment. Not included in the census returns for Britain were a very significant 'expatriate' community, colonial administrators in all four corners of the globe, railway engineers in Argentina, tea planters in Assam, rubber planters in Malaya; doctors, teachers, missionaries and assorted farmers, traders, bankers, etcetera, wherever you looked. Additionally there were many more born in Britain during the years covered by the censuses who emigrated voluntarily to the colonial territories, as well as the United States of America.

The German population in 1914 was over sixty million and in France, thirty nine million. Germany was however in alliance with the Austro Hungarian Empire/Kingdom forming the majority of the armies of the Central Powers with additional resources of manpower. Britain also was able to call upon additional manpower resources from its overseas territories. Australia, Canada, India, New Zealand and South Africa as well as the smaller countries that made up the British Empire.

India was the source of the most immediate significant reinforcement of Britain's Army. The Indian Army equipped for war, was embodied and trained to be compatible with European/British procedures. Additionally, and strangely in the perceptions of today, soldiers of the Indian Army were loyal to the British Crown and the military ethic of the British Empire. That was the first piece of good luck for the Western Allies. To the credit of the soldiers of all ranks, the units of the Indian Army fulfilled their obligations as the King's Soldiers and served with distinction, strengthening the remains of the army Britain could deploy during the crucial months from November 1914 onwards until the new armies could be trained and deployed.

There is no easy comparison of the relative population strengths of the Allied powers and the enemy Central Powers. On first examination Britain and France were outnumbered but the comments above are an indication that the comparison is not that simple. Then, the Allied powers included Russia with a population probably equal numerically to the combined strengths of all the other nations with the exception of India, whose population has to be taken into account when considering the numbers theoretically available to Britain. I told you didn't I, the bare essentials of information are complicated enough before anyone has fired a single shot.

The second piece of good fortune for Britain and France, the Western Allies, was that Russia had not the means, the ability or the inclination to get mixed up in Franco/Belgium/British operations. There were no viable means by which the ramshackle army of the Tsar of all Russia could integrate their command and operational procedures with those of the Western Allies. Better by far that Russia was left to do its own thing in the East, worry the Kaiser and the Emperor Franz Joseph with the weight of numbers and crumble into revolutionary disorder in 1917. Russia's contribution to the fray was to divide the attention and armies of the Central Powers and force the German High Command to divert forces to the Eastern Front. Had this diversion of effort to the East not taken place, in all probability the Allied armies in France would have been overwhelmed by the German attack through Belgium and the whole event would have been a re-run of 1871 with Britain implicated in the defeat as well.

That takes us some way from the population and people of Britain who were to fight the war. The difficulty is that with an amateur in charge of this project, separation of politics, strategy, tactics and military objectives, from the real people whose efforts were needed to complete the task are too easily confused. One consequence of this situation is repeated by more experienced commentators, as I read the accepted versions of events. There is a generalised assumption, it appears, that the professionals of the armed forces and the British Army in particular, who went about their tasks, were somehow not people. Automata were conjured from some distant, abstract place to undertake tasks others would not carry out. The actuality was that the professionals of all ranks, suddenly faced with an aggressive enemy and hundreds of thousands of volunteers, had no option but to build the new armies as the mirror image of the regular forces. The time had long past for planning and introducing a new model; war had been declared and the shooting had begun. The enthusiastic recruits and the later conscripts had no option but to fit, very uncomfortably, into the system the army already had in place. A system that had never considered the implications of combining the vast range of abilities, education, physique and achievement deployed by the population at large into the regular army.

The automata model of the British Army is misconceived, the army as a volunteer force serving in dispersed locations worldwide had to be careful of its soldiers, there was no endless supply of recruits coming through on the next draft. The planners and organisers* of the British Army were and remain, regimental officers, or from a corps such as Engineers, carrying out a tour of staff duties usually for three years in peacetime. There was an understanding that whilst the enemy must be defeated, casualties must be minimised. As a contrast, the German Army of the day had the elite 'General Staff' with distinctive, and envied, double carmine red stripes on the side seam of their trousers or breeches. They also alternated with regimental duties but took with them the aura and the stripped trousers of the elite. They also took field command responsibilities with their military ideology conditioned by the knowledge that the conscription system would replace losses. This subtle distinction meant there was always in the mind of the British planners the consequences of asking too much of their regimental fighting colleagues. That is not to say that there were not, during the Great War, many times when too much was required of the fighting units. Nevertheless the function of the 'Staff', who, despite all reports to the contrary, were real people; trained soldiers, mindful of the consequences for their friends in the firing line, was to produce, against the odds, a winning formulae. Our friend Murphy then had numerous opportunities to demonstrate the application of his well known law. Plans, ideas and orders are of no consequence until somebody does something in war situations or indeed in any other aspect of practical affairs. Then however, people, in particular the enemy, all make their contribution and before very long the whole idea has changed radically. Moral: when up to your waist in a swamp with crocodiles snapping at your backside it is difficult to remember that the job is to drain said swamp. In the context of war you have to accept that the enemy will use his best efforts to defeat your plans. Especially if the enemy is the German Army; defeat was not within the schedule of options of the German nation, even as late as the spring of 1918.

Nothing is as it appears for this conflict. This was the very first time

---

(*see also Pg 125 for the views of Field Marshal Earl Wavell.)

total war was fought in ways that affected the lives of virtually the whole world and in its outcome changed the government of nations great and small. It was indeed a Great War, the first industrial war! This was the very first time that the entire population of Britain had been committed to wage war. One hundred years or so after Napoleon introduced the idea to the French. From that we need to consider the strengths and weaknesses of British society and the preparations, or lack of them, that preceded the decision to join, sustain and lead the Allied forces to the defeat of the pre-eminent European army in November 1918.

Whatever else is disputed about the Great War, or any other war, victors or vanquished; people are the casualties: killed, maimed, dispossessed, widowed, orphaned. The lives of generations of Europeans were lost or damaged by the conflict of 1914–18, all at the behest of a vainglorious charlatan and his military sycophants.

The incomplete table of population details on pages 34 and 35 of this section gives a small and selective insight into the extent to which Britain and its population changed in a century and a decade. Population expanded almost three fold, converted from a largely rural agricultural society to a dynamic, world class, manufacturing economy, dominating some sectors of economic activity, backed by banking and commercial sectors, such as insurance of unrivalled global consequence and with the benefit of a merchant shipping fleet beyond comparison.

The drama of the epoch was the Industrial Revolution, spinning Britain to a position of international significance. This change has within it a curious contradiction. Unlike the Florentine Renaissance that flourished on the genius and talent of a relatively small number of gifted artists and bankers under the patronage of the Medici family, Britain and its population took opportunity by the throat and fashioned success on the contribution of the entire community. That is not to say that there were not hardships, deprivation and poverty but there were counterbalancing opportunities for improvement and wealth open to society as never before. Here was the moment in the national history when the enthusiasm and enterprise allowed the development of a counterbalance to the established order of political power through the wealth of the landed gentry and political patronage. Nothing in a nation speaks louder than wealth and within a generation there were sufficient 'new men' of money and no allegiance to the establishment, to alter the balance of political and social perceptions and power. The Liberal reform acts of the 1830s and Sir Robert Peel's repeal (no pun intended) of the Corn Laws were such signs of the times!

The blunt speaking people from Lancashire quickly summed up the way things could change with the wry observation that the self-made 'went from clogs to clogs in three generations'. It was the opportunity of personal improvement in Britain that probably contributed to the dilution of revolutionary zeal that ran riot in continental Europe in the nineteenth century. This factor was paralleled by the effect of Charles Wesley and other evangelical nonconforming Christian churches that so influenced the lives of the new working class, particularly in England and Wales. That was the second aspect of the social change wrought by the Industrial Revolution, the creation of social mobility. Very quickly the ability of people to carve out their own prosperity improved dramatically. This opportunity was enthusiastically adopted by the expanding industrial workers of all degrees. No yeoman farmer, however diligent and talented, could expect to own, in one generation, the wealth accumulated by the men of enterprise who drove the industrialisation of Britain.

The unanswered questions concerns how and who became the 'drivers', I hesitate to use the word 'managers', of these burgeoning enterprises. For example Matthew Boulton and James Watt went into business making steam engines, moving in 1795 to Soho Foundry, Aston, at that date next door neighbour to burgeoning Birmingham. Very successful they were too, so much so that it was quite impractical for them to supervise every detail of their business. Based as it was in the centre of England they could not give personal attention to the installation of their machinery in Cornwall, Yorkshire and numerous other locations whilst, at the same time, managing the daily affairs in the Soho Foundry. This is a lone example but it must have been replicated in every successful enterprise in the land. Suddenly the nation had a need for designers, organisers, engineers, clerks, accountants, draughtsmen, and a legion of other specialists. Such people had to be competent, independent, commercially adept and technically effective. There is no easily found explanation for this development; but happen it did, to the credit of the people of the day.

The equation's solution is in part due to the expansion of the population, the 'X' factor, but the second part of the conundrum is the 'Y' factor, where did the population acquire this knowledge? In 1801 reading and writing were, to the bulk of the people, a dark art, the population was largely illiterate and yet by 1851, railways were being built during railway mania. In 1825 there was about thirty miles of railway track for steam trains in Britain. By 1850 there was more than 7,000 miles and still growing. Iron steam ships from Britain were trading the world, pottery, textiles and numerous other manufactured goods for use in the domestic economy of Britain and abroad; wherever the flag went trade was bound to follow. All this in addition to the huge commercial and financial operations of the City of London, and, businesses and the economy went on growing. Where did the resources of a competent, trained professional, commercial and technical class of 'tradesmen' (women were as yet outside the reckoning) originate and acquire their expertise? Yes I know, I have repeated the question, but in my defence to emphasise the point.

The huge discrepancy between the near threefold increase of the population in general and the increase in the number of soldiers referred to above disguised many associated problems. Not least the issue of senior commanders. Whilst industry and commerce was breeding managers and specialists of any and every description to run and promote businesses of great influence, the army, though reformed, was operating on 'cadre'* establishment. These circumstances ensured that only the very minimum of officers could progress to the higher levels of command and gain the experience of planning and deploying significant land forces in a war situation. In 1914 the French found more than sixty general officers wanting in the discharge of their professional duties and relieved them of their commands. I would very much doubt that the British Army had many more than sixty generals of all ranks on the active list in 1914. Britain had no option but to use all its generals plus others recalled from retirement, good and otherwise, it was all that was

---

* cadre, a unit of the armed forces maintained at a minimum manning level, to allow for the recruitment and training of additional soldiers for war establishment strength.

available. Perversely this situation protected Haig and Robertson in 1917 when Lloyd George was actively working for their removal. He then found to his horror that there was no alternative to the team in place. No one else was of the stature or experience, able to command the respect of subordinates and deal with the French competently. That comment is not intended to detract from the achievements of such men as Plummer and Maxse. These and other officers were competent above their rank, their most effective contribution was to continue in their appointments and set an example of excellence for the remainder of the army.

A retrospective view suggests very strongly that Britain in common with the rest of Europe had not paid too much attention to education. Three universities, Oxford, Cambridge and London in England, a clutch of grammar schools, in particular those founded and endowed in various parts of the country by Edward VI, plus establishments we now recognise as major public schools, founded in Victorian times, provided for the education of the sons of the merchants, landed gentry and aristocracy. The recognised professions were essentially those of the law, the Church, the army, the navy and medicine, as a physician. Surgeons, 'sawbones' were yet to become respectable. These needs could be fulfilled from the established resources and provide for the higher education of those needed for administering colonial affairs, all in the classical tradition as widespread education in 'natural sciences' was something for the future.

Inheritance law in Britain had always required that the eldest son acquired both title and land on the death of a father. Money could be willed to other children, sons and daughters, but land, the estate, was the right of the heir. The nurture and expectations of the sons in a family with title and estate paid close attention to their potential inheritance. The eldest son and, often if available, the second son were not expected to put themselves at too much risk. Heir and spare was the policy of numerous families; at a time when even the most privileged were equally at risk from the diseases of the day. These were the children whose education through the schools and universities of the day were to maintain the family inheritance. If the elder brother survived into adult life, by no means a certainty, the younger of the two sometimes found his way in to political affairs. Sons of lesser significance, numbers three, four etc., were a different matter. They had to make do as best they could; the Church was secure, comfortable if supplemented by a modest private income and preferment was possible, perhaps to the bench of Bishops. The law had similar attractions; medicine, unless for the fashionable portion of society, was not of high standing or great attraction; the army and navy, risky, but with the potential for significant rewards to the successful. Hence the armed forces of the Crown drew many of its officers from the younger sons of the aristocracy and landed gentry. The Duke of Wellington when he joined the army was the Hon. Arthur Wellesley, younger son of the Earl of Mornington. His career in the army was not only successful in military terms it produced an addition to the wealthy, landed dynasty. Whilst this was a comfortable arrangement that suited the needs of the time for Britain's volunteer army, it was not a system to support a military caste in the style of Prussia. Yet the outcome of the army's campaigns bore favourable comparison with the other European nations, most of whom paid much more attention to the cultivation of the military elite in their societies.

Education was not a high priority in the perception of many who exercised influence in affairs of the nation. Schools provided an understanding of the classical civilisation and their language, history, divinity, mathematics, geometry in particular, were the core of most school learning. The beginning of the nineteenth century saw the foundation of the Royal Military Academy (RMA), eventually Sandhurst, to educate young men in military matters and to place these aspirant officers in suitable regiments. Between 50% and 60% of the officers who joined the regiments of the line did so by purchasing their commissions. The remainder came to appointment as an officer by promotion from the ranks or by a peculiarly English arrangement. A young man hopeful of making a career in the army could, if his family had suitable contacts, join a regiment in an unpaid capacity, known quaintly as a 'volunteer', and serve in the ranks whilst living with the other officers when off duty. By this means a commission could be secured without purchase, when a vacancy became available as an ensign, cornet in the cavalry, the ranker would take his chance and apply to be appointed to the vacancy. The mess toast to a "short war and a bloody one" defined with precision the prevailing promotion opportunities.

That was the system, as Napoleon made his mark on history. Over the next hundred years, Britain refined and developed a procedure that eliminated the purchase of commissions, advanced the status of military education for young men at the RMA, Sandhurst, and also introduced specialist training for Artillery and Engineers officers at Woolwich. The responsibilities of the Secretary for War, the Horse Guards and the Board of Ordnance were combined, the appointment of Commander in Chief abolished, a Staff College founded to develop the abilities of officers for senior appointments and so on. The army of 1914 was a very different organisation from that which defeated Napoleon Bonaparte at Waterloo in 1815.

Britain did not 'do' revolution, by a narrow margin the upheavals experienced by other nations of continental Europe were avoided. Changes came by argument, necessity and the influence of social progress in the nation as a whole; the need for reform was agreed, however reluctantly, and the army also moved gradually to became a modernised fighting organisation. The British Army had, since the restoration of the Monarchy in 1661, reflected the national conditions of the day, unlike other nations the military did not set the agenda for the nation, rather it adapted the aspirations of the country to the exigencies of military service.

Insofar as education was concerned, by the 1870s governments of the day were finding the resources, support and leadership needed to improve the education of the population at large. First Gladstone then Disraeli introduced legislation to establish an entitlement for the education of children. Initially this was for children up to the age of thirteen, twelve for those who could read and complete simple arithmetic tests. But it was a fundamental change, the state for the first time passed legislation insisting that part of the population must undertake an obligation, funded by taxation to improve individual and social standards; one of the earliest examples of social engineering. More importantly legislation at about the same time introduced the concept of formal education for apprentices additional to the master's responsibilities under the terms of the indentures.

'Mechanics Institutes' were established to provide formal instruction in technical subjects for the apprentices under indentured service, particularly those in the engineering trades. The institutes were organised at the initiative of local towns and cities which were empowered to finance the facility by levying a local tax on the sale of spirits to the amount of one penny a bottle. The colleges were sometimes known colloquially as 'whisky colleges'. This is an unusual example in Britain of a 'hypothecated' tax at local level for a national scheme. Amongst the first, if not *the* first, to open under these provisions was the Mechanic's Institute in Whitehead Road, Aston, now a suburb of Birmingham, then an independent borough. The building was still in use as part of a Technical College with the legend over the portico 'Mechanics Institute' as recently as 1965. Education for the people had arrived. I don't think there was any consultation with the army or the navy on the purpose or content of this monumental social change.

Hindsight enables us to see one of the errors inherent in this failure. The armed forces, army and navy, had been gradually isolated from the mainstream of general life as society changed during the nineteenth century. As a proportion of the population, as each year passed, the army represented a smaller and smaller percentage of the total; the armed forces were marginalised by the birth rate. The obligations of defence and colonial control required by the state were undertaken by volunteer professionals as discussed above. The government saw no purpose in seeking the opinion of the professional soldier or sailor on matters that concerned the education of John Citizen, neither for their part did the armed forces, army or navy, show any interest in the matter. This omission further increased the gap in the perceptions of the professional thinking of the command structure of both the army and the navy and their appreciation of the changed social structure of the nation. Eventually, when there was a need to mobilise a citizen army, the discrepancies between the recruits of the past, and the expectations of service life of the 1914 volunteers with the enthusiasms and opinions of a literate society, took the army by surprise. There was a gulf between the perceptions of the citizens who joined to fight a war against the Kaiser and the professional army who delivered success their way using long term regular service as the bedrock of its thinking and training. This gulf in all probability helped provide the seeds which when cultivated in academic hothouses gave rise to the 'Butchers and Bunglers' school of military criticism.

Germany and France with their conscription of young men for army service had already addressed this issue and arranged their affairs to combine both sources of manpower. Britain had, for reasons previously described, abstained from conscription even in time of war. There was also another good reason for the government to steer clear of such a radical change. The legal system of the nation included the concept of common law, an element quite unknown in continental Europe. The awkward truth was that conscription into the army might be found illegal at common law if tested in the courts. Only those who of their own freewill volunteered to submit to the additional legal commitments of military law should be accepted for the sovereign's service was the argument. A concept not always scrupulously observed by the recruiting sergeants of some periods of our history.

Now to cut to the chase and look at Thomas Atkins and his like, of whom the Duke of Wellington observed "I don't know what effect these men have on the enemy, but, by God, they frighten me". Earlier in the text the trite observation was made that armies are people within a command structure. What was the source traditionally of young men who made the army their life and what was the comparison with those who in 1914 set aside their previous plans and enlisted, initially as volunteers and later in the war by conscription? Make no mistake, soldiering is for the younger man. Capt Dunn, M.O. of the 2nd Battalion, Royal Welch Fusiliers makes the point well in his diaries of the Western Front war (Chap XVII), that infantry soldiers over forty years of age need particular attention if they are to be effective. Attention that is not necessarily available when enemy shot, shell and other 'nasties' of fighting a war are being exchanged to some purpose.

Typically for 250 years the army recruited for the rank and file those left over from the annual hiring fairs for agricultural workers, the prisons, fugitives from family responsibilities or debt and boy soldiers from the foundling hospitals for orphans. There was another small elite group, the sons of soldiers, serving, discharged or dead. Regiments were responsible for finding their men, when and where they could and the opportunity to enlist a young man into a regiment who was already familiar with army life was a bonus. In particular if the father of the recruit had served with distinction. August 1914 found the army dealing with recruits from every portion of society and adaptation had to be the order of the day.

The description frequently applied to the other ranks of the British Army, as the 'crude and licentious' soldiery was probably accurate. The description however brings those who use it face to face with this uncomfortable issue: what was the alternative? If you demean any assembly, use the individuals badly, pay them poorly, allow their exploitation and yet expect them to serve in dangerous conditions in an occupation you are not prepared to undertake yourself, disillusion will surely follow. The expectation has to be that several outcomes will result, additional that is, to the crudity and licence mentioned above. These include introversion and contempt for those who use them badly. That however was, and remains the perception of soldiers by society at large. Read Kipling's *Tommy* and reflect. Occasionally though from the army's other ranks appeared a man of note, William Cobbett who obtained his discharge from the army in the rank of sergeant major was such a one, progressing to a notable political career becoming the Member of Parliament for Oldham.

Yet, with this unlikely foundation of haphazard officer recruitment and other ranks from the 'also rans' of society, an army was fashioned that fought on its own, and in coalitions, to beat the best in Europe, eject the French from Canada and India, see Napoleon sent packing from Egypt, Spain and Portugal, win in the Crimea against Russia despite the appalling mistakes of the commanders and get the best of most of the sovereign's enemies, with whom numerous governments took issue. The army did badly against the citizen army of the United States and made other mistakes in the Low Countries at the end of the eighteenth century and South America at the beginning of the nineteenth, on balance though the ledger showed a very creditable balance in favour of success. How, by what process of alchemy, was it feasible to produce an all purpose, go anywhere, winning team generation on generation? No other contemporary nation achieved such success, even Frederick the Great and the Prussians served and succeeded only in Europe. In 1914 when the Great War began, the army of Rome seems to be the only previous example of a military organisation, soldiering on so many frontiers with a comparable record of success over at least 250 years.

The secret of the British Army was to produce the regimental family that took for its other ranks; the dispossessed, the fugitive and the orphan absorbing each into a community that valued them for what they did, their endurance and discipline, not their morality or paternal influence. The system provided certainty of rations, clothing, food and accommodation. The provisions were both mean and mean spirited, but were consistent and bore favourable comparison with the expectations of an agricultural labourer or a mill hand in Lancashire. In return for the protection of the regimental family the discipline was draconian, the conditions anywhere uncomfortable and risks awesome. The alternatives were also seriously unattractive.

This was the system through the nineteenth century, until in 1881 the reforming Mr Cardwell as the responsible minister set about making the uncertain amalgam of individual interests into an effective, modern army, using the best features as a firm foundation for this achievement. The inheritor of Mr Cardwell's initiatives was Sir Edward Haldane, in 1908 his reforms concentrated upon the militia and Territorial Force as reserves and a home defence force. They knew they had opportunities to use the army's traditions to create an organisation that would be able to defend the realm when it was needed. Neither of the reformers took the opportunity to widen the social basis of the army's recruits. That was a serious mistake as the nation's population was achieving great things personally, socially and economically but the army was isolated from the effects of these changes. Generals of the Napoleonic era would have recognised officers and men of the regular army of 1914, the same Napoleonic Generals would have been astonished at the scope and achievements of the society outside the army. Cardwell and Haldane were also uncompromising believers in the advantages of the British way. A very Victorian attribute and the Achilles heel of the British Army in 1914.

Underlying the result of the reorganisation the army itself remained steadfast in maintaining the precept 'officers will lead and the men will follow'. Of the French Army it was said 'if the men will follow the officers will lead', not the same thing at all.

The raw material of the organisation envisaged by Cardwell and Haldane would still be, so far as they could see, the men recruited from the margins of society. Going for a soldier, never was and never will be a comfortable option. The changes they put into place were to ensure that those who made the choice to serve in the army before the emergency of 1914 should be treated reasonably, accommodated healthily, fed, clothed and equipped according to the demands of the soldiers' trade. August 1914 changed everything. Under peacetime conditions the army dealt with about 30,000 recruits annually. The first ten days of August 1914 brought 100,000 recruits, the second half of the month another 100,000 and by the middle of September a further 100,000. Britain had no experience of such frenzied military activity. For the army it was, 'make it up as you go along' time.

They built better than they knew, for when the time came the British Army, regulars and volunteers, created on the achievements and the regiments of the past, fell in, marched to the sound of the guns, halted on the command, formed line, dressed by the right, held its fire until the whites of the enemies eyes were visible, then fought with such ferocious intensity that the ambitions of Kaiser Wilhelm II were thwarted and the long march to the defeat of Germany's military ambitions began; a tragedy to be played in two acts and not completed until 1945.

For the first time in the history of the nation the butcher, the baker and the candlestick maker, as well as the clerk, the draughtsman and the solicitor rubbed shoulders with the professional army and, together, as the British have always done, made things work. Given the conditions and danger it was a monumental achievement.

CHAPTER 3

The Military; Industry, Supplies and Manufacturing

The demands of the army on industry and technology during the prolonged period of small scale operations were not intense. The Royal Navy took pride of place for effort and expenditure; in particular the conversion of ships from wooden hulls and sails, first to steam for propulsion, then to iron clad hulls, followed by iron then steel hulled vessels each to superseded Nelson's Navy. For the army the procedure seemed to rely upon the recognition by the army and its suppliers that a worthwhile idea for weapons improvement had become available. It was evolutionary not revolutionary change. Rifled guns not smooth bore; muzzle loaders out, breech loaders in, black powder replaced by cordite and so on. Equipment could then be put on trial to develop handling techniques and tactical methods before the government was encouraged to find the will and the resources to provide the new weapons or other new item. After introduction, supply and demand could be adjusted by using the war emergency reserves and making good excess usage in a later year. But when all is said and done, a gun is a gun. Battlefield movement remained dependent on horse power and the sweaty feet of Tommy Atkins. Railways improved the deployment of men and supplies behind the battle zone and came to dominate military planning in Europe.

The Industrial Revolution and the subsequent progress of industrialisation in Britain had provided the nation with an incomparable manufacturing and communication system that included a merchant shipping service that reached into every navigable corner of the world. Trade on an international scale not rivalled by any other nation and a national credit rating for the Bank of England that was the envy of the world. Each, in some way a factor in the tensions leading to the events we now address.

The manufacturing businesses of the nation included numerous concerns whose speciality was armaments. Vickers, and its rival Armstrong, were pre-eminent in the field, others were close on their heels though, Birmingham Small Arms (BSA) and the Royal Ordnance factories for example, plus unrivalled steel making facilities in South Yorkshire, Wales and the North East; each were important components of the army's supply chain. The weapons from Britain were able to keep several armies, additional to Britain's own, supplied with equipment at peacetime rates of usage. There were numerous nooks and crannies throughout the land with nice little earners in their product line that were armament related. With the exception of the ordnance factories the businesses were commercial concerns, they made what a customer was asking for and at a price that allowed a comfortable return on capital. Essentially they established an operating policy that measured supply and fulfilled demand using minimal resources, good sound business economics. Not by any means a suitable preparation for an all out, high intensity, lengthy international war in which one of the protagonists had the clear intention of finishing up as 'head honcho' for continental Europe; which another, offshore participant, was equally determined not to allow. 250 years of foreign policy scheming, several wars, a global empire and a place at the top table of international affairs was not to be sunk between the Dogger Bank and the Heligoland Bight of the North Sea on the whim of Wilhelm II.

The demand change that developed following the initial encounter battles of 1914 needed volume; every type of armament and defence item, including the obvious need for weapons and ammunition, other war like stores such as barbed wire, water pipes, shovels and field telephones anything and everything the soldier needs to hold his ground and defeat the sovereigns' enemies; in quantity and at once. And these needs come after men and animals have been feed, clothed and accommodated. This was not only the war to end wars, it was to be the war in which the moral and physical courage of men dressed as soldiers was to be tested to the limits of experience in the Western world.

In the period since Britain last found the need to deploy her army in continental Europe, the contrasts of technology had sharpened. Breech loading, rifled weapons had become the standard for both infantry and artillery, black powder had been superseded, recoil systems had been introduced for artillery, automatic weapons had been adopted and alternative ammunition types invented. The guns remained guns, it was the range, velocity and destructive effect of shot and shell that changed. The sword had been discarded for the private soldier although officers retained them for a time after the whistle blew for the kick off in 1914, but not for long. Armies moved about by railways when such useful systems were available, otherwise they marched on their booted feet or if they were very lucky, or sufficiently senior, on horseback. Exactly as the armies of Alexander the Great and Julius Caesar, *et al*, had progressed on their expeditionary conquests.

The stores needed to sustain the fighting men about their business followed on carts drawn by horses. Motor transport was making spasmodic appearances by 1914. London Transport sent a fleet of their pretty red omnibuses to help out with troop movements, for this reason at the annual Remembrance Sunday service in Whitehall, a representative of London Transport lays a wreath at the cenotaph.* I wager some Tommy to lighten the mood called out the bus conductor's refrain "only five standing, move down the gangway please". As a generality the rate of advance remained the speed at which a trained and equipped soldier could progress on foot, across a piece of ground, usually under fire. The cavalry moved quickly but no role could be found for them in trench warfare. Tanks when they arrived could manage three miles per hour. In short the technology of destruction and defence had moved more quickly than the technology of movement and attack. The British infantry tactics had developed the simple concept of fire and movement, for aggressive or defensive actions, whether on foot or transported. This concept though was unsuitable for trench warfare well supported by artillery. As the conflict progressed tactics were developed to cope with the consequences of a conscripted and, by extension less experienced, army facing and using greatly increased fire power. It is true that these tactical changes were not always welcome or completely successful. Some of the few

_____

(* Cenotaph, from the Greek word, meaning empty tomb.)

regulars who remained as senior NCOs and warrant officers as Kitchener's battalions joined the fight expressed the view with some force that the British Army fought at its best 'In Line'. Sentiments founded in the experience of past campaigns were not confined to the officer class!

The British Army had developed a stores and supply system for an army posted throughout the world in locations that varied from the pleasant, spacious conditions of South Africa, the hot, varied and unusual conditions of India, as well as the difficult and hostile environments in places such as Sudan and Burma. Supply to such a widespread community of units had, by its very isolation, to be sufficiently flexible to allow local sources to provide essentials where practicable. As an example, feed for the animals used by the army has to be acquired locally unless there is absolutely no alternative. There were various other ways that the army could use local resources for its day to day requirements, but there are limits; replacement for bedding and clothing alright, spades and other basic tools possibly, but not always practicable, weapons, never. Military weapons must be manufactured to standardised tolerances and the last detail of design, supplied only by approved manufacturers to the field army. The supply system created by the army to look after its own approached the outbreak of hostilities better placed than other participants to keep its forces in the field. Not because it was better planned, or of adequate size, but because it had much practice in dealing with the unexpected in unpredicted circumstances and was able to improvise successfully when the enemy was doing his best to get in the way of proceedings.

One of the defects made by bean counters of the treasury is the failure to grasp the idea that the military needs supply lines full of all the goodies needed by the fighting man and the supporting services such as engineers, ordnance and the like. When the enemy is coming over the horizon, delivery in ten days will not suffice; wars are lost when supplies fail. Despite the adverse comments surrounding the supply of ammunition, in particular for the artillery in the early months of the year, the existing arrangements produced a nineteen fold increase, before Lloyd George became the responsible minister! But you wouldn't realise this was achieved; such is the strength of mythology that now surrounds the events of the Great War.

The British Army also appreciated that an army in the field must be self reliant; there is no corner shop at which the quartermaster can call for bread. Field bakeries have to be provided, likewise laundries, mobile bath units, hospitals, workshops and other essential services; each of these units creating their own demands for food, accommodation, pay, post and the other essentials of daily life. The army knew this simple fact of soldiering, politicians either do not listen or ignore the advice they receive.

This is the point at which the reader needs to take account of some of the most obvious differences between the events of daily peacetime life. The retail services provide for the needs of the nation's daily life. A British Army on campaign in the twentieth century could not live off the land it occupied by force, as was common in earlier wars. The needs of military operations had reached a degree of complexity that necessitated a dedicated supply train for all its material requirements. The Army Service Corps, (Ally Slopers Cavalry), Royal from November 1918; the corps initial becoming RASC, quickly translated unofficially as (Run Away Someone's Coming) came of age and delivered the goods despite the dangers. The ASC increased in strength by 2212% between 1914 and 1918. It is not to say that that there were not instances of private enterprise by individuals; some chicken foolish enough to stray could well have improved the diet of Tommy Atkins occasionally. The authorities though did take a dim view and in blatant cases soldiers were punished; Wellington, in the Peninsula a century before, hung some looters, as an example. The situation in France was different to that of many previous campaigns; the British Army was fighting on the territory of an allied country. Plunder was off the agenda, supplies had to be paid for, even the weak French beer cost Tommy some of his pay.

The essential lesson to be absorbed is that the military supply train must deliver to the consumer. The fighting units have to be supplied right to the front line by a system that meets daily and even hourly needs, water for example. The customer is much too busy making mischief against the enemy to collect the goods and will not accept a charge for delivery.

The supply system has to be filled from end to end to deliver requirements consistently. Unfortunately in 1914 there were some pretty awful gaps in the appreciation by politicians, civil servants and soldiers of what we now call logistics. The appreciation of the acquisition system seems to have operated initially on the basis of sending an order from a government organisation and expecting the demand to be fulfilled. The action could of course usually deliver the goods once, perhaps twice before raw material stocks were exhausted. There seems to have been no understanding that stocks of material at whatever stage of the supply train must be balanced down to the last detail. This means if the circumstances demand, tin and rubber from Malaya, coal from Wales and high grade iron ore from Sweden all have to be at the point of manufacture when needed. In this particular war volume demands suddenly expanded by a factor of ten, twenty and sometimes a hundred times, for many of the necessities of war, industry was overwhelmed. Within the first few weeks of the war orders for 3,000 machine guns had to be placed with manufactures in the United States.

By way of examples only, to highlight the type of problem that can arise when demand is expanded to an unlimited extent, consider the issues of the production of thousands of new rifles, if you are unable to make and assemble simultaneously all the components from stock to firing pin the rifle is useless. The raw wool for uniforms had to be delivered from Australia, tin, bauxite and manganese had to be mined and shipped to the smelters, rubber had to be tapped and treated before forwarding for further processing. The supply train requires high level management skills to operate successfully, as well as sophisticated control and planning systems. The organisation for the change to war conditions needed concentrated effort, talent and above all time, time however was against Britain and her allies.

The Government of Herbert Asquith approached the early stages of the conflict with the motto, 'Business as Usual'; heaven help the poor soldier.

The pre-eminent trading position and the national wealth and credit rating allowed the government of Britain to turn to overseas sources, the United States of America in particular. This nation did a very good line in personal weapons and was pleased to be able to make a quick buck out of the European situation. The Central Powers, Germany in particular, would have liked access to American goods, the Royal Navy thought otherwise; just another complication to Willie's plans to put the rest of Europe in its place on the back of a minor political event distorted by the bumbling oligarchy of Austro Hungarian aristocrats, overcome by their own self importance, to justify their arrogant assumptions.

In 1914, as described, Britain knew how to supply a widely dispersed imperial/colonial army at considerable distances from their home base. The supply and equipment of a mass army of untrained recruits on home territory and the provisioning of the BEF, a few miles away on the French/Belgium border was something new. That it was achieved at all from the starting position was remarkable in itself. The other European participants had all wrestled with the problems of supplying a mass army in a full scale, high intensity war for many years with varying degrees of success. The Germans knew what they had to do but forgot to consider how to proceed if the enemy did not accept the inevitability of Teutonic hegemony and give up quickly. The French did some things well, their 75mm. was an excellent gun, the red and horizon blue uniforms of some troops sent to war in 1914 was an unforgivable mistake, as also was the inability of the Serbians – remember them, they were our allies – to supply all their troops with rifles.

The BEF went to France fully supplied and the front line continued to be supported throughout the war. (Rudyard Kipling in *The Diary of the Irish Guards* (pg 288) records with some asperity that only when hostilities had ceased in November 1918 did the breakfast rations fail to arrive on time.) This meant that the shortfall of accommodation, clothing and equipment had to be borne by the volunteers who had flocked to the colours in the autumn of 1914; Kitchener's New Armies. It was these men who drilled in their own clothes, lived in leaking tents (all tents leak, don't let anyone tell you otherwise) and put up with numerous other shortages, to say nothing of the quality of the catering. There is a well established summation from this period of soldiers' opinions of cooks that goes as follows; Orderly Sergeant, "Right listen up, who called the cook a b*****d?" Reply from the ranks, "Who called the b*****d a cook."

Eventually the enormity of the problems created by the unexpected arrival of a major war thirty miles from the front door step was recognised by government and the Ministry of Munitions was created, and to this key role came the Welsh wizard, David Lloyd George. Given the needs of the time he was a success at the job, he was also a manipulative politician, cunning and spiteful, eventually meddling in military affairs properly to the concern of the General Staff. The CIGS from 1915 ('Wully' Robertson who rose through the ranks from cavalry trooper to Field Marshal) told him so and eventually was sacked for his pains. In the post war period LG fell from power and grace and it was commented that from that date forward, he (LG), was unable to make the job of mayor of a small Welsh seaside town in a poor year for candidates, or so it was said.

Given the circumstances however, what was the alternative? Once the conflict began, to withdraw from the alliance because of problems with the supply system was not a tenable political option for one of the world's leading industrial and commercial powers. From a military standpoint it would be an admission of defeat and disgrace. Again we run into the cul-de-sac of pre 1914 thinking in Britain that ignored the political possibility of a European war; maintaining an army establishment and organisation that had insufficient resources to provide a field army 'en masse'. The army itself is not without responsibility in that despite the staff work undertaken with the French to provide the BEF, the planning stopped at that point, no one would look into the abyss of all out, long term, high intensity conflict. Perhaps there was sufficient realism amongst the senior generals of the day to appreciate that it 'would be the end of civilisation as they knew it', and so it proved to be.

The follow on consideration from the issues concerning the arrangements to get the supplies to the right place at the right time comes back fairly and squarely on to the industry of the day. Manufacturing is not of itself a difficult task. After all since early times in man's progress, people have been acquiring the skills to make goods other people will need and buy. The complications begin when the product being made is successful and the maker has to produce several all at once, all to the same quality standard. The Industrial Revolution solved the problem by creating the factory system. Putting lots of people able to do a small part of a job in one place with some machinery and organising the jobs so that raw material could be fed in at one door and the finished product leave the factory by the opposite door was a logical step. The procedures were analysed and improved over a couple of generations by several prominent industrialists and a group of early 'management consultants' known as Scientific Managers, pre-eminent amongst these was the American, F. W. Taylor, whose ideas were to influence Henry Ford; by 1911 Henry had applied the notions to his model 'T' motorcar ("Only way to build a car is, 4ft off the ground and keep it moving"). Significantly the most successful early factories based on these ideas were breweries and flour mills.

The snag is that the bigger the factory, the more complicated and expensive the equipment and the more specialised the jobs of the work force, as a consequence the adaptability of the workforce and indeed the organisation is reduced. The factory may be able to increase its production but if the output is not a product needed by the market – in war time situations the armed forces – the product is without purpose, it is a waste of effort to make it. Another issue arises with installations such as furnaces and smelters for iron and steel, production has to operate on a continuous basis twenty four hours each day, producing the refined metal. Such equipment has a fixed output the only way volume is increased to any significant extent is to build more furnaces. This requires a protracted lead time, substantial capital investment and a skilled workforce that will include strong young men!

Industry therefore faced two different requirements: expansion of manufacturing resources to meet greatly expanded consumption of highly specialised products such as, shells, guns, aircraft and so on, this alongside the conversion of existing resources to make general purpose items such as clothing to military (and naval) requirements. The two tasks are not the same although there may be common elements. The expansion by conversion of existing manufacturing resources from consumer goods to armaments is complicated and time consuming. The machine tools, lathes, millers, extruders, drillers, power presses etc. all have to be converted to new set ups, equipped with new tools, patterns and jigs. All these later items made by the elite tradesmen of the day, pattern makers, toolmakers and machine fitters working on one job at a time often using hand tools for the final exacting stages of manufacturing. As an example, the production of just one of the colossal lathes needed for the machining, to exacting tolerances, of gun barrels for the large artillery pieces must have been reckoned as several months. These issues are neatly summarised in a book recently published privately by the Birmingham gun makers, Westley Richards, to celebrate the company's two hundred years of business life; four times the work force, training of unskilled employees for skilled tasks, buying up patterns and building their own machines to acquire additional capacity and modifying other machines to their own design to increase capacity. And this was a company whose business for the military was the manufacture of small arms! The nation as a whole was on the back foot.

Another conflict of interest now appears round the corner (Murphy again). The most adaptable, dexterous and productive workers are the young men about twenty-five years of age whose eyesight is still keen for such demanding tasks and who are capable of sustaining a high output level each day. And who are the most likely quality candidates as good reliable soldiers? Why young men aged about twenty-five, adaptable and with good eyesight, etcetera.

Now the nation faced a real dilemma, quality volunteers were rushing to join the colours, mainly the army, but the nation needed to expand manufacturing activity with an urgency of which no one had any experience. Yet another circle that had to be squared. Schemes had to be introduced that released skilled men for industrial work either to their original employers or a particular concern producing armaments. Such men retained their status as members of the armed forces and could be recalled to service if it was deemed necessary. The problems inherent in a 'helter skelter' expansion of manufacturing facilities including the absorption of an inexperienced, untrained workforce were dramatically demonstrated by the explosion on 21 January 1917 at the Silvertown explosives plant on the Thames Estuary. More than fifty were killed and over one hundred injured, many of them young women recruited specifically for the expansion of explosives production. The damage was so great that no specific cause was identified. My money though would be on careless procedure, short cuts, bad practice by the inexperienced management and workers. There are some substances with which no risks can be taken; high explosives are one of them!

The issue here comes back to consumption as the army fights harder and expands to fulfil its role in the war time emergency, then the amount of 'war like' stores grows without reference to any predetermined political ideas, the demand must be measured by the amount of equipment needed to overcome the enemy and win the battle and the war. To the armchair expert the opportunity to put the issues to rights in retrospect is too good to miss; it is not they, however, who had to deal with the hierarchy of demands and priorities as the economy was shifted onto a war footing. Consider the situation in respect of the development of the Artillery, the key to eventual victory; in 1914 the BEF held on charge 486 guns and howitzers, by October 1918 this had raised to more than 6,700 an increase of almost fourteen times the initial holding of such weapons. This concentration of guns enabled the Commander, Royal Artillery (CRA) a usage of shells amounting to 12,000 tons in twenty-four hours. The final total of guns in service at the end of hostilities takes no account of the introduction of new versions of the weapons, loss through battle damage or indeed the necessity to repair and overhaul the weapons as the bores and breech mechanism wear through heavy usage. All the components of the increased equipment had to be manufactured, all the replacement items had to be added to the manufacturing load, together with optical sights, gun carriages and ammunition limbers. Such an expansion took a massive effort and commitment of time as well as resources and whilst this was being organised the army did the best it could with what was available.

Note: Anthony Bird in his account of the two day engagement at Le Cateau reminds us that the hard fought action cost the artillery thirty-eight guns lost: the manufacturing output of the British armament industry in the three months, August to November 1914 amounted to fifteen field guns and thirty one field howitzers.

Then we have to consider the expansion of resources by building new factories on green field sites to make more of the armaments needed by the soldiers. Starting from the ground works, foundations and drains, brickwork, wood and steel work, roadways, conveyors, machines, toilets, boilers, and so *ad infinitum*. It all takes time, organisation and effort that in the short term provided nothing for the fighting man. Rome was not built in a day, neither were the new factories!

To illustrate the point in respect of the increase in the use of existing resources there are below details of the amount of additional traffic generated for the Great Western Railway during the years 1914-18 as a guide. Resources for these additional trains would have to be found by working all the rolling stock, engines and staff of the railways more intensively. The special trains detailed* are additional to the usual railway service whose traffic volume did not diminish! In reality the number of passengers carried in 1916 was greater than the immediate pre war year of 1913.

Year	Troop Trains	Admiralty Coal	Munitions, Guns, Stores..	Totals
1914	3,376	309	1,460	5,145
1915	9,077	1,729	5,478	16,284
1916	7,904	2,454	8,941	19,299
1917	6,681	3,421	13,201	23,303
1918	6,577	5,763	12,232	24,572
Totals	33,615	13,676	41,312	88,603

Great Western Railway, Additional traffic.
* Source, *History of the G. W. R, Vol. 2, 1863—1921*. E. T. MacDermot, revised by C. R. Clinker.

All this before we even get to consider the need for explosives. Germany had, as a nation, become during the second half of the nineteenth century, pre-eminent in the branch of science known as 'organic chemistry'; essentially the science of the useful and widely available element carbon. This predominant position of academic and industrial life seems to have no rational explanation, in much the same way that there seems to be no obvious reason for the number of acclaimed German composers of classical music. Nevertheless the Germans were superb industrial chemists. One quick glance at the list of reactions named after German researchers is enough to prove the point. So what? Well you need to understand organic chemistry very well to make the substances that go BANG inside a gun, shell, bullet, etc. Britain was not as good in this vital branch of science and business and was forced to improvise, import and eventually expand its industrial competence to catch up, but of course slowly. One unfortunate effect of this process was that later in the war (1917) a ship carrying several thousand tons of explosives blew up in the harbour of Halifax, Nova Scotia, devastating the town, killing many and providing the world with its very first example of a manmade multi kiloton explosion, fortunately without the problem of radioactive fallout of subsequent bigger bangs.

Once again we find ourselves up against the maxim; we make war as we must, not as we would. Theorists should note that the task set in 1914 was not within the scope of pre 1914 political appreciations. The ships of the Royal Navy, so dear to the nation, were ineffective as a means of dealing with the offensive campaigns of the German Army on landmass of continental Europe. Only by blockading tactics and maintaining open sea ways to the UK could the navy influence events, when all the time the enemy was knocking at the door of the democracies who had challenged the Germanic hegemony of Europe. Or, more accurately, the Allied nations had sent their soldiers, officers and men to withstand the assault on the gates of freedom and correct the view of the Kaiser, his Chancellor and assorted Generals.

That awkward question keeps returning, what was the alternative? Once war began only the Central Powers could return the position to the *'status quo ante'* without defeat being forced upon aggrieved and invaded nations such as France and Belgium. Even Britain in all probability would have had its wings clipped and forced to concede naval limitations and overseas colonial territory to a triumphant German Kaiser.

CHAPTER 4

Technology and Military Operations

This is the point where the obvious must be argued to a position of precedence over the preferred options to which some critics resort, when offering their own solutions to the defects, mandatory in their opinion, of the conduct and thinking of the British General Staff responsible for the participation of Britain in the Great War. The application of advances in technology by the army receives little attention generally. The developments in just three aspects of warfare: artillery, air power and armoured fighting vehicles, allow an inference to be drawn, that all is not as it first appears to be.

First we all need to remember that armies of the time were not organised to produce original inventions. The armies of the day could only use the technology and equipment available to them from the industrial sources of their nation. They could also of course buy naturally occurring materials such as timber, coal, stone, meat, fish, cereals etc. as well as employ men and horses. The military organisation has only the most limited resources to originate, design or produce manufactured items, and it is not their job so to do. The army can specify a need, whether it can be satisfied is a very different matter. Once again the precept about war needing to be fought as it must, not as we would like.

To digress and provide an illustration of wishful thinking by some commentators, more than once I have found an opinion expressed in respect of the Battle of the Somme in 1916 that the infantry should have been provided with the body armour as protection, from which planet were such suggestions coming from? Metal (steel) body armour had been abandoned for soldiers in Europe in the seventeenth century with the advent of reliable (fairly) fire arms. The weight of the protection was too great when matched against a musket ball. Nothing changed in the next couple of hundred years or so, there was no viable protection for a soldier in the open. Not until the advent of 'Keflar', a light plastic material, in the last quarter of the twentieth century was there a material that could be utilised for personal protection (nb, plastics at the time of the 1914–18 conflict were confined to a limited range of 'thermosetting' compounds invented by the Belgian chemist and businessman Dr.L.H.Bakeland and independently in England by James Swinburn (later Sir James Swinburn FRS) the invention became known, unsurprisingly, as Bakelite). A few synthetic fabrics such as 'rayon' and the flexible nitrocellulose (celluloid) material used for the recently developed cinema films were also available. The latter invention was to be of great value for the camera roll films, although glass plate negatives continued to be widely used. Polymers such as Nylon and polyethylene were for the next generation, just.

The second issue for thought is concerned with the relationship between origination and application. Academe makes a clear distinction between pure and applied issues. The pure aspects of science are in the realms of abstraction and intellectual reasoning, such matters as Newton on gravity, Einstein on relativity or Faraday on the phenomenon of electro-magnetic induction and electromagnetic rotation. Whilst two of the three quoted examples help us to comprehend the influences affecting our universe there is no immediate practical use for the knowledge, after all, things have been sticking to mother earth for many millions of years and are likely to continue to do so. Michael Faraday and his understanding of the subject is a different matter, observation and understanding enabled theoretical considerations to become practical equipment with real utility in every field of human activity. Another platitude for consideration, invention is 99% perspiration and 1% inspiration.

The intention of these early paragraphs is to emphasise the anomalous position of the military when it comes to the use of technology. As an extreme example the much loved science fiction device of the 'Death Ray' was only feasible in the novels of Jules Verne and H.G. Wells, the technology did not exist to provide the devices visualised however much the military and/or the naval authorities may have wished for them. The technology of manned, powered flight was a different matter, empirically this conundrum had been solved by the Wright brothers, on 17th

December 1903, only a decade before the outbreak of war; their day job was more prosaic – they were bicycle mechanics. Between 1914 and 1918 the aeroplane as an instrument of war moved from the use of fragile single engine machines for limited spotting and reconnaissance tasks, to the creation of an independent fighting service capable of waging war on its own terms. This advance did not take place overnight and the substantial resources had to be allocated, including an intellectual commitment, to the development and application of the nascent opportunities before air operations became both technically and operationally effective.

On analysis it appears that there were for the British three main aspects of technology which they applied and expanded to achieve the defeat of the German Army; air operations, mentioned above, the use and improvement of artillery and the introduction of Armoured Fighting Vehicles (AFVs); tanks in non military terms. Chemical warfare, gas, never quite made it as a reliable weapon. The use of gas, certainly on the Western Front, although helpful as a shock tactic often got out of control because of climatic conditions and turned on the troops of the instigator; an outcome that is unhelpful for morale at the very least. Wireless (radio) was also a technology which did not advance military operations to the extent it might have been anticipated, although line based telephone systems were an essential part of army communications, wireless though was used at base headquarters despite concerns about security.

The arrival and development of aerial warfare in this conflict was not to bring about significant material losses to enemy forces, any loss suffered in air combat operations was and would continue to be insignificant in comparative terms to the damage inflicted in the war on the ground, throughout the Great War. What was achieved was that rear areas and even civilian locations could become targets for interdiction. There was consequently an affect on the morale of the non combatants. The objective and indeed the eventual success of the Allies was one of control. The Central Powers, the Germans, were denied freedom of operations in the air including air space behind their own lines. The enemy were denied a vital initiative, their planning as the war entered its final year had to be based on the assumption that air superiority or even parity would be denied by the Allied air operations. Air reconnaissance, target and artillery spotting, bombing raids and aerial photography were used by Britain and France to modify and organise their offensive and defensive operations on the ground. The generals of the day accepted and developed the use of a brand new concept to the operations of war in Western Europe. The intrepid and visionary commanders, such as Major General Hugh Trenchard, John Salmond and Hugh Dowding risked their professional careers to establish the new resource of air power and made a signal contribution to the war in which they fought and should be allowed more credit for their achievements.

Artillery forms a neat counterpoint to the introduction of the aeroplane based on the new technology of powered manned flight. Artillery had been around in one form or another for many centuries. The Romans had their siege engines, the Chinese invented gun powder, and cannons had been used on land and sea but not always to the best effect. The Royal Navy, experts in the use of cannon, preferred to rely on massed, close quarter broadsides until the breech loading rifled barrel arrived and could be combined with newly invented hydraulic recoil dampers. These innovations were to be combined to produce a mounting system allowing a gun to return to a fixed alignment after firing; the accurate use of artillery weapons of various calibres on the battlefield in modern warfare became achievable.

Naval gunnery has suffered from a difficulty that technology strove to overcome. Ships on the move mounting guns, fired at the enemy on the move. Not so the army who fired from static emplacements. Ships would be following their own course but affected by pitch and roll at sea, to some greater or lesser degree. The target(s) also would usually be on the move following a different course and also changing position with the movement of the sea. To overcome this inherent disadvantage to accurate shooting, the technology of the naval construction industry, following the introduction of steam power, eventually favoured the use of several large guns in huge ships (the bigger the ship the more stable the gun platform, theory), who all sailed along in a nice tidy line, training their upmarket cannons on the enemy and hoping that the gods of war and some smart calculations would do them a favour and let a few of the explosive shells disable the enemy before the same fate befell them. That was the way the Royal Navy went about its affairs in 1914, almost but not quite oblivious to the introduction of sea going submarines equipped with Mr Whitehead's torpedoes

In 1914 the Royal Artillery was divided into three groups, the smart, high profile Royal Horse Artillery (RHA) very dashing, lots of horses to make a fuss about and nice small guns to rush into action behind the PBI (poor bloody infantry). Firing their weapons at visible targets and correcting their shooting by observing the fall of shot, then making individual adjustments for each gun to hit the enemy target. Just to make sure everyone knew that the RHA were a cut above the common herd the buttons on the jackets of officers' mess dress were round, almost like a musket ball, other gunners were referred to as 'flat buttons'. A bit foolish really when all portions of the Royal Regiment were carrying out the same task of bringing confusion to the enemies of the sovereign.

The second group of gunners were the Field Artillery, much less glamorous, heavier weapons of larger calibre, pulled around by tractors or heavy horse trains, sweaty soldiers in shirt sleeves serving the guns which, generally speaking, were fired at targets on an area basis hoping that there would be a detrimental effect on enemy positions. The third part of the gunner's empire was the Royal Garrison Artillery (RGA); these were the specialists who manned the guns of the fortresses in stations such as Malta, Gibraltar, Dover and so on. The guns used by the RGA were large calibre, eight inch was common, as much as twelve or fourteen inch sometimes, in fixed and reinforced emplacements. In most cases the only way for the gun teams to practice live firing was for the gunners to be embarked in capital ships of the Royal Navy and sent to ranges in the open sea and this is what they did each summer. Service in this part of the artillery was not much sought by ambitious officers. During the 1914–18 war these were the men who operated the giant 'Railway Guns', the siege guns used to reach far behind the enemy lines with their barrages. The Germans also used weapons of this type and famously during the Great War shelled Paris from positions located in the occupied portion of France.

The appreciation of the general principles of artillery work had progressed significantly as the technology of the guns and the explosives used had advanced over a fifty year period immediately prior to the outbreak of war in 1914. The technology that lagged was twofold, fire direction and control and secondly, ammunition and fusing.

In 1914 the gunners still needed to see their targets, line of sight was vital to bring effective fire to bear on specific targets. (The Royal Navy also had to continue with observed fall of shot even on capital ships, equipped with fire control towers and high resolution range finders.) That is not to say that area bombardment was discarded, but the effect of this method of bombardment was more concerned with damaging morale or fixed installations such as railway junctions and important bridges, than ensuring that specific damage was achieved to a military formation or emplacement. Hence in 1914 the horse drawn gun batteries rushed into action behind the infantry, shelled the enemy who were foolish enough to show themselves, laid a bit of smoke then hitched up and nipped behind the nearest cover before they received repayment from the opposition, in kind*. Lovely horses, polished brass work on the guns and limbers impress the locals in a colonial outpost, but the procedures were not organised to operate in the context of the warfare of the trenches; hidden targets, well dug in and protected with earth works, sandbags, etc. Should the army have anticipated the need? Yes, most certainly it ought to have looked ahead and anticipated the need for indirect fire control. There was though one link needed to allow such technology to be introduced, instant communications, hence field telephones were brought into use.

A little excursion is needed to explain the idea of indirect fire. The first issue to accept is that artillery pieces (guns) are very valuable items of kit to the army, loss or damage to even one of a battery's guns is a serious business amounting in some circumstances to disgrace. As the range of

---

* This is a small exaggeration, The Royal Regiment of Artillery had learned from the events of the Boer War; indirect fire was in the process of introduction using the 'clock card' and field telephones, but old habits die hard. So it was on 1st September 1914, 'L' battery, RHA arrived to support the fighting at Nery, it did not flinch in the face of the enemy, Captain Edward Bradbury, Battery Sergeant Major Thomas Dorrell and Sergeant David Nelson earned their place in artillery legend for their heroism and determination, each was awarded the Victoria Cross. Bradbury was killed in the action, Nelson was commissioned, achieved the rank of major and was killed in action on 8th April 1918, Dorrell survived both wars of the twentieth century and died in 1971. 'L' battery now bears the title 'Nery' as its battle honour.

guns increased with technology the opportunity to damage and even destroy the guns of the opposition increased, guns therefore had to be adequately protected. This was done best if the enemy could be prevented from knowing the position of your gun emplacements, such as placing the battery on the reverse slope of a hill and firing the gun over the summit of the slope. The problem is, of course, the gunners are unable to sight their weapons. Now some of the gunners were a bit special, understanding subjects such as surveying and trigonometry. This knowledge allowed the gunners to calculate range and trajectory as well as making allowances for wind deflection and correct for the curvature of the earth. The guns of a battery could therefore be aligned with great care and when fired the shot would fall very close to the target, but not necessarily close enough.

The next step was to introduce a specialist officer called a Forward Observation Officer (FOO). The job of this intrepid man was to take up a position sufficiently far forward to be able to see the target at which the guns had been directed to fire. He would have a telephone link back to the Battery Commander and a routine, called registration, was introduced to make sure the guns were correctly aimed to the last yard. Early in the process FOO had to make himself comfortable in a suitably waterlogged ditch, tasks such as this one always lead to a close encounter with water, mud, manure and other undesirable materials. The telephone link is then cranked into action and all the guns set to the calculated alignment, the order would be given for one of the pieces to 'fire for registration'. Initially two or three rounds, FOO observed the fall of shot and sent a message back to the battery, giving details of the amount of correction that should be made to the range, bearing and so on. A couple more rounds to ensure all was well and the aim was perfect, the remaining guns of the battery aligned to the revised data and then the whole battery would be ordered to blaze away for the stipulated number of rounds and destroy the enemy position. The registration procedure allows for adjustment to be made for other factors which affect accuracy such as barrel wear.

Easy when you know how, there was of course a catch to the execution of this cunning little plan. The field telephone link from the hapless FOO to his Battery Commander was a vulnerable piece of cable, passing along hedges, fences through an assortment of middens, pig sties, road junctions and so on, between the two points. Vulnerable to the destructive attention of passing vehicles, animals and irate farmers, if all else failed the opposition did not have to try too hard to break the connection by casual gun fire and then the system falls flat on its face. Not until the arrival of field radios was fire direction a more reliable procedure. It is unfair of me not to acknowledge that considerable effort was expended to bury the telephone cables, however warfare being what it is, even the best efforts were confounded and the wire damaged by one means or another. Additionally FOO had to hide himself very thoroughly if he was not to attract the attention of enemy snipers or machine gunners. Officers and their signalmen who undertook fire direction duties were men of courage.

At this point the nascent Royal Flying Corps (RFC) found ways and means to come to the aid of the gunners. Before the war was very old it became clear that airmen could see what was going on below and spot the fall of artillery shot as well as identifying targets in advance when the enemies' guns had a pop at the British or French positions. This, it was realised, must become part of the fire control procedure for the gun batteries. To begin with communications were, to say the least, haphazard: messages dropped in weighted bags, Morse lamps, hand signals and later the first airborne Morse transmitter, able to send simple messages to gun batteries tuned to the transmitter's frequency and corrections made enabling indirect gun fire to fall on a predetermined target. How was the target identified? The RFC recognised the opportunity for aerial photography as their skill in reconnaissance work developed and the techniques were quickly developed to match maps with photographs and then use aeroplanes with trained observers to correct the shooting until the target no longer presented a threat. Problem was of course, the Germans did the same thing. Solution, shoot down the reconnaissance planes, using other planes, fighters, or anti aircraft fire from ground batteries. Then it all gets complicated with fighters flying as escorts to reconnaissance planes as well as other fighters trying to shoot down enemy reconnaissance planes escorted by more fighters; a very confusing introduction to warfare for the fledgling RFC. It was the fulfilment of the adage 'cometh the hour cometh the man'. The previously mentioned

Maj. Gen Hugh Trenchard, in 1914 holding the rank of colonel, was the man who took the forty-eight planes that went to France in 1914 and inspired the RFC to greatness. The enemy had within a short time better aeroplanes but the RFC and the French air corps had more planes. The policies and techniques that were developed as the war progressed by Trenchard enabled the Allies to gain superiority in the air and impose their authority on the Germans, this despite such 'aces', as von Richtoffen. The Germans were again tempted down a cul-de-sac, priority went to the destruction of enemy planes not the development of the reconnaissance and fire control role emphasised by Trenchard. A decision it has to be said that cost the RFC dear in human terms. In April 1917 aircrew casualties in some squadrons were exceeding 100% in the month.

Ammunition and fusing is yet another vast subject for specialist analysis, the casual observer, you and I, need to remember that an artillery shell has in addition to the fuse two main components: the projectile, the pointed bit that should damage the King's enemies, and the casing that contains the propellant material. Both components are required to go BANG but not at the same time. The explosive in the casing is detonated by a percussion cap in the base which contains a very uncertain material, Mercury Fulminate or something similar, even the boffins who make this stuff treat it with care. When the percussion cap is detonated by loading the shell into the breach of a gun, closing the breach and administering a smart tap with a pointed steel rod the main propellant charge in the casing is exploded, this generates a lot of hot gas and the projectile is forced up the barrel of the gun towards its target where the fuse will be activated and the resultant second explosion will do damage to the enemies of the Crown. The essential part of this routine is to make sure that when the shell is fired from its gun the fuse is not activated and a premature explosion take place on home ground; all a bit tricky and in 1914 even more so because Britain did not have sufficient manufacturing capacity for one of the essential explosives. The dilemma was resolved however by the arrival on the scene in the nick of time of Dr. Chiam Weitzmann, yes that's right a German, of Jewish origin who was able to offer an alternative manufacturing process for the production of acetone, a solvent necessary to the manufacture of the explosive Cordite, essential for the Allies' war effort.

As with all newly established manufacturing operations there were some problems, initially the artillery had a nasty outbreak of 'prematures', 'shorts' and 'duds', until all the manufacturing problems were resolved, not I am sure without much grief in the factories. At the Somme in 1916 the estimate was that about 30% of the shells fired were affected by one of the shortcomings. The design, manufacture and use of artillery fuses were the cause of many problems to all the national armies in this war. Artillery fuses are items of precision engineering in which the components have to be machined to exact dimensions, within 0.0001" (one thousandth of an inch). Now put this requirement into the context of the rapid expansion of the armaments' industry and the introduction of workers, unfamiliar with the manufacturing operations, but required to work to these exacting standards and the problems become more apparent. Small wonder there were difficulties. The trouble is that an artillery shell is fired once only, recovery and repair are not options and guess who gets the blame for failure, the poor sweating 'squaddie'.

This was not a problem for Britain alone, both the French and German gunners, it is reported, had at least the same number of defective rounds. Never though is there a word of such shortcomings by others allowed to dilute the virulence of the critics of the British achievement. There is also the issue of the ammunition type to be used in a particular operation. Shrapnel, named after the eponymous colonel, no use against fortifications, high explosive works OK against fortifications, but has limited radius of effectiveness against soldiers with their heads down. So the complications mount.

As we have now introduced the fearless FOO to our narrative this is probably the place where it is appropriate to look at the non appearance of radio. At the time this equipment was known as wireless, we will for the remainder of our deliberations use the current term, radio. Radio was a practical operating system by 1914, the navies of the world including our own Royal Navy were well equipped to take advantage of the new technology. There were two aspects of the systems available that militated against widespread use by the army. Size was the first and this included a requirement for gigantic amounts of power, requiring noisy generators for the current with attendant fuel supplies, plus the cumbersome aerial displays needed for transmission and reception of signals. There was no suitable installation for trench warfare. In 1918 an experimental army radio 'set up' needed seven men to transport the components.

At this stage of development ships were ideal users, 'man pack' sets were a dream for the war of 1939–45. And before anyone says how ridiculous the situation was that the bright boys of the new telecommunications industry could not do better, remember please neither could their peers in Germany, France or Italy. The problem was the power needed to transmit signals on the wavelengths then used and the efficiency of the newly invented thermionic valve, many of which were the size of an inverted flower vase of reasonable capacity and rather more fragile. Aerials also were large and obvious, as noted above, look at the wire festooned from the masts of any ship equipped with radio systems, you take my point. As also did the enemy who would have a jolly time with machine guns and other trench weapons cutting the masts down to the ground, foot by foot as target practice.

This goes some way to explain the dangerous nature of communications between formations, in particular the troops holding the front line trenches. The men at risk were the 'runners' who had to rely on good luck as they dodged through the broken ground of the battlefield to relay a message back to a commander, field telephones' cables were so frequently broken, pigeons got lost, dogs and men who were wounded or killed. Please explain, what are the alternatives missed by the men on the ground?

The third example of new technology that found its way to the battlefield as a consequence of the Great War was the Armoured Fighting Vehicle (AFVs) aka tanks. As with artillery the basic idea had already received some attention. In the fourth century BC the Persian King Senacharib devised a mobile, wheeled cart in which bowmen could be pushed closer to the enemy under protection from arrows fired by their opponents. Leonardo da Vinci left records in his notebooks of his suggestions for an equivalent machine. These early propositions suffered from two significant disadvantages, though mobile they were cumbersome and they depended on the muscular effort of a crew of men who were at least equivalent in number to the bowmen to make progress. In simple terms, as an equipment for mobile warfare, they were none starters.

Come the Great War technology had moved on, the internal combustion engine had arrived and was used in various haulage applications, including continuous track drive systems for heavy work and agricultural tasks on adverse terrain. The proposal to develop a 'land ship' came to the attention of that energetic, maverick politician Winston Churchill and before you can say "Attention this day" Britain was leading the field to invent a vehicle by combining tracks, armour and engines with a gun or two for good measure. In the light-hearted way the military has with these things they were developed at the instigation of the Admiralty under the cover of a project for the Russian Army to transport water, hence 'tank'.

The development of this machine was by no means straightforward; carried out under the pressure of events and casualties on the Western Front. Companies, their design teams, production engineers and the specialised tradesmen all had to find solutions to a range of new problems for this innovative equipment, without the assistance of computers. Enter the armchair critic, again equipped with hindsight and preconceptions, "Ah," say the critics, "obviously the generals got it wrong, they should have thought of the problem and the solution before battle commenced." Well perhaps they should but if that is the case what were the generals in Germany and France doing? It really is very unrealistic to point fingers of accusation at the generals of the British Army without acknowledging that others much more concerned with large force, high intensity conflict had also failed to get to grips with the problem, before the first shot was fired.

In the end it was the British Army and its commanders who sought, found and introduced to the battlefield an innovative machine, incorporated it into their order of battle and devised ways to supply, maintain and use the new weapon.

The received wisdom is that the British command structure, rooted in its affection for horses, rejected innovation and when forced into accepting new equipment wasted and misused the opportunities so created. The examples above suggest that this is not the case. Rather it seems more probable that those looking for scapegoats are prepared to overlook the complications that accrue when an impasse is reached for which the solution is innovative. Think again about the difficulties of ensuring that the use of gas as a weapon of war was effective.

The general outcome of reading and analysis of information on the use and development of new technology is that when a system was seen to be realistic and effective the generals would take it into use and make the most of the advantages provided. The point of failure or neglect in technology terms is, I think, to be found in the low technology aspects of life, in particular the support and care of the soldiers in the line. Much more should have been done to make conditions bearable in the trenches. Primus type cookers available at platoon level to ensure that a hot drink and basic meal, such as a stew, could be supplied during the day; waterproof wrap over sleeping covers; prefabricated trench support and footway systems; grappling iron systems attached to hand operated winches to pull away enemy wiring systems, all these and many more would have made the life of Thomas Atkins that little more bearable.

From whichever way the issues are considered, the front line soldiers in the fighting zone, and his officers, had conditions in which to operate several degrees of magnitude worse than any rear area soldier of whatever rank and nothing should be too good for those whose task it is to prevail against the enemy in the name of the sovereign.

CHAPTER 5

Military Considerations, Reconnaissance

Attention now has to be paid to the nature of war. The armed forces of Britain once committed to war by Parliament are required to win the conflict. Nothing can be more misguided than to ignore this fundamental obligation that the military takes on when war arrives. The utter defeat of the enemy using all the resources the state makes available is the task. Nothing else will do, there are no prizes at all for coming second. When making this position clear there must be acceptance that the term winning includes participation as a partner in a winning alliance. Victory does not always need to be achieved on the basis of single nation combat, although that is a situation with which the British forces are not unfamiliar. In this comment I have assumed for the sake of charity that writers and historians were too polite to frighten their readers with the hard fact that military adventure is about winning, no more, no less. Military writers probably do not wish to look foolish by stating what to them is too obvious to require repetition. Civilian and academic writers seem reticent, avoiding this essential requirement of a military dimension to events. Unable maybe to confront their own consciences and realise that although they must be free to criticise, it was not they who faced demanding and dangerous decisions, day in day out, twenty-four hours a day for weeks on end. Decisions that the commanders knew would cause the deaths of many, including their friends. Several senior British officers, and the Prime Minister Asquith as well, had to come to terms with the death of one of their sons as part of the toll of casualties.

Historically speaking wars have the tendency to provide surprises for the participants. The eponymous Captain Jenkins must have been surprised to find the nation at war over his amputated ear. (Statements of the blindingly obvious are the admitted mark of a writer who is a desperate beginner.) Even for those who have made some plans and preparations, events during a period of conflict have a nasty trick of producing an unexpected sequence of events or requirements. The Government of Britain under Mr Asquith was profoundly shocked by the sequence of events. The whole fabric of their defence and foreign policies was destroyed by the escalation of event from a nasty spat in the Balkans into a full blown European war, all in a few weeks.

Essentially the issue is summed up in the previously quoted dictum, 'We make war as we must, not as we would'. Both Wellington and Kitchener are credited with this aphorism. General von Clausewitz made the second point of note when he reminded the German General Staff that, 'No plan survives the first contact with the enemy'; one of the certainties of war, is that it is uncertain; another is that casualties will be suffered. Two or more parties, nations or alliances are engaged in armed conflict with the specific objective of imposing a particular policy, ideology or practice on another, or defending themselves from such an imposition. One party or the other has to be victorious; each must therefore create conditions that will put their enemy at a disadvantage of such severity that defeat must inevitably follow.

In retrospect the impression given by contemporary accounts of the incidents of the day in Sarejvo were not recognised as a moment of significance, the spark that would ignite the European powder keg. Austria/Hungary could have another local dispute with the Serbians, though that would be nothing new. Then Willie handed over the 'so called' blank cheque to the Austrians and the fat was in the fire. Effectively Germany agreed to underwrite any risk that the Austrians took to seek satisfaction for their grievances following the assassination of Franz Ferdinand, however unreasonable the demand. Suddenly after a state funeral, Europe was looking into the abyss of war. Russia went for partial mobilisation as a 'precaution', Germany let Russia get ahead by a few hours, before putting the full mobilisation plan of German forces into effect. France joined the rush and Britain sent her fleet to its war station at Scapa Flow. The fleet had actually got together for one of its periodic parties, alternatively known as a review. Winston Churchill (First Lord of the Admiralty) was then able to get ahead of the game by telling the admirals to put the party hats and fancy dress back in the locker and prepare for war. The army left for France and the Foreign Office rolled up the maps and put the lights out, on the instructions of Sir Edward Grey, Foreign Secretary.

Mobilisation is the arrangement of the armed forces of a nation to institute a plan of attack or resist such an incursion. This means in very simple terms calling on all the trained reserves of manpower to supplement the existing embodied force, providing all the equipment needed to sustain the planned operation and moving the formed units to their war stations; all to be done in a few days. In the case of Germany there was a complicated plan using the national railway system on a precise timetable to move the army to the prearranged positions preparatory to opening the offensive against France, Belgium and Russia. The essential to grasp at this point is that although mobilisation is serious, it is not of itself, war. War requires further steps, a declaration, serious shooting, which could be at sea, and/or invasion of territory to cite a few. In theory at least, two opposing mobilised armies could face each other for years without firing a shot.

In the 1870/71 Franco Prussian War, one contributing factor in the French defeat was poor supply arrangements. The lesson was not lost on the military establishment of either nation as well as others who observed the events. The Germans further refined their supply arrangement and built large parts of their railway system specifically to supply and transport their army at war in Europe. The French made vast improvements to their supply arrangements as well. Both of these nations were clearly anticipating the possibility of a conflict to come. This they could see would be fought on the old battleground of northern Europe, using short and secure lines of communication. Armies organised for war on this basis have the luxury of planning their operations on a generous scale of supplies. This is in marked contrast to those armies operating with extended supply lines over territory with only minimal road and rail facilities and sometimes dependent on supplies travelling by ship as well; the common condition under which the British Army served with its worldwide commitments.

Supplies, the perennial dilemma, for the British Army; successive governments of Britain and their 'bean counters' at the Treasury have always had difficulty understanding the use of equipment and supplies in times of war. It seems inconceivable that after so many conflicts in all four corners of the globe that the British Army always ends up with inadequate equipment and supplies. Soldiers are just cannon fodder if they cannot use their weapons. It took just twelve weeks of war in 1914 to reduce the artillery to an allocation of four rounds per gun, per day. Soldiers on active service also need every piece of their kit in reserve: socks, towels, soap, shirts, boots, etc. all have to be available on demand, not next week when the Pickford's van comes by. To say nothing of the daily demand for ammunition, food, and in 1914-18, fodder for the numerous animals, all forming part of the army's establishment. Equipment scales as discussed earlier reflect the defence policies set for the army prior to the conflict. The Imperial Police role required of the British Army was not an ideal preparation for a continental European war. By way of example consider for a moment the criticism made that British infantry battalions began the 1914 war, established for only two of the Vickers .303 Medium Machine Guns (MMGs). Both the British and German armies nominally deployed two guns per battalion. The German Army in 1914 concentrated its MMGs in a company of eight weapons per regiment of four battalions (the equivalent of a brigade in the organisation of the British Army). These weapons, introduced from 1908, were some of the first battle worthy automatic weapons available for infantry use. This was a weapon for defence, as explained below. The man portable light machine gun, the Lewis, was not to become available for general use by infantry battalions until 1916.

The MMG itself is not easily moved; manhandling over any significant distance required the gun to be broken down into three loads. The barrel/water jacket and breech mechanism weighing about 45lb (20kg) can be carried by one soldier. The mounting tripod, weighing about 30lb (13.5kg), carried by a second man and the one gallon cans of water necessary to provide cooling for the barrel during firing, hoses and ready use ammunition by a third. Only for a short distance is this practicable. Then of course the gun has to be reassembled, coupled to its cooling water cans, loaded, aimed and firing commenced. All whilst the enemy sits and watches, in all probability the said audience will bring down a steady drizzle of rifle fire, not applause. For the more remote corners of the imperial estate two weapons of this description were valuable additions to the offensive capacity of the battalions. More, and the supply overload was probably too great. The 'Home Army' could have accepted a more liberal scale of equipment. That would have financial implications, for which political will was needed.

The cyclical rate of fire of the Vickers was 500 rounds per minute. Normal rate of fire was 250 rounds (one belt) per minute. Two such weapons could require a thousand rounds a minute, for a continuous fire tasks. Every last round of which has to be brought to the firing position, by somebody, from somewhere at the rear. Not an easy task in a benighted corner of the Hindu Kush. When the supply line is well served by transport facilities and good roads such ammunition consumption can be contemplated. If though the supply train depends on bullock carts, mules and pack horses over rocky, muddy tracks, which is also bringing up rations, replacement boots and spare weapons, different assessments are made.

Supplies (now known as logistics) were to become a recurrent nightmare for the infantry soldier of the 1914–18 conflict. The only way front line soldiers could be supplied was by the unrecognised efforts of working parties, usually found from the battalions in reserve who had just completed a stint in the line. It was they who carried food and supplies forward through the trench system at night to their fellow soldiers. This task done against a background of mortar and machine gun activity, artillery fire put down to disturb planned reliefs and re-supply efforts and the sheer misery of carrying forty or fifty pounds of supplies in sandbags, through mud, in the dark, filth and disorder created by trench warfare. This was the only way this essential task could be undertaken.

The armies mobilised and moved to the start lines, the world held its breath but not for long, the Napoleonic dictum 'march divided fight united' was adapted by the complicated plans of the German General Staff's interpretation of Schlieffen's master plan. Developed as a plan to make the most of the element of surprise by a march through neutral Belgium and the speed with which this initial phase would be achieved: would that the reality of events as they were accomplished were as straightforward as the concept. Concentration was the second essential ingredient of the plan after surprise. In this scheme for German success, the weight of the action would be on the right of their advance. Allowing the German force to march through Belgium across northern France, then swing to the west of Paris and trap the French Armies between this advance and a second advancing German force, deployed originally as a blocking force, to defeat a French advance through Alsace and Lorraine; the classic hammer and anvil offensive. This plan needed the German force in the north to be successful quickly, and the blocking force not only containing but also forcing the French advance through Alsace into retreat. This created two competing requirements for the German Army, the concentration of fighting resources and supplies. The German plan hoped to make a virtue out of this situation and incorporated the idea of a 'revolving door' into the scheme. Essentially this would mean the French using too many resources in the east, Alsace and Lorraine, allowing German efforts to the north in Belgium to gain the benefits of surprise and speed. Neat thinking but did the good Field Marshal Schlieffen have a word with the Belgian and French generals to explain the part they were expected to play? I think not. Re-enter our friend Murphy.

The French Army stayed a few kilometres west of their border with Germany during the early days of August 1914. The Austrians had already had a poke at the Serbians and come away with a bloody nose. The Russians put their team together faster than anticipated and the Germans swept into Belgium and Northern France. The BEF (British Expeditionary Force) made its way, by cross channel ferry, to the northern flank of the Allied line and found itself once again on the familiar territory over which many of its previous campaigns had been fought by regimental ancestors. The Belgian Army, outnumbered, fought tenaciously, with the BEF on its eastern (right) flank retreating towards Ypres and the channel coast, fighting all the way. The German Army, high on early success, was delayed and deflected from the plan brought by Willie from Herr Schiefflen as a consequence of the combined efforts of these two forces and a shortage of supplies. The French despatched their army into the ceded territories of Alsace/Lorraine to implement Plan XVII, their campaign plan, and were severely mauled. Falling back towards Paris and the River Marne and exposing the British right flank to danger.

Fortunately the deflection of the German advance and the decision of the German commander, von Kluge, to follow a line of advance east of Paris exposed the flank of his own forces and the Governor of Paris, a perceptive old soldier, General Gallieni, scraped together a force of sufficient size and sent much of it in a fleet of Parisian taxis, with their meters running, to take advantage of this mistake, saved the day and prevented a repetition of 1871. This forced the German to battle on Allied terms in the first Battle of the Marne.

The German commander, General Helmuth von Moltke (the younger), was dismissed and replaced by General Erich von Falkenhayn, the Minister of War, on 14 September, six weeks only after the outbreak of this unnecessary war. Von Moltke was the nephew of the victorious Prussian commander of the same name in the 1871 'set to' against France, hence 'the younger'.

The German High Command now faced a situation for which it was unprepared. The Western Allies were undefeated and showing serious signs of continuing the fighting. In the east the Austrians had had a few inconclusive scraps with the opposition, the Russians remaining unbeaten. Willie ought to have been appalled; there was no Plan B. This was war on two fronts, plus a full-scale naval blockade by the Royal Navy. The late Otto, Prince Bismarck was vindicated, to the last detail. The British Army had been launched on a European war for which it had not been organised, trained or equipped in recent times, now it had to make the best of the situation to provide the successful outcome required by the political leadership. One major issue for any small army that has to undertake a large scale operation is that it is a one shot campaign. Unless there is the desired outcome in the first engagements there are few if any reserves that the army can use to mount repeat actions and offensives against the enemy, so it was for Britain. The campaign was to be over by Christmas, claimed popular sentiment; the commanders knew they could not sustain a long campaign with the existing forces. Few reserves either of men or equipment were available to the field army. The planning and financing of the pre-war force did not match the circumstances faced by commanders and the army when war was thrust upon them. As the poet observed of another military adventure, 'Someone had blundered.'

The French Army went to war in 1914 with more than fifty divisions; the Germans, eighty in the west, and more deployed on the Eastern Front. The British Army deployed five infantry divisions and one cavalry division in August 1914. If every depot/cadre battalion in Britain and Ireland had been incorporated into war establishment divisions the total would still only have been seven divisions of infantry and at most three of cavalry. The recall of every battalion from its overseas station would not have doubled the size of the available force and time was not on the side of such a re-deployment.

There is also the issue of practicality. In addition to the infantry battalions of a division, there are the troops who form the divisional regiment of Artillery, another of Engineers, Service and Ordnance units as well as medical and veterinary services and other support services such as pioneers and military police. The problem is not confined to the available weapons and manpower. There is the need for transport and tents, horses and harness, rations and fodder, and almost anything else you can think of in quantities not previously imagined, because the army will need it. None of which had been incorporated into the provisions of the military or their political masters on a scale that matched the needs of the war that broke out in August 1914.

Above all there is an overwhelming need for manpower, trained, experienced, fit and available. The ex-warrant officer urgently needed for training new recruits who is farming in New Zealand is no use at all in the short term. The same goes for every other rank, including generals.

A division at war establishment in 1914 totalled around 16,500 men, of whom the fighting infantry totalled 7,800 in round figures. (There will always be a shortfall through sickness, injury, training etc.) To this must be added the gunners and engineers who are also classed as 'combatant arms'. Put in simple terms, every fighting soldier needs the support of one other on the divisional strength to undertake his role effectively. That ratio takes no account of the troops who form the line of communications, supply depots, hospitals, railway operating units, pay and record units, mobile bakeries, laundries, hygiene units and so on. Total war has an insatiable demand for men, money and material. When the first movements of the 1914 campaign failed to produce a winner in the enclosure to grandstand the crowd, the alternatives became fewer and less attractive as time passed, whilst the demands increased on an exponential scale. Virtually all of the enthusiastic volunteers of 1914/15 had to be trained from scratch in every aspect of military affairs, whatever the branch of the army to which they were assigned.

Once the first phase of the war was completed the relative military positions could be evaluated. The Germans had not achieved their objective and could from one standpoint be said to be in the least satisfactory situation with war on two fronts. On the other hand the German Army had invaded and now occupied virtually all of Belgium and a significant slice of Northern France. Additionally with her ally Austria/Hungary, Germany had dealt the Russians a thoroughly good beating on the Eastern Front; in all for the Germans a negotiating position of some strength. Their army despite losses, was confident and aggressively positioned to pursue campaigns that could deliver Willie the victory he so desired. The French Army had lost badly in the opening moves and battles of the war in Alsace and Lorraine, over 300,000 casualties, including 20% of the regular officers, in the first few weeks of the conflict. It was though in a position to draw upon reserves of colonial troops and was also fighting on home ground.

The British Army was seriously depleted, digging into all its reserves, bringing battalions from overseas postings, mobilising portions of the Indian Army to fight in Europe and looking to the Territorial Forces for replacements of all ranks, before committing the Territorial units as formed battalions and divisions. The Minister of War (Kitchener) is reported to have had a low opinion of the volunteer Territorial Forces and had to be persuaded by necessity and events to deploy the units in France from March 1915. A small number of Territorial battalions were deployed in the autumn of 1914 and some, mainly from the West Country, were sent as relief for the regular units in overseas postings now required for service in France. However, as in the past, when Britain fought a continental war, not one single acre of British ground had been conceded, the national integrity was intact; Britain, if it so wished, could walk away from the war and have no more to do with the land actions. That was a viable military option but politically untenable.

Almost by chance in the four years leading to the outbreak of war in 1914, the initiative was taken by a British general on the make, Major General Henry Wilson, later Field Marshal, by all accounts a schemer and Francophile, but on the evidence, a superb staff officer. With few resources and it seems even less authority, he prepared the brilliant plan used in 1914 to mobilise and deploy the BEF to its war position on the left flank of the French armies, thank heavens for the mavericks.

Criticism of the army's preparation for a continental war needs to focus on the apparent lack of planning for the expansion of the army to meet the requirements of a continental war. The dilemma faced by both government and military planners was that to provide an army with a European defence dimension would require a two part force, one for the Empire and one for Europe. Nobody it seems was willing to grasp that nettle. Although the politicians were not making funds available for actual increases to the establishment, detaching six or eight bright younger officers in twelve month stints to prepare the blueprints for a rapid increase in strength was an essential, and low cost, responsibility the War Office failed to undertake. The governments of the ten years prior to the events of 1914 allowed the nation to sleep walk its way to Armageddon. The possible solution of up to sixteen British based divisions formed, trained and equipped for a war in Europe would have been too awful to contemplate. In particular this would mean the navy would have had to do without some of its big ships to help finance the army's expansion. The navy though was the darling of the nation, whilst Thomas Atkins needed to kept in his place until, that is, there was 'trouble in the wind' and 'the troopers on the tide'.

These defects meant that the enthusiasm of the volunteers of 1914 was degraded by the poor conditions they found waiting for them. Living in tents without uniforms or equipment under instruction from cadres of elderly reservists, the surprise is that their morale held together at all. Additionally no serious enquiry had been instituted to establish how national manufacturing and economic resources could be brought into action to equip and accommodate the expanded army. When this omission is added to the poor appreciation of the methods that would be used to fight a major European land war, the outline of the bleak conditions that Kitchener and the generals were to face in August 1914 begin to fall into place.

The commanders who faced the need to fight the war with Germany picked up the pieces with which they were presented and made war as best they could with the components available. The shortcomings with which they were faced were not of their making, the mistakes had been accumulating for three decades and more, Robertson, French, Haig, *et al*, are the names laid out in the history books for criticism, these were the fall guys who did their duty: to wage war, trust the fighting qualities of their armies and with their Allies win the war.

Odd that the critics are very strong on Allied, and in particular, British defects and failures but nip smartly round the need for comment on the eventual outcome; that the Allies, having recovered from the early reverses, were victorious. The Germans and Austrians who engineered events to achieve their own objectives were defeated, in both military and political terms. I will repeat that in case anyone missed it the first time; the Central Powers, whose responsibility it was for setting the whole miserable train of events going, then lost the war? Remember that inconvenient reality the next time a commentator spouts the received wisdom of waste and failure.

The issues for all the participant armies now reverted to the classic requirements of military doctrine; definition of the objective, concentration of effort, surprise, maintenance of the initiative, economy of resources, reinforcement of success. Easily said, but solving the issues of what to be done and how to focus the attention and minds of some very experienced soldiers and politicians as realism dawned and winter drew in on the Western Front; revealing through the fog of war an untidy placement of armies, ill equipped for the position in which they found themselves, dug into trenches as protection from artillery and machine gun fire; to say nothing of political cross fire of a different variety. A complicated debate that continues to this day.

The greatest enigma that occurs to me from my superficial amateur analysis of the events of the summer of 1914 is quite simply put. What on earth possessed Willie, the German High Command and the nation at large to initiate a strategy to which such colossal risks were associated? The price of failure was always going to be enormous, militarily, economically and politically. Yet ahead the German nation went. It makes the 'Charge of the Light Brigade' appear to be a well planned and brilliantly executed action. Was this war of 1914, ostensibly a war against France and Russia, in reality a means of drawing the real enemy, Britain, into a major European conflict? If it was, then the stakes were raised to stratospheric heights.

Britain's Army was by continental standards a 'contemptible little army', but it had a lot of fighting experience, and above all made a culture of the use of high quality small arms (rifle) fire. These attributes coupled with a nasty habit of coming through on the rails at the last minute and winning the battle that mattered, the last one. Any half decent bookmaker would think long and hard about the odds he would offer on the outcome of a campaign which would include the British Army.

One aspect of the British Army that attracted unfavourable comment from, it is alleged, the German High Command, was to the effect that it was 'an army of lions lead by donkeys'. Some considerable effort has been made over past years to attribute this quotation to a particular source, to no effect unfortunately. The sentiment has however been picked up and adopted by the armchair critics to prop up their prejudices and condemn the casualties sustained. Superficially the comment has some attractions, but what of the French whose casualties amounted to 5.6 million, killed and wounded, Germany six million, Britain and her imperial partners by comparison, three million. More detailed thought on this vexed question will follow in Chapter 9.

At this point in the review it is worth putting the question, who were the guilty men of the 1914–18 nightmare? Nothing is as it seems; beware the glib, the censorious, and the politically expedient comments. The real issues have been buried by three generations of propaganda and axe grinding.

Now on to some further complications to confront the platitudinous pundits' preconceptions.

CHAPTER 6

Soldiers, Officers, Leadership and Discipline

Soon after beginning an appraisal of the 'Great War' references will be found critical of the British military organisation accused to some greater or lesser degree of compounding the difficulties of fighting the German Army by perpetuating the 'class' system. Separating worthy rankers from officers of dubious merit based only on such criteria as school attended, family background, title, estate or the old favourite, contacts in the 'establishment'. Any attempt to argue that the officers of the regular army prior to the 1914 war were representative of the social structure of the nation would be nonsense, it was not; but as so often in this expedition through the jungle of social myth, all is not as it seems.

As recorded in an earlier section, at the time of the 1801 census from a total population in Britain, the army and militia amounted to a few hundred short of 200,000 from a population of close on eleven million, 1.7%, or thereabouts. Immediately prior to the outbreak of the 1914–18 war the regular army and Territorial Forces totaled half a million from a population over forty-five million 0.14%. These figures can be used to support various contentions, my offering is one culled from the experience of commercial life, simply put it is that any organisation not subject to the pressure of competition will continue to practice its trade in ways with which it is comfortable and meets the demands of the consumer. In this case the consumer was the British government, a customer who was delighted to spend as little as possible on the army or its reform, reforms cost money, always. Defence of the realm was left to the Royal Navy, look at all those lovely big ships the nation provided. The army was marginalised and therefore continued to recruit its soldiers from the dispossessed, the rejects of the population, when the requirements of the new industrial society had been satisfied. Officers came as they had for generations from the nation's gentry, some sons of the newly affluent portion of the commercial and industrial community and from the ranks. For the very simple reason that it had no requirement to change, it could do the job asked of it, in ways found successful in the past. Is this a further example of the defects of a policy that left continental wars to the continentals, until it was too late, almost?

We do have to adjust our focus as well and recall that in the way the British Army was integrated with the social structure of the nation, the army reflected society and attitude; it did not set the pattern. This, in case you wondered, was quite the opposite of the situation that prevailed in Prussian dominated Germany. In the newly created Germany, post 1871, the Prussian Junker style of military attitudes dominated the scene. Young boys and adolescents of the aristocratic families of Prussia and other German states were processed through a network of military schools and academies to supply the officers to meet the needs of the large conscript army. The badge of status for a young cadet officer in the Prussian tradition was the duelling scar, the more visible the better, not a pretty sight. The German Army in the Prussian tradition occupied a position of privilege in the government of the nation, answerable to the Kaiser. Let the elected representatives of the Reichstag think what they like, the army and navy were the personal fiefdom of the Kaiser. For the less privileged men of the nation, there was conscription, the obligation for a majority of each age year to undertake a fixed period of military training of two years, followed by a continuing liability to service in one of the reserves until the age of fifty-five. France was a republic and should have been more egalitarian, but 'L'Affaire Dreyfus' suggests all was not as it should have been. As for Russians and the Austro Hungarians each of these nations had forgotten more about class distinction than the British ever contemplated.

Poor Britain and her army, castigated again as the source of an alleged social injustice when the nations that got Europe into the mess and then lost the bet, had even more reactionary habits, such an embarrassment never gets a mention. If you have a case to argue then accept that there are two sides, at least, to the considerations.

On the issue of 'class' and its place in the events leading up to and during the Great War, this is another minefield of opinion and myth that will explode in the face of the amateur commentator, usually from most unexpected circumstances. Let me demonstrate. The Industrial Revolution created many things; the *'piece de resistance'* of the drama was the introduction of the unique and modernising railway system that dated from the opening of the Liverpool and Manchester Railway in 1829. This was the cutting edge technology of the day. Not an improvement on existing ideas, as for example in the mechanisation of the textile industry. Railways powered by steam engines were wholly new as a means of transportation on land. It was the creation of inspired men such as; the Stephensons, father George and son Robert, Brunel, Crampton, Gooch, Hawthorne and many others. An industry ready to accept the talents of the entrepreneur and the inspired practical men who became the engineers, organisers and controllers; social class and parentage were not an influence, achievement was the key to success. Indeed three General Managers* of the GWR in succession, Potter, Aldington and Pole between 1911 and 1932, each began their career as junior station clerks aged fourteen years. The industry had achieved a life span of eighty-five years only, when war commenced. Yet we find in an account of the operation of the GWR's Swindon works employing 14,000 people that a fourteen-year-old year old boy joining the workforce as an apprentice would be allocated to a trade based on the trade of his father. If Dad was a skilled craftsman, then the son could follow in his footsteps. If, though, Dad was lower in the food chain, a son of his would be trained for a more ordinary job. Why I ask myself, in a new industry such as railways, owing nothing to the past did the old bogy of 'class' find its way into the affairs of the railways. Was there within the cultural ethos of the British, a predisposition to accept a hierarchy in society? A replacement perhaps for the Norman feudal system of administration that collapsed in England in the fourteenth century following the outbreak of plague, the Black Death, that forced landowners into paying wages to labour recruited at annual hiring fairs.

---

* The present day job title equivalent would probably be Chief Executive Officer (CEO). A few years after the Great War, the railway employed more than 85,000 people.

Having made the initial point we now need to look at what in general terms are the roles of the players on the field of battle, the profession of arms including the exercise of command. The British Army has numerous precepts by which it distils the essence of its skills, some are quite unrepeatable and these we will avoid.

What the army could not do in 1914 was to reinvent the wheel and develop a new approach to the command structure, there was no time. The barbarians were at the gates. Wilhelm II, despite being cousin to George V, the reigning King of Britain, would not get back in his box for a couple of years to enable the future ambitions of social scientists to be realised. Willie was playing for real and playing to win in August 1914.

Now to move on; in the list of precepts underlying all officers' training is the dictum that soldiers win battles, generals lose wars. Direct and to the point, Tommy Atkins is not to blame because you as the commander get it wrong, whatever 'it' may be. Secondly, officers are responsible for leadership, warrant and non commissioned officers are responsible for discipline. For confirmation of this distinction ask anyone who has faced the ferocious attention to detail of a Drill Sergeant from one of the Regiments of Foot Guards when a major event is in preparation.

To explain the subtle distinction in the relationship between these two aspects of army life another diversion is needed. The issue of 'orders' and their place in the conduct of affairs need some explanation. There are clear procedures for issuing the instructions to officers and other ranks. At the time under consideration there were variations of practice in different units but the intention was identical. To take an example from the campaign experience to which the British Army was well accustomed, in this case a battalion, 2nd Green Howards (19th Foot), in the North West provinces of India, now part of Pakistan, in 1936. The column reaches the objective for the day's march, halts and makes camp with all round defences, just as the Roman Army did. Within a few minutes the company commanders will receive a message, brief and to the point; COs (lieutenant colonel) order group, 17.00hrs I.O. and T'pt officer to attend, no move before 04.30 hrs. The company commanders, majors, will in turn straightaway issue their own warning order company 'O' group at 17.45 hrs, no move before 04.30hrs.

These simple instructions tell all concerned that the battalion will be continuing to move and has about twelve hours to clean weapons, refuel transport or alternatively feed the animals of the pack train, eat, sleep and pack up for the next stage of the expedition. The instructions for the following day will be brisk and to the point, situation, objective for the operation, axis of advance, disposition of forces, command and communications procedures, attachments and detachments and all the necessary minutiae to accomplish the task set for the formation. The company commanders then at their own 'O' groups pass on the information to their own team of officers, each in turn giving appropriate orders to the sub units of their company.

The army has by this procedure given orders to the officers and men which have the authority of military law. To disobey or fail to undertake an instruction given at such proceedings is an offence under military law for which the consequences following conviction by court martial can be extremely severe. There is then a second communication system through the battalion. This is how it works, after the colonel's 'O' group the Regimental Sergeant Major (RSM) will be told by the CO of the substance of the following day's operation. The CO may well then go on to say to the RSM something along these lines, "Mr Green some of the field craft looked slipshod today, have a word with your sarn't majors will you and get them to work with the sarnt's and section corporals to get a grip on the slackers, officers can't be everywhere you know and I will not accept casualties if the cause is careless soldiering. Also, keep your eye open for the good corporals and encourage them. If this chap Hitler goes on as he is doing now, we shall be back in France again and you know that means we shall need all the well trained NCOs we can lay our hands on."

The task has been set, orders given and the need for discipline reinforced. Nowhere in a conventional manual on management theory will you find a similar system, but it works. All the above is a possible scenario and is much abbreviated, but the outline is a valid description of how things were organised. Although the events above were after the Great War the model is relevant to the discussion. The officers did one part of the task, the warrant and non commissioned officers undertook the second portion of the responsibilities and together the army fulfilled its role. There is a continual undercurrent of criticism directed at the army that went to war in 1914 to the effect that it would have been better 'managed' if more 'other ranks' had become officers. I have great doubts about this proposition; a soldier who rose through the ranks to warrant officer became a person of significant consequence in his unit whose experience and opinion is recognised by his officers: to transpose him on promotion, to that of a junior officer in a different unit, is a significant cultural shock. Junior officers aged between nineteen and twenty-four are needed in units for their enthusiasm, daring and sense of adventure, that is what many young men are good at and soldiers expect it of them. A warrant officer of the time would have been at least thirty years old and out of his depth as a carefree spirit, looking for trouble.

The core of the difference between the methods of the army and civilian activities, finds expression and emphasis in the expression 'The Military Imperative'; there is no room for compromise when the order is given in terms such as: "The battalion will advance and capture point 142 by 08.00hrs on 12 February." That is the task for the unit within the overall operation. The objective will be achieved, casualties are a secondary consideration.

After the confusion of the first few weeks of the war, the army had to make emergency arrangements for the recruitment of officers and NCOs. Reservists reporting after the first few weeks, usually when they reached Britain from some distant part of the world, were combed for talent; the Officer Cadet Training Units of universities, the territorial and special reserve battalions, all had to give up valuable trained or part trained men to fill the ranks in France as well as supplying the cadre needed to train the units of Kitchener's new armies. The dilemma remained as ever when resources are scarce, do you use a good sergeant as a sergeant major, or promote him to be an officer and accept that he must be retrained to do his new role adequately before he is of use to the organisation. This is another example of the penalty that the nation paid for running its army at a minimum manning level. Pragmatic solution to the problem, as practiced, promote the man to sergeant major and tell him that if he makes a good job of training the new recruits and his junior NCOs he will be given the opportunity for promotion to commissioned rank which as I have commented above was not always an easy transition.

To restate the situation in the decades prior to August 1914, the army had not sought recruits with education; it took what it could get and then trained the men to be soldiers of outstanding quality. After twelve or so years in the ranks, a worthwhile soldier could be suitable for promotion to warrant officer rank and capable of maintaining the discipline of his company. Such a soldier in his progress through the ranks will have become a complete expert in the minutiae of fighting, no detail of surviving under fire and giving the enemy a hard time will have been too small to have escaped his attention. All this skill will have been used to train the soldiers who are his responsibility in a regular unit. In a similar manner a subaltern joining from Sandhurst (Royal Military Academy) would, by the time he was thirty-two, have gained the experience to command a company. An officer suited to this level of responsibility would have acquired the skills to control the tactical operations of his command, understand the role of artillery fire control, field engineering, staff work to feed and supply his men and more besides. Most important of all he will have acquired the skill to put himself in the place of the enemy and therefore develop his tactics to defeat the foe.

Whatever the armchair experts might think officers have a different role to the warrant and NCO ranks, their tasks are though, mutually dependent. No wise officer ignores the advice of a good sergeant major. The impression of so many of the accounts and commentaries on the events of the Great War is that the authors do not want to understand the complexity of fighting a high intensity conflict in the conditions and on the terms presented to the British Army in August 1914 and lasting until November 1918. That little imp of mischief that sits on my shoulder can imagine such veterans of the graduate school of second guessers meeting Caesar in the afterlife and giving him a hard time for defective operations during the Gallic Wars, based on at most one reading, in translation from the original Latin, of the historic literary account of that campaign.

It is difficult to be brief on the social implications of the situation in which the army found itself in August. Suddenly, not only was it recruiting huge numbers from traditional sources and was shocked at the condition of the health and physique of many, it was also taking recruits into the ranks; men who were from the professional, commercial and industrial resources of the nation. The motives and experiences of this second cohort of recruits being as different as chalk from cheese by comparison with traditional recruits, to both the army and this innovative group of recruits there was a profound culture shock, which when you think about it should surprise nobody.

The contrasting roles and attitudes of the officers and the other ranks leads conveniently into one of the other more regular complaints, in particular, generals, of whom a criticism is voiced that such senior officers were never seen by the other ranks; therefore could not understand the conditions in which they were expected to serve. Hmmm, from my small experience, the mere suggestion to Thomas Atkins that a general is to make a visit to the unit was enough to see the doctor inundated with complaints needing immediate treatment, the applications for training courses would soar, as also would the leave requests. In other words, for soldiers to complain that they had not seen the general recently was a pretty uncommon event.

Digressing again, but briefly, to the reaction of Mr. Atkins on learning of the general's intention, the comments that would flow around the dug outs, canteen and billets would all have the same theme. For example; "Bleeding 'ell Chalky 'ave yer seen part one's [orders], the bloody general's doing annuver visit, annuver bloody quarter guard, out of me scratcher [bed] at five o' bleeding clock, an' no 'ot water from the cooks fer shavin' an' more bull fer us in the ranks." The visits of senior officers were not events greeted with unalloyed enthusiasm by Mr Atkins, believe me.

The diary of Capt. F. C. Hitchcock, M.C. 2nd Battalion the Leinster Regiment, 29th Division is a useful point of reference here. The earliest part of his diary covers the period from the middle of May 1915 to early November 1915, the first of his three tours of duty in France, when he served as a subaltern in the front line, records five formal inspections and one unscheduled visit, these in a period of about seven months by the divisional major general or the brigade general. One swallow, as they say, does not make a summer but it seems probable that this pattern of personal encouragement was used as a means to keep in touch with the front line units. Just as a reminder the divisional commander, major general, would be in overall command of twelve infantry battalions, three batteries of artillery, three field companies of engineers, plus, a cavalry detachment, service corps, ordnance and medical services and other smaller formations of specialist troops such as police, vets and the like. For each to be visited, judged, encouraged and advised on a monthly basis, together with all the other requirements of his command responsibilities sets a cracking pace for the diary. A history of the Royal Flying Corps records that prior to the Arras offensive in April 1917 Major General Hugh Trenchard, who was supposed to be confined to bed with a combination of rubella and bronchitis, flew himself, on the day prior to the attack, to visit twelve of his crucial aerial artillery spotting squadrons. I worked for a managing director who reckoned to see his depot managers, of whom there were no more than twenty, at their locations in Britain, once a year.

Taking up this point, the enormous problem with this subject is that so much is recorded it is practicable to cherry pick material to support or disprove virtually any contention. I would suggest however that a complaint by some soldiers that they never saw a general, in support of a claim by a commentator, *post hoc*, of poor generalship is taking things too far. As indeed is the projection of the pattern of visits in one division, to the army in France as a whole.

The diarist cited above, served in a battalion in one of the two wholly regular divisions in France, the other was the Guards division, provides rare insights into how the junior officers whose training and ambition was for service in the army viewed their task. As a young platoon officer he expected to know not just his own men but the remainder of the men in the company, referring to them throughout the diary using their name and the four last digits of their regimental number. In many cases he knew of their homes and families and where other relations were serving. He grieved when his men were killed or injured but without sentiment. The constant theme of his diary was the importance of the task set to beat the German enemy whose actions had caused the war, he and his troops were sharply focused on this aspect of events. The demands of the fighting are recorded and seen as part of the job. Particular distaste is recorded for the effect of the enemy's mortars, aerial darts and the 'minenwerffer' (mortar). Each of these weapons having a missile with a trajectory that fell almost vertically towards the ground and therefore into a trench, which had no overhead protection. Interestingly, the account by Lieutenant (later Captain) Ernst Junger of the German Army, records the same sentiment for the mortar fire of the British. The Germans also had a serious dislike of the British 'Mills' bomb, hand grenade. This aversion came about because unlike the German 'potato masher' grenade which was a blast weapon, the Mills* bomb, with its cast iron case which on explosion produced a nasty shower of shrapnel with a danger range of twenty yards or so (eighteen metres), when treated like a cricket ball could be thrown accurately for up to forty yards; a skill commonly available within the British Army and the imperial contingents who also served in France. The Germans, unused to the game of cricket, were at a disadvantage particularly so when combined with the long wooden handle of the 'potato masher'. The phrase 'it's not cricket', took on a whole new meaning.

It is necessary now to look with some care at the issue of discipline and military law as so often in a discussion it is usually not too long before the issues of military justice and the misconceptions of this issue surface to muddy the waters of sensible argument about military discipline. In an excursion such as this only the most cursory account can be given of the significance of 'military' law in the conduct of the army's affairs, in particular to the importance of 'orders' to the chain of command. Not everything that is done has the authority of an 'order', the technical and administrative procedures by which daily affairs are organised are only orders when specified. Military law is derived from the Army Act passed by Parliament from time to time as required to introduce necessary changes. Included in the legislation is a portion which deals with the enforcement of matters of military discipline and criminal law. It is by means of the Army Act that the concept of the 'military offence' is introduced to the life of serving soldiers. Issues of civil law, tort, probate, divorce, etc. are not within the competence of the army's judicial procedures, members of the military must pursue action for such matters through civil proceedings in the same way as non military personnel.

---

*The British Army adopted the hand grenade known as the 'Mills' bomb in 1915 and used the weapon for about fifty years, there is some doubt though that Mr Mills of Birmingham was the true and original inventor of the device, a very similar item was designed by a Belgian Army officer, Capt Leon Roland, I have not traced the outcome of a court case on the issue.

The first aspect of the authority exercised by the army that everyone should have clear in their minds is that all the requirements of common and statute law relating to criminal conduct, the whole lexicon of crime continues to apply to soldiers, non commissioned officers or officers as it does to civilian equivalents. What is different is the procedure administered under the Army Act, providing that the persons concerned are subject to military law, they are dealt with under the military disciplinary system. As a simple example any member of the army who steals from another soldier or the army itself is dealt with by the army's system of justice. As a matter of information; there is a well established tradition within the army of 'winning' army property by nefarious means either from another unit or from a careless QM, the distinction here is that the acquired goods are applied to the common good of your own unit, not to an individual and the items are of no great consequence, polish, bath plugs, rifle oil were commonly sought items. This activity is not thought to be of significance to the maintenance of good discipline by the powers that be.

The situation can become complicated if, for example, there is an instance of fraud which involves both civilian and military personnel. Additionally a member of the army who commits an offence outside military jurisdiction, car crime perhaps, will unless there are unusual circumstances be dealt with by the civilian courts; though just to confuse things, military personnel driving an army vehicle on military property (an exercise range) could be the cause of a traffic accident and be dealt with by the military authorities for this matter. This just sets the scene and when there are no active hostilities to give the army something to do, great attention is paid to the minutiae of proceedings under the provisions of the Army Act and the strictures of the manual of military law.

There seems to be general acceptance by the public that providing criminal law is applied with justice, army personnel should have the same treatment as their civilian counterparts. The misunderstandings arise out of the requirement that additional responsibilities are required by those persons subject to military law. The Army Act introduces the concept of the 'military offence', something which has no equivalent in civilian life, obedience to orders, the military crimes of mutiny, desertion, cowardice, the casting away of arms, sleeping on sentry duty, striking a superior officer and more besides. There is then the catch all section of the Army Act; when I had something to do with these matters it was section 69. This section allows for military personnel to be charged with the offence 'Conduct prejudicial to good order and military discipline'. A typical charge dealt with under this section, the miscreant having been identified by number, rank and name, could be phrased as follows on the charge sheet (AF [Army Form] 252): "That on the 23rd May 1960 at 2350 hrs outside the NAAFI premises, Anglesey Lines, Catterick Camp, he did urinate on and over the dog 'Bonzo' the property of the Regimental Sergeant Major, using the words 'and that goes for the both of you'". The outcome of such a grave offence when everybody had stopped laughing might not have been too serious. All these requirements are additional to the criminal law and there are penalties for those found guilty; after due process has been completed that could include trial by court martial; reprimands, imprisonment, reduction in seniority and/or rank, dismissal from the army or, until many years after the Great War, execution, usually by firing squad.

The implementation of both the conventional criminal law and these additional responsibilities of military law are dependent on the authority granted by the sovereign to the officers appointed to a commission. The wording of the sovereign's commission specifically provides officers with the authority to require the obedience of those under their command. The soldier on enlistment takes the oath of allegiance and agrees to carry out the orders of his superiors. This is the concept of 'original authority', it is not unique to army officers who can only exercise this delegated responsibility within the military context and for military affairs. Matters such as; entertainments, are outside the scope of this authority, unless and until the activity affects the performance of military duties. Others to whom the sovereign grants this significant responsibility are police officers, judges, magistrates and other like officials; those in other words who have responsibility for the realm and its safety.

The system of military law administered under the provisions of the Army Act is a carefully structured system, regulated by the 'Manual of Military Law'. It allows minor crimes to be dealt with at unit level and is specific of the maximum extent of punishment that can be imposed by unit commanders. There is no such thing as summary justice at the whim of an officer or NCO, the charge can be a whim, the outcome of due process is another matter. The authority of unit commanders to deal with more serious offences are proscribed and limited to forwarding the matter for trial by court martial. There is also provision in the proceedings at unit level allowing an accused soldier to refuse to accept the decision of his unit commander and elect for trial by court martial. A nightmare scenario for a unit adjutant is a number of 'squaddies' returning late to billets drunk as skunks and when apprehended and charged all the accused decide there is nothing to be lost for their misdemeanor by exercising their right for trial by court martial. Little would such miscreants appreciate that the board of a court martial would take serious exception to such time wasting and could well use their additional powers of punishment to teach them a lesson.

The inattention to the precise details of military affairs continues to lead to mistakes which have the result of perpetuating myths of arrogance of attitude by and amongst the officer class. A well known television series included an installment in which a soldier of the 1914–18 war, in full kit and uniform, within the sound of front line action is found wandering by a senior officer. According to the script he was arrested, dealt with summarily and executed by firing squad. Such a representation is a travesty, a soldier in uniform with his rifle, close to the front could not be treated as a deserter, a charge of cowardice was notoriously difficult to sustain and as he was in possession of his rifle he had not cast away his arms, the most likely charge was that 'he was absent from his place of duty'. Another example which made me cross, and unfortunately I did not record the details of the source, was in a novel of the 1939-45 war and has an officer in 1940 reducing a sergeant in a regular battalion of an infantry regiment to the ranks on his say so. Such an action could not occur, the unit adjutant, fearful for his own reputation, would act immediately to quash any such attempt to impose summary retribution. For such punishment there must be a charge brought under the Army Act, dealt with at unit level by the commanding officer. If the commander believes a suitable punishment is beyond his powers, as would be reduction in substantive rank, a court martial must take place, a guilty verdict returned and the punishment awarded by the court including the loss or reduction of substantive rank.

In the context of the Great War, much controversy and incalculable rivers of ink and media time was utilised in a campaign of misinformation during the last twenty years around the 346 military personnel, not all soldiers, who were executed, of 3080 sentences handed down by court martial, for various crimes during the war. There are two very helpful sources of advice on this difficult subject; Gordon Corrigan in *Mud, Blood and Poppycock*, (Chap 8) and the essay by John Peaty (Chap 12) in the collection, *Haig*, edited by Brian Bond and Nigel Cave; both are good starting points, for those who have an interest in taking their knowledge further. Modern day politicians though do not understand the mood within the army of the day when the decision to carry out the death penalty was made. Casually it would appear, under media and campaigning pressure for reasons of expediency, a general pardon for those who did suffer for their crimes was granted.

The crux of the matter is that under military law all ranks of the army are obliged to obey orders. Orders are not a basis for negotiation they are the expressed command of the sovereign and there are penalties for those, who having sworn obedience, do otherwise.

This synopsis of the fabric of military affairs has to consider the issue of leadership and this is the point where I take risks of significance with any sympathy that I have accumulated with the earlier sections of this excursion through this alternative assessment of the Great War. Offering others firm opinions on the scope, style and influence of the talent, or lack of it, referred to as leadership is about as dangerous as Cardinal Wolsey telling the good King Henry VIII that Catherine of Aragon must remain his wife.

Nevertheless duty must be done, here goes. Dictionaries are quite useless, providing anodyne definitions that tread with consummate skill round the issue of what leaders and leadership achieves, so no help there. There has to be a starting point and for the purposes of this analysis consider this suggestion. Leadership is the ability of an individual to influence others to combine and cooperate in the achievement of some common purpose, and in unfavourable circumstances to use reserves of skills and ability to succeed in the common aim in ways which may be to the detriment or personal loss of an individual. The key issues that have to be addressed are the role of an individual working with a group to succeed. The defect of most considerations of this difficult aspect of life is that few, if any, who look at the subject acknowledge that situations demand different repertoires of abilities. As an extreme example of this contention consider Isambard K. Brunel, brilliant engineer, entrepreneur and leader as creator of the original Great Western Railway, accepted as such in this context simply because he had no rival, his leadership depended on his unusual combinations of talents which no one else replicated. There were though, in his personality, elements common to those we expect a leader to demonstrate: enthusiasm, determination, imagination, specialised knowledge and courage, the list goes on. The final attribute quoted is the block against which many stumble, the reckless bravado of those who lead the way into physical danger of any description is of a different character to that of the calculating risk taker of an enterprise, such as Brunel; who could have had common cause with the strategic requirements of Haig's command.

So it was in the British Army of the Great War, the demands for reckless enthusiasm needed by the junior company officers in the trenches were not those needed by Haig as Commander in Chief. There is a difference in the roles fulfilled, generals do not belong in the front line, they get in the way. The German General of the 1939–45 conflict, Erwin Rommel, is often singled out for praise by commentators for his front line leadership in North Africa. In the accounts by German officers of the campaign there are strongly expressed views that Rommel's frequent absence from his headquarters, partying around the Western desert, was very detrimental to the overall direction of the campaign and this, with greatly improved radio communications. Such officers do have to have the courage to stand up for their men and the units to which they belong and prevent them from being over exposed to risk, taken for granted and unfairly treated so far as training, supplies, leave, luxuries and awards are concerned. In fulfilling this role they put themselves at risk, as, although they may not be killed, they can if defeated on such matters be finished professionally, as was Lt. Gen. Horace Smith Dorrian, of whom more later.

The issue of 'The Generals' is at the core of most individual perceptions of the Great War and the issues arising from the conduct of the conflict; almost without exception the myths used by those who comment centre upon 'unthinking waste of life'. Not for one moment should that generalisation go unquestioned. Already we have recognised the consequences of expecting an army of half a million, including reserves plus the part time Territorial Force to expand by a factor of ten at least, the impracticability of the tiny officer pool building this enormous new army, the quantum differences in strategic and tactical concepts and so on and soon. Yet we find criticism of generals on the grounds of their upper class style, names for example; Adrian Carton de Wiart, his family was of Belgian descent by the way, or the honours granted for past service such as Companion of the Bath (CB). If you make the comparison with the German Army there were just as many generals with funny long names, what about, 'von Prittwitz und Graffon'(commander of the German Army on the Eastern Front), and a chest full of orders and decorations? The Prussian enemy loved nothing more than a well decorated chest, very manly. Another who should have known better, pours scorn on generals for the nicknames they attracted claiming the names given demonstrated the contempt in which the officers were held. Nicknames were part of the culture of the day, boys expected to acquire them as well as award them. This particular critic also condemned one corps commander as 'a very stupid man'. Reading between the lines I suspect that this opinion could well be a reflection of the general's lack of enthusiasm for the colonel's proposals. My question is, if the good colonel was so competent, why wasn't he at least a brigadier general at the time? Subsequently he did achieve the rank of major general. After all one of the Bradford brothers reached the rank of brigadier general at the age of twenty-five, having started the war as a lieutenant in the 2nd Battalion the Durham Light Infantry. He was killed in 1917 when on an excursion from his HQ to visit one of his units, a stray shell splinter found its mark!

Once again the critics are matching the selection of facts in support of their preconceptions. An astonishing example of this process is the quote by one historian of the comment of a staff officer, undefined by rank or function, who when viewing the battlefield of Passchendaele is reported to have said "Good lord did we send men to fight in that." The criticism being that the remote staff had no idea what was being asked of the troops. Remember this, if you will, there were many on the staff who quite rightly did not know what was going on on the battlefield. For example an officer on the staff of the Royal Engineers, Railway Staff Corps was in France to run the railway system used by the British Army. He would have had more than enough to do with his responsibilities to be able to find time to get himself up to the front line. If this unknown officer ranks for criticism then his formation, rank and appointment ought to have been quoted.

It is worth reminding ourselves, as we follow the procession of information in this review, of one component to making a good case from an apparently confused mass of detail and material. As a concept of logic an argument must be constructed from the particular to the general. Argument should not proceed from the general to the particular.

The question of leadership as I see it, in particular for the events of the Great War, circulate round the published expectations of individuals, not what was possible in the conditions of the fighting. Some of them, opinion formers who experienced the conflict first hand, such as Blunden, Graves and Sassoon, have the authority of their experience on which to draw. Others, though, deploy arguments that rely on hearsay and selective examples to make their case, usually to dismiss the effect of the leadership exercised by the various ranks within the army, claiming as they do, that in the winning the 'sacrifice was too great'. Their case rests on the flawed concept that lives were wasted. Such reasoning has failed to grasp the fundamental difference of this war. This difference was that winning was an 'at all costs' requirement. For the first time in a hundred years democracy and the independence of nations was at stake. This was no sideshow colonial war in a far off province which if unsuccessful had no significant effect on the nations of Europe; the outcome of the Great War was crucial to the way that the majority of people in Europe would live their lives in the future.

Was the concept of the leadership exercised by the British Army from 1914 to 1918 unsuited to the task? Some leaders certainly will have failed to discharge their obligations adequately but show me any organisation of equal size and complexity and there will be leaders who will be found wanting at critical moments. The difficulty is that trying to define leadership is about as easy as putting your thumb on a blob of mercury; there is nothing there when you lift your thumb. We all know what leadership is and recognise it when we see it, few if any can provide a satisfactory definition. The benefit the army derived from the network structure of ranks and leadership roles described above was that as the tasks unfolded and leaders were found wanting or lost as casualties, others exercised their judgement and initiative and filled the gaps. What is more the leadership of the British Army was an essential part of a winning team.

In the context of the foregoing paragraph there is one enigma that can never be solved now but leaves unanswered questions on which to reflect. In August 1914 the BEF comprising two corps, a total of six divisions, was on its way to France as we know. The C in C was Field Marshal Sir John French, Sir Douglas Haig commanded I Corps and a General Grierson had been given command of II Corps. As the army made its way to the front line our interfering friend Murphy made a contribution to events, Grierson died of a heart attack. A replacement had to be appointed instantly and the choice fell on Lt. Gen. Horace Smith Dorrian; a respected and experienced infantry soldier. Here was Murphy's second chance to make a contribution to the difficulties created by the sudden change of commanders. French disliked Smith Dorrian intensely. Smith Dorrian had succeeded French in the prestigious Aldershot command and promptly revised the training systems and objectives, in particular turning the cavalry units into mounted infantry; anathema to French who was a 'dyed in the wool' lance and sabre cavalryman. French did not forgive and forget and Smith Dorrian in turn was known to have a fiery temper.

As the BEF engaged in the early days of fighting in France, II Corps was competently led and fought well as the pressure of the German advance became more and more acute and the French Army gave ground. II Corps was seriously exposed, Smith Dorrian recognised the danger and with a bold Nelsonian touch reinterpreted the orders of his commander, French, the C in C. II Corps then fought an effective stopping action at Le Cateau, eventually withdrawing to safety, continuing the retreat from Mons.

Field Marshal French was not a happy man but had to leave the errant Smith Dorrian in position as his actions were clearly correct. He did not survive for long however and in the spring of 1915 was transferred to Britain to take up command in East Africa. French was found wanting in due course and was replaced by Haig later in December 1915.

The issue raised by this clash of personalities, because that is what it was, is could Smith Dorrian who had proved he was a competent commander have made a successful army commander under Haig or even challenged Haig for the top slot as C in C?

The French/Smith Dorrian disagreement was a loss to the army and its officer corps which might have been corrected by some imagination. The losses to the officer corps in general revealed in the diary of the Irish Guards, 1st Battalion, records the names and ranks of those killed from the regiment. The losses of junior officers, subalterns and lieutenants as a ratio were one officer for twenty-six other ranks. The establishment ratio of a rifle company for junior officers was one to thirty other ranks. Life was 12.5% more dangerous for junior leaders than it was for other ranks. Officer casualties were numerically fewer than other ranks but as detailed in an earlier section less than 5% of a battalion's combat strength were commissioned officers.

There is however no room for argument with the proposition that all the casualties of the Great War were an appalling and grievous loss to the wealth of the nation. As to the question of necessity my argument in this examination of events is that the Allied governments had no option but to take up arms to defend their societies. Their success depended on leadership just as much as it required *materiel,* finance and the achievement of soldiers to defeat the intention of the Kaiser and the German High Command.

One critic of the Passchendale offensive which was plagued by bad weather was to the effect that when the going got tough in October, Haig should have realised how unpleasant things had become for his troops and called a halt to the operation. The C in C did not have the luxury of this option; the battle had to continue until it was certain that the Germans would not launch an attack against the French lines, whilst Petain was completing the task of rebuilding the army following the mutinies after Neville's failed spring attack. What was the alternative?

Certainly there are no credible ones encountered in the literature I have seen. To sustain the operation in the face of the enemy and the conditions required leadership from the C in C, Haig, through every rank and formation, this was delivered by the men of the day.

At this point there is some value in looking briefly at the rewards for service during the Great War, some seem obvious, others more subtle. In respect of the latter category good unit commanders used the opportunity of training courses to protect and rest both officers and men from the daily effort of life at the front. Four weeks at the corps Bombing School improved the skills available to the unit and eased the strain on the soldier. Regular officers were still being processed through the promotion system and would be posted back to Britain for the appropriate courses. There were also opportunities for postings as instructors at the training schools. Both of these arrangements were rewards as well as the protection of experienced men. Then of course there was leave, local leave in France or an opportunity for a return to 'blighty' for home leave. The granting of leave was of course at the discretion of unit commanders but it was a right and many soldiers were able to return to their homes for a few days. Not surprisingly there were mixed feelings, the contrasts were too significant for complete adjustment to the unthreatening environment of home life. It is worth remembering that one of the complaints made by the soldiers of France who mutinied in 1917 was that leave was an illusion never in practice realised.

Britain also paid her soldiers of all ranks*, not as much as they were worth but paid they were, and, better paid than their French equivalents. There was a small group of officers who were always welcome when one of them arrived at a unit as it rested from front line action. The field cashiers who went round paying out money and cashing cheques, often at no small risk to themselves, they never had a frosty reception.

Then there was promotion, the change in rank was not always an incentive as it usually involved additional duties, but there were advantages as well not just pay. Admission to the sergeants' mess, after life in the ranks was a respectable perk. Morale could be improved in a unit when a recognisably good soldier achieved promotion. Promotion during war

---

(* see Annex 1 for full list of army ranks)

time operations on the scale of the Great War are not at all straightforward but some effort must be made to put the issues on record. The regular army went to war knowing exactly who held what rank and the seniority of that person in his rank, usually by date of promotion but not always. All that had to change, rapidly, as the army expanded. Officers and other ranks of the regular army and recalled reservists had to be promoted quickly to fill vacancies created by casualties and new appointments. Now we get the outcome of making things up as you go along. An officer could be given acting rank, for example from captain to major, and go off and take on responsibilities and serve as a major and he would be employed as such as long as needed. The service in an acting rank though did not count for the purposes of seniority. The demands of the war were such that appointments above the officers' substantive rank were virtually guaranteed. That was for the regular officer establishment including those from the pre war special reserve. Now to the temporary soldiers, officers and other ranks the whole scheme was a bit academic. Their ranks were all temporary and had no regular army seniority attached to them; so far as they were concerned, come the end of the war they were intent on leaving the army, alive and in one piece. They soldiered in the rank required and left after the war some retaining the honorary rank achieved during their war time service. Many regular soldiers were promoted several steps above their substantive rank. Major generals under war time conditions who, when the fuss died down, had to face the possibility of reversion to their regular army rank of lieutenant colonel for example. There was also an *'ad hoc'* system of 'local' rank which was unpaid but required the lucky recipient to do the dirty work of the rank. That is why Corporal Lucas A. M. was discharged on expiry of his service as a member of the Territorial Forces in 1917, during a time when he with the battalion were busy in action on the front line, was on immediate recall to the colours, recommended for promotion to the same rank, but local and unpaid. He quite rightly invited those concerned to visit the taxidermist and continued his service as a private soldier. Ranks, seniority and service are not at all a straightforward subject!

Morale was also one of the essential considerations of the awards and medals system. The morale of the soldier who deserved recognition and the improvement of the unit's self-respect by the recognition of the contribution and bravery of its members. Orders, decorations and medals in itself are an absorbing and intricate subject on which acres of print have been expended; for the purposes of this discussion brevity must be the watchword or else we shall end up with another 50,000 words. Essentially, orders are the ancient chivalric awards in their various degrees or classes awarded by the sovereign for particular and loyal service to the Crown, for the armed forces the Order of the Bath and from 1916 the Order of the British Empire, Military Division, were and remain the mark of distinction for soldiers. These marks of service are not intended to recognise acts of courage although often the service recognised contains continuous requirements for the courage of one's convictions. Courage in the face of the enemy is recognised by the medals awarded for specific acts of gallantry. The system was regularised during the Crimean War and the pre eminent award of the Victoria Cross was instituted, until recently the only award common to all services their officers and other ranks. There were 627 VCs and two second awards, one to a medical officer and the other to a chaplain. For the army, during the war of 1914 to 1918 there was the introduction of two new awards. For officers and warrant officers the Military Cross (MC) was instituted in 1914 and for other ranks the Military Medal (MM) in 1916. These awards supplemented the Distinguished Conduct Medal (DCM) for other ranks and the Distinguished Service Order (DSO) for officers as recognition for gallantry which had been introduced after the Victoria Cross. In all for gallantry the King authorised the award to army recipients of 135,723 medals and more than 48,000 'mentions in dispatches'. Service on campaign was marked by campaign medals with the addition of clasps for special actions or particular years. The three common campaign medals for Western Front service were nicknamed after cartoon characters of the day, 'Pip, Squeak and Wilfred'.

The pre eminent award was then and remains still the Victoria Cross. 'For Valour' was the choice of Her Majesty and the conditions of the warrant of the award have if anything since the inception of the award become more rigorously applied. The young airman who, during a flight back from Germany in 1943 in a badly damaged bomber, crawled onto the wing of the damaged plane with a fire extinguisher to deal with a fire in one of the engines was awarded the Victoria Cross. To which the uninformed, quite rightly would say "I should think so too." Not so the awards committee of the day who expressed serious concern that the airman's bravery was compromised by the self interest of saving his own life. The majority of the 627 awards of the VC during the Great War were posthumous; what of the remainder, the bravest of the brave? Several others died as a consequence of other actions. The award of a VC did not see the soldier treated as a special case and withdrawn from action. Of those who survived the conflict some carried on being soldiers, Gort, Freyberg and Smyth all achieved much in the 1939–45 war. Others became civilians again and made successful careers, one such was a civil engineer who won his award in the final days of the autumn advance to victory in 1918. After leaving the army he eventually established a practice as a consulting civil engineer in the Midlands. Subsequently he was knighted for his services to the construction industry. In his later life he was not always meticulous about wearing his decorations when there was an official function. A custom developed amongst those friends and colleagues who met him regularly at such events. The precaution taken by his friends was to keep their own lesser decorations in the pocket of their suit and only if the respected knight had remembered to wear his decorations would the remainder of the party find the opportunity to put their lesser medals in place on their lapels. (That anecdote was provided by the late George Marsden, served RNVR 1917/18, who was associated professionally with this holder of the VC.) Of the others they appear to have become what they had previously been, Tandy, VC, DCM, a gate keeper at the Triumph motor cycle factory, Garforth VC, War Department Policeman, another Edward Foster VC, a Refuse Collection Supervisor.

The combination of awards, campaign medals and rank enabled the old and bold soldiers to recognise quality when they saw it, the ribbons above the left breast pocket the rank and the regiment or corps told a story and provided fair warning, to those who knew how to read the code, of the discretion that ought to be exercised when dealing with someone unknown. Let me quote an example. The diary of the Medical Officer of the 2nd Battalion, (His Majesty's 23rd of Foot), The Royal Welch Fusiliers,

Captain J. C. Dunn, DSO, MC and Bar, DCM, RAMC, with the campaign medal awarded for service in South Africa during the Boer War, has been a valued source of information. The award that would attract the attention of the regulars of the Welch Fusiliers when he joined the battalion in November 1915 was the Distinguished Conduct Medal (DCM) and the South Africa ribbon. The DCM was the award for bravery for other ranks, but the good doctor was forty-one in 1915, the dates did not make sense, the reason; although qualified as a doctor, Dunn volunteered his services in South Africa as a Yeomanry Trooper, aged twenty-six in 1899. He earned his award during service in the ranks. Later in that war he took an appointment as a civilian surgeon. He would have been received with respect by all ranks of the battalion in 1915 when he joined and would have accorded equal respect to the members of the regiment for whom he was responsible. There was a subtlety in the method which is at odds with most perceptions of military interpersonal relationships, now that's an oxymoron if ever I saw one. The old and bold soldiers of all ranks could read the ribbons on a man's chest and at once recognise the quality of the stranger.

Another with the same pedigree was Major General G. F. Boyd C.M.G., DSO, DCM who commanded 46th Division in the last weeks of the war. He also earned his DCM in South Africa. This example illustrates another valuable lesson. General Boyd was commissioned from the ranks and must have been not only an exceptionally good soldier but also exceptionally lucky. If he commenced the war as a company officer and served in line regiments earning a DSO on the way, clearly there was never a bullet with his name on it. He was able to serve long enough without significant injury to learn the business of command and generalship, others for sure were not as lucky. He understood the military task to a degree that enabled him to lead his division to attack German positions astride the St. Quentin Canal and wrest the Riqueval Bridge from the determined enemy, an achievement of great significance in the advance to victory. Another instance that suggests that all the accusations that the British Army was in thrall to a self serving, introverted military caste was not quite the case when considered in detail. But then any respectable preconception can 'out bid' a decent fact whenever you like.

Finally in this section I would like to turn to the record of one family of four brothers. So far in this review of the Great War I have deliberately avoided detailed consideration of individuals and their contribution to the outcome of events, large or small. I did not know the men concerned and to become consumed with the details of individuals and their talents or defects was not the way I wished to develop my theme. I must plead your tolerance for my limited comments on some historical personalities such as Bismarck, William of Hohenzollern, Gavrilo Princip and their late Majesties Victoria and Edward VII, and some others. It was I think essential to place these and other personalities in their historical context. I make no apology for approaching these luminaries with less than due reverence.

Now to the Brothers Bradford; the family lived mainly in the North East of England, Northumberland and Durham was their home territory. The boys' father was a mining engineer who not only worked in Britain but also abroad, he was by all accounts an extremely tough, hard and unsympathetic man, even by the standards of Victorian England. The boys' mother was the moderating influence; the family was completed by a sister. The eldest son Thomas Andrew, was born in 1886, the second son George Nicholson, was born in 1887, followed by James Barker the third son in 1889, the youngest, Ronald Boys was born in 1889.

The eldest son Thomas had aspirations for a career in the Royal Navy but did not progress beyond the stage of cadet. In 1906 when he was twenty he was commissioned as a second lieutenant in the 4th Battalion the Durham Light Infantry (DLI). In 1914 he was OC 'D' Company as a captain, 1915 saw him in France at the second battle of Ypres during which he was twice mentioned in dispatches. In 1916 he was a major commanding 'A' company of the combined 6th /8th battalions DLI and awarded the DSO, thereafter he served as a staff officer and as an instructor.

The second son George, joined the Royal Navy as a cadet in 1902, commissioned as sub lieutenant, served on HMS Orion in 1916 at the Battle of Jutland, promoted to lieutenant commander 1917, he volunteered for duty on the Zeebrugger raid (see Chap 10) on St George's Day 1918, awarded Victoria Cross, posthumously, gazetted 17th March 1919.

James the third son joined the Northumberland Hussars in 1913 and went to France with the BEF in 1914, commissioned in 1915 as a subaltern in the 18th Battalion of the DLI he became a specialist bombing officer, awarded the MC, he was wounded and died on 14th May 1917.

Finally there was Ronald who also first joined the DLI in 1910 as a territorial soldier. In 1911 he transferred to the Special Reserve before being granted a regular commission in the DLI, 2nd Battalion, in 1914 he also went with the BEF to France. In 1914 he was mentioned in dispatches, in 1915 he was a captain with temporary rank in the appointment of adjutant, first with the 7th and then with the 6th Battalions of the DLI. He then took a staff appointment as brigade major before becoming second in command (2i/c) of the 9th Battalion as a major before promotion as lieutenant colonel (acting rank) as he took emergency command of the combined 6th and 9th Battalion of the DLI. On 25th November 1916 he was gazetted with the award of the Victoria Cross. In 1917 he was promoted brigadier general commanding 186 Infantry Brigade at the age of twenty-five. He was killed on 30th November 1917 when undertaking one of his regular excursions to visit one of his units. He had also been awarded the MC during his service but I have no note of the date.

Four young men, two Victoria Crosses, one Distinguished Service Order, two Military Crosses, a clutch of Mentions and one survivor.

Footnote; the most decorated non commissioned soldier in the British forces was a stretcher bearer, Lance Corporal Coltman VC, DCM and Bar, MM and Bar, 1/6th North Staffordshire Regt.

Dedication.

E. H. Robinson. Esq. DSO, MC and bar, MA.

This portion of the expedition is dedicated to E. H. Robinson. Esq., Headmaster, Moseley Grammar School, Birmingham, 1923-55, previously Major, King's Shropshire Light Infantry; a Kitchener soldier.

The text of the commission issued to an officer newly appointed in 1960, signed by the sovereign and impressed with the seal of the Realm. The archaic wording emphasises the scope of the authority the officer accepts.

Elizabeth R

Elizabeth the Second

by the Grace of God of the United Kingdom of Great Britain and Northern Ireland and Her other Realms and Territories Queen, Head of the Commonwealth, Defender of the Faith. To Our Trusty and well beloved..Greetings

We reposing especial Trust and Confidence in your Loyalty, Courage and Conduct do by these Presents, Constitute and Appoint you to be an Officer in our Land Forces from the ...... day of .... 19... You are therefore carefully and diligently to discharge your Duty as such in the Rank of Second Lieutenant or in such other Rank as We hereafter may from time to time hereafter be pleased to promote or appoint you to, of which a notification will be made in the London Gazette, or in such other manner as may for the time being be prescribed by Us in Council, and you are in such manner and on such occasions as may be prescribed by Us to exercise and well discipline in their duties, such officers, men and women as may be placed under your orders from time to time and use your best endeavours to keep them in good order and discipline.

And We do hereby Command them to Obey you as their superior Officer and you to observe and follow such Orders and Directions as from time to time you shall receive from Us or any superior Officer according to the Rules and Disciplines of War, in pursuance of the Trust reposed in you.

Given at our Court of Saint James's, the ....day of ....19... in the nth Year of Our Reign.

By Her Majesty's Command.

Name,
Rank.

114

CHAPTER 7

Army Organisation and Operations; Advance to Contact

The next necessity in this expedition into the achievements of the British Army during the Great War is to remind ourselves of the structure adopted by the army to undertake its responsibilities. In an earlier portion of the text the establishment of the English Army on a permanent basis after the restoration of the monarchy in 1661 was explained. The fundamental aspect of the change was the introduction of a standing army; an army as a permanent feature of the organisation of the nation, raised, officered and financed to give effect to the policies of the government of the day. Prior to the appearance of Oliver (Olly) Cromwell on the political and military scene English armies had been raised on an *'ad hoc'* basis for defensive or expeditionary purposes, by a similar process the Kings of Scotland put troops in the field. Cromwell changed this cumbersome arrangement that owed its existence to the medieval monarchical government and the earlier feudal system and in Scotland to the Clan system that dominated the nation in the Highlands, north of the country. This arrangement for raising of armies, 'contracted out' responsibility on a feudal basis to the landowning aristocracy, who, dependent on such individual matters as; personal allegiance, health, wealth, age and so on would appear with their 'regiments' of armed followers, who may or may not have been trained as soldiers. This was a handy arrangement for the sovereign who by this means didn't have to stump up and pay for the troops on a regular basis; but it provided absolutely no guarantee as to military fitness for purpose. All this changed with the 'English Revolution'.

The 'standing army' was not the invention of 'Olly' Cromwell. He just knew enough of his classical history to realise that the Romans were on to a good thing. The Army of Rome was, for the period in history that it existed, a 'wonderous' thing. This army was a permanent establishment of trained, uniformed soldiers allocated to membership of identified units, each formation increasing in size by combination of smaller sub units. A command and rank structure to allocate responsibility, promotion on merit and service, standardised equipment, tactics, pay, and for those who survived the fighting and tough service conditions, a pension; often by way of a grant of land in some of the newly conquered provinces. The units of organisation were allocated to specific commanders by rank with defined functions. Infantry and cavalry as the fighting elements, engineers and artillery in support, supply trains, messenger and medical services all deployed to implement the policy of the state, republic or empire, independently of the individual personalities currently holding the reins of power. A senior commander from the Roman Army would have recognised the way in which the British Army of 1914 was organised.

The Roman Army was good enough to conquer, on behalf of the state, a swathe of Western Europe from England's northern border with Scotland, south through Gaul, modern France, to the Mediterranean coastline and westward to colonise the Iberian Peninsula, modern day Spain and Portugal; eastward to the Sea of Galilee in modern Israel, as well as northern Africa and as Shakespeare explained, Cleopatra's Egypt. The extension of the Empire even further east, towards the Persian Gulf, was not altogether successful. In Europe the Germanic tribes to the east of the Rhine rejected the virtues of being conquered by Rome with violence and success. Maybe that is why they ended up with Bismarck and Wilhelm II. This was the army that stayed in business for more than 400 years; a record yet to be equalled.

It is not the function of this review to look at the route by which the English Army of 1661 developed into the organisation that took the field in 1914. There are too many factors and personalities who made contributions to the structure that produced the mobilised army of the Great War to weigh and explain the issues, within these considerations. The need is to understand the organisation that did do the fighting during the period 1914–1918.

First a detail of nomenclature, in these early sections reference has

116

been made at several points to 'the army' or the 'British Army'. These have been used as the generic term for the entire organisation from Chief of the Imperial General Staff (CIGS), as it was titled, to the most junior soldier. Now we need to be more specific in organisational terms for the purpose of command responsibilities, an 'army' is a field formation consisting of a minimum of two Corps, with additional headquarters and army designated formations e.g. heavy artillery, the whole commanded by a full general; a ration strength of approaching 200,000 all ranks. In the portion of this review dealing with organisation and operations the word 'army' will mean this command formation. Here is a suitable moment also to look at the word 'establishment' as it is used in the context of military organisation. Establishment means for this purpose, the authorised numerical strength, detailed rank by rank, of all the units and formations within the army. There are usually two establishment figures, one for conditions of peace time operations, the second when the 'blast of war blows in our ears' and soldiers must be about their business. On mobilisation in 1914 reserves were called to the colours and units went to France at 'war establishment'.

The Commander in Chief of the British forces in France, in 1914 Field Marshal French and subsequently his successor from December 1915, Field Marshal Haig, eventually held responsibility for five full fighting armies plus what is known as Line of Communication troops (L. of C.), railway engine drivers, road builders, prisoner of war guards, field bakeries, mobile bath units, laundries, battlefield clearance units and so on. Additionally he also commanded the Royal Flying Corps (RFC) until the 1st April 1918 when it combined with the Royal Naval Flying Service (RNAS), not commanded by Field Marshal Haig, and became the Royal Air Force (RAF), a new and separate service. A total ration strength in France of over 3,260,000 men and a small number, comparatively, of women, as nurses and drivers.

Now having made these preliminary points we can go back to the beginning and describe the organisation that performed the task of ensuring Mr Atkins citizen, became Thomas Atkins private soldier, and then combining him in teams and formations capable of turning defeat into victory. Tommy exists in various creations, as infantrymen, troopers in the cavalry, gunners, sappers (engineers), drivers, cooks, clerks and so on. To deal with all these manifestations is a task on which we will not embark. Our attentions will be confined to the infantry formation with only passing reference to other soldiers of equal worth.

To become a soldier training is a prerequisite, the profession of arms for war is like no other, men and only men in 1914 had to be trained together to the common aim of defeating the enemy which will mean killing fellow members of the human race, an act that the process of civilisation has rejected in the conduct of social life. It is a culture shock of enormous significance to become a state executioner. To accomplish this role the recruit soldier has to be converted into a committed member of a fellowship of comrades in arms who undertake the hazardous business of war. For this each member needs the utmost confidence that his comrades and commanders can be trusted and in turn they value the efforts and dangers required of the individual soldier.

The training of Kitchener's volunteers in 1914/15 was far from straightforward, everything except the enthusiasm of the recruits was in short supply, officers, NCOs, accommodation, equipment and of course, time. The pre-war recruitment procedures were used to dealing with about 30,000 selected recruits annually, now it had ten times this number in two months. Additionally to the horror of commanders at all levels the physical standard of many of the men who rushed forward for service left a great deal to be desired. The health and physique of many, the products of poor housing, diet and conditions in the industrial cities of Britain had not fitted the volunteers for the extreme physical demands of army life, despite the hard manual work of many. Before anything else the poor physique had to be remedied and that took time of which there was not enough. Once again the unreality of the pre-war governmental defence policy was revealed as hopelessly flawed.

Army training generally falls under one of three broad headings, physical, personal and the all important 'military skill', that is to say field craft, fighting skills and skill at arms. The object of the physical training is to produce soldiers of great stamina, strength is not the same as stamina and when push comes to shove, soldiers must endure and if necessary march their boots off, as many did in the retreat from Mons in 1914.

Some units marched fifty miles, each man carrying his personal kit and rifle and ammunition, in twenty- four hours. The personal requirements a soldier has to learn is the essential of caring for himself in difficult conditions, preserving his weapons, kit and the effects needed to take an equal part with his comrades in the tasks set for his unit, be it his section, his regiment or his army. The equality of contribution is built of many parts not the least of which is the acceptance and obedience of orders, in this aspect of conduct parade drill is an essential element of the training. Then there is skill at arms, the ability to use his fighting equipment to full effect and act in concert with his fellows to defeat the enemy. A trained infantry soldier needed to be able to fire fifteen aimed shots per minute under battle conditions, including the reloading procedure for the incomparable bolt action Short Magazine Lee Enfield (SMLE) .303 rifle. None of these requirements are easily accomplished, for some, one part may be easier than another but to all, it is a challenge the like of which few if any had previous experience.

In 1914/15 what resources the army could scrape together for the training of the volunteers, achieved a result that bore favourable comparison with regular formations and amounted to an achievement equal to the feeding of the five thousand with five loaves and two small fishes.

The smallest recognised unit to which 'Tommy' belongs is the section: eight men including a corporal in command. The step to the substantive rank of corporal, wearing two chevrons on his sleeve as mark of his rank, is significant. This is the point where a regular soldier gets onto the promotion escalator of seniority. Time served in the rank, depending on vacancies, will ensure advancement to the next higher rank. Field Marshal Sir William Robertson (CIGS from 1915) made it from trooper (the equivalent of private in a mounted regiment) to the professional Head of the Army in the rank of Field Marshal. The first step was his advancement to corporal. The corporal may be a lance corporal who is somebody who it is expected will hold, some day, the substantive rank of corporal. Until that time comes he holds the appointment of lance corporal, with one chevron on his sleeve; an appointment confers no permanent seniority within the army. A lance corporal getting himself into a spot of bother over a pint too many can be relieved of his stripe by his commanding officer. A substantive corporal committing the same mistake has to be convicted by court martial, to be punished by reduction to the ranks.

A section lives, together trains together, drinks together and looks out for the errors of each of the comrades that could incur the wrath of the platoon sergeant or someone even more awesome such as the company sergeant major (CSM) or, perish the thought, God's assistant the regimental sergeant major (RSM). Four sections make a platoon, commanded by a 2nd/lieutenant (the most junior officers' rank) four platoons make up the strength of a company when the small company HQ is taken into account. The HQ consists of a major, commanding the company, his second in command, a captain, the CSM, the quartermaster sergeant (CQMS) plus three or four soldiers who have sufficient experience to be jacks of all trades as clerks, store men, messengers etc. A total, if all the company is on parade, of 150. It needs to be said that units are rarely if ever at full established strength. Soldiers take leave, are sent on training courses, break their legs playing football and so on. That however is the establishment of an infantry company. Four such companies, usually identified as A to D, are the fighting strength of an infantry battalion. Added to this is the headquarters and here we find a mixture of soldiers with skills needed to support the men of the other companies. The strength of HQ is divided sharply into non combatant and combatant members. Dealing with the former as a first step because they are straightforward, the 'non combs' are confined to the chaplain (Padre) and by association his clerk, and the medical officer and the orderlies who man the Regimental Aid Post. Their duties are recognised and protected by the Geneva Convention and it must be recorded this protection was generally observed during Western Front operations by all the armies. Stretcher bearers have split functions carrying the wounded under the protection of the Red Cross they are non combatants, also, they are trained soldiers as well and can function in this role, providing they abandon the protecting insignia. In the regular battalions of the army that went to war in 1914, the bandsmen usually doubled as stretcher bearers.

The combatant soldiers of HQ again fall into two groups, those who the battalion hope will fight like demons, the commanding officer, usually of the rank of lieutenant colonel, sometimes as an expedient when the colonel is injured or absent on other duties the battalion commander will be a major, as usually the second in command takes over; the adjutant, a captain, and the regimental sergeant major (RSM), plus the pioneers, the machine gun section, prior to 1916, with its Vickers MMGs and the intelligence officer with his marksmen snipers. The sergeant of pioneers is by tradition the only rank of the army who has approval to wear a beard. All these have vital roles to play in the fighting operations of the battalion. The second portion of HQ company's strength are combatants, if though they are found with rifles engaged on matters of serious intent in the firing line, their comrades will know that desperate measures are needed. These are the soldiers on the strength of the HQ who do all the jobs needed to make things work, transport drivers, in 1914 mainly for horsed transport, cooks, a farrier for the horses, clerks for the orderly room, quartermaster and his team, armourers, an additional 230 soldiers; a battalion strength of 830.

The battalion is at the heart of the fighting organisation of the army, large enough to be allocated tactical objectives of significance in attack or defence, organised to look after its own affairs on a short term basis, large enough to make a difference when used as reinforcement. This is an example of the best of any management situation, a component of an organisation that delivers results. A battalion must however be supplied and receive support in such aspects of warfare as artillery and engineer services, it is of insufficient size to be self sustaining. Regular and reliable replacement of the essentials of the soldier's life must be provided: food, water, ammunition, battle stores such as barbed wire, forage for the horses and more besides. Four battalions were in 1914 therefore combined into a brigade. This formation adds to the fighting effectiveness of the infantry by providing artillery support from a field battery Royal Artillery (RA), engineer support from a field squadron Royal Engineers (RE), signals, transport, medical and stores from units of relevant specialists; as well as lesser units providing police, postal and in 1914, important veterinary services, in total more than 6000 men.

In 1914 the fighting components of the army were the Infantry, Cavalry, Artillery and Engineers, these are known as 'The Arms'; the supporting formations formed the 'Services'. The eventual battlefield conditions in which all the Western Front armies found themselves meant that Cavalry had no means to exploit its traditional role as a mobile and powerful force to overwhelm the enemy. The fighting arms were effectively reduced to three.

The mobilisation plans for a six division expeditionary force prepared in 1913 provided for the deployment of a field army that included the following.

Cavalry Division,	467 officers, 9,412 other ranks, 10,327 horses, 24 guns, 24 machine guns, 582 horse drawn vehicles, 23 motor cars, 18 motor cycles, 371 bicycles.
Six Infantry Divisions.	3,558 officers, 108,342 other ranks, 36,750 horses, 456guns, 144 MMGs, 5,034 horse drawn vehicles, 54 motor cars, 54 motor cycles, 1662 bicycles.
Army troops.	219 officers, 3,847 other ranks 2,285 horses, 2 MMGs. 286 horse drawn vehicles, 24 motor cars, 8 motor vehicles, 35 motor cycles, 48 bicycles.
L. of C*. troops.	34,653 all ranks.

A total when the RFC and nursing staff are included of 166,653 officers and soldiers, 60,638 horses, 492 guns and 190 machine guns. This gives a strength for the infantry division of 18,650 and a brigade strength of 6,216.

It is worth remembering here the importance of horses to transport services in 1914. The British Army's transport services in 1914 were organised into fifty columns using horses and twenty-two using mechanical transport (lorries and tractors). Before anybody raises the usual red herring of reactionary forces at work preventing modernisation, take into account if you will that in 1939 the German Army went to war with all its second

---

* Line of Communication: rear area formations needed to supply the front line units, run hospitals etc.

line units dependent on horsed transport. Only the elite 'Panzer' formations were fully mechanised.

In 1915 the divisional strength had increased to 19,614, but the amount of artillery had remained unchanged. (Gordon Corrigan, *Mud Blood and Poppycock*, Cassell 2003.)

The army formation that was to make the most significant change was the Artillery. The BEF went to war with 492 guns. In November 1918 the British Army in France deployed 6,406 guns of all calibres, a thirteen fold increase.

There were other changes to the fighting organisation of the formations in France as the war progressed, the introduction of the man portable 'Lewis'* machine gun enabled the Medium Machine Gun (MMG) the 'Vickers' to be redeployed, from the infantry battalions and consolidated into a specialist corps, the 'Machine Gun Corps'(MGC). This enabled the battalions to maintain their fire power with the new more manageable weapon and carry it with them during attacks. The specialised unit of the MGC also enabled divisional commanders to deploy the intense fire power of the MMG in concentrations that would enhance the support needed by fighting units for both attack and defence. Contrary to some opinions the MGC was not an easy option for the tired and weary. Overall it suffered four times the casualties sustained by the Royal Engineers, a corps with four times the number of soldiers in its ranks.

The British Army also formed and introduced into the Order of Battle (Orbat) the armoured fighting vehicle (AFV) referred to as the tank, organised eventually into a separate formation, initially designated Heavy Branch, Machine Gun Corps, and in 1917, The Tank Corps. This major weapon was originated by the British Army and, driven by the enthusiasm of Winston Churchill, arrived on the battlefield in September 1916, achieving its first notable success at Cambrai the following year,

---

* As a contribution to this appraisal of the war by a family member, Albert Lucas MM, who fought in France from March 1915 to October 1917, he was not enthusiastic about the Lewis Gun. The mechanism had numerous moving parts and unless kept scrupulously clean would jam, usually at a crucial moment. You try keeping the mud out of the breech of a gun when it's pouring with rain, dark and under fire from the enemy! The 'Bren' (light machine gun) of WW II was a great improvement, he said.

1917; a clear indication of the way ahead. Pause for a moment there, which nation invented the tank and brought it into use? Surely not, Britain, oh yes it was! Not Germany or France who had been considering the requirement of a large scale European war for forty years or more. Somehow it slips the mind of the armchair critics who complain that the machine should have been available when needed by Britain in 1914, that the two opposing armies of northern Europe had not seen the need for such a machine and done something to bring it into operation.

In 1914 the BEF took the aeroplane to war as part of its 'Orbat', four squadrons, forty-eight aeroplanes, plus a few spares, ninety-eight officers and 685 other ranks. The RFC was incorporated into the operational requirements of the BEF to such good effect that by 1st April 1918 it could stand on its own as a fighting arm of the nation and formed with the RNAS, the RAF. The RFC/RAF learnt its trade the hard way, trial and error in every aspect of the tasks allocated to it, reconnaissance, aerial photography, air combat for air defence and bombing to name but a few.

The army also found ways and means to form specialist units for mining, digging tunnels under the trenches of the Germans, filling them with explosive and blowing up sectors of the enemy's fortifications. Units for using chemical (gas) warfare against the German originators of this tactical weapon, mechanising the army transport system, running railways using the expertise available from the management and staff of the companies who operated the railway system in Britain.

Such dramatic changes as are outlined above do not bear the imprint of an organisation moribund and unable to initiate change and innovation. To labour a point the commanders had to find alternatives to the preconceptions of 1914; if only their critics were equally open minded.

At this point we need to give some consideration to the army's organisers, 'the staff'. There is often within the numerous comments and critiques of the Great War an antipathy towards this element of the army. There is a parallel within industry and commerce which bears examination to make a point. Manufacturing and sales functions have an affinity believing that it is their achievement that together keeps others employed. To a large measure they are right; usually however the people who undertake these tasks are unskilled planners, poor purchasing specialists, unimaginative designers, lousy accountants and inferior organisers. All of these functions requiring their own skilled and competent employees; only the pay office is loved by everyone. The unfortunate truth is that there is a symbiotic relationship, each needs the other to survive to enable a viable concern to operate. The same is also true of the armed forces, without organisation the fighting man will fail, his supplies, ammunition, food and yes, his pay, will not arrive when and where needed. The development within the British Army to train officers for staff responsibilities following the Haldane reforms of 1881 had improved the effectiveness of both the staff officers as individuals and the function of staff work within the army as a whole.

It is worth at this point quoting verbatim the view* expressed by Field Marshall Earl Wavell GCB, GCSI, GCIE, CMG, MC, C in C Middle East, August 1940 to July 1941, C in C. India 1941- 1943, Viceroy of India1943-1947; one of Britain's most cerebral soldiers to whose knowledge and judgement I willingly defer.

"The feeling between the regimental officer and the staff officer is as old as the history of fighting. I have been a regimental officer in two minor wars and realised what a poor hand the staff made of things and what a safe and luxurious life they lead; I was a staff officer in the Great War and realized that the staff were worked to the bone to try and keep the regimental officer on the rails; I have been a Higher Commander in one minor and one major war and have sympathized with both staff and regimental officer. Shakespeare's description** in this passage of the fighting officer's view of the popinjays on the staff is extreme, but amusing. Hotspur, by the way, described poetry contemptuously as 'mincing poetry, like the forced gait of a shuffling nag'."   A. P. W.

---

* see, *other men's FLOWERS* Pg 131, an anthology of poetry by Earl Wavell, it is a startlingly varied choice of verse worthy of more attention.
**see, Henry IV, Pt I, Act I, Scene 3.

The answer is, there is no answer, the staff have the responsibility to give effect to the orders and plans of the relevant commanders, orders that usually cause at least inconvenience and often much more, the staff ensure the supplies, ammunition, maps and much else are at the right place at the right time, but in the last analysis the army maxim, 'If you can't take a joke you shouldn't have volunteered' sums up the reality, particularly when combined with the nugget of old soldiers wisdom, 'orders is orders'. British Army staff officers from fighting arms rotated between staff and regimental duties until seniority, usually at the rank of colonel, forced a more 'arms length' relationship. The animosity extended to specialists, some brought direct from their civilian operations to organise and operate docks, railways, workshops and other newly necessary services were understandable. Such men, officers or otherwise, would never see the firing line and would, unless circumstances were exceptional, know where to find their bed when the time came. They were nevertheless essential to the operations in France.

The criticism that can be made of the arrangement for the staff during the Great War is that the differences were too obvious and emphasised to too great an extent. A regimental officer transferred to a staff appointment could not avoid the facts that his personal comfort would improve significantly, suddenly he would have a clean bed, baths on demand more or less, food at regular intervals etc. Remember if you will the envy of the PBI for the Army Service Corps (ASC) personnel who were generally thought to have an easy life, something far from the reality of getting supplies to forward units under fire.

Such considerations were not the essence of the issue in my opinion; it was the insignia of difference that exacerbated the complaint. A captain, in army parlance a company officer, low in the food chain as we would now say. On taking up his new job, suddenly wore on his uniform collar the distinguishing red gorget* patches, universally referred to as 'tabs',

---

*Gorget, originally the part(s) of a suit of armour that protected the throat of the wearer, usually a mounted knight. The British used and still use, the gorget patch as a distinguishing mark, described above, for officers. The German Army retained a metal gorget collar on a chain worn around the neck for their military police until as late as 1945. The military police are by tradition, in any army, even more heartily disliked than the staff.

red bands on his uniform cap and a distinguishing arm band known as a brassard. For specialist staff, tabs and cap bands came in colours other than red, medics, crimson, intelligence, green, others had their own versions and there were more than fifty varieties of the brassard for the numerous formations, HQ's, Arms and Services. Rightly or wrongly these distinguishing marks, however necessary they were thought to be, created a belief that each did not understand the other and the 'Them and Us' attitudes became a source of irritation that the army would have been better without.

Moving on from the animosities of the army's organisation, more serious issues had to be addressed. As the war progressed and the replacement of killed and injured became more problematic organisations were changed, brigades, significantly, were reduced to three battalions instead of four. Fit and able older men in the support services were re-mustered as infantry to provide essential reinforcements from the troops already in France. Frank Aldington was one such; he was reported missing presumed dead in October 1917 as the 3rd Battle of Ypres was drawing to its close, the battle in which Albert Lucas was awarded his MM. The losses were becoming unsustainable and the politicians and commanders knew this. Nevertheless the British Army deployed sixty divisions in November 1918.

Initially in August 1914, it was the peacetime army plus reservists that went to the war, supplemented in the autumn of 1914 with reinforcements from the Indian Army, regular soldiers, every last man, plus a few volunteer Territorial battalions. Available in Britain were the Territorial Forces created out of the Haldane reform in 1908. Earl Kitchener, Minister of War from August 1914, did not favour the deployment of these units to reinforce the depleted ranks of the formations in France. His opinion seems to be summed up by the term 'toy soldiers', which was a slur on the enthusiasm and effort displayed by the young men who had volunteered their service and joined these units. Putting no finer point upon it, it was a mistake to overlook an embodied reserve whose members had experience of the basics of military life, knew how to care for and use their weapons, were already in possession of their equipment and formed into units with officers and NCOs of some experience. All that was required was several weeks of battle training, at the very most and the reserve could take its place in the line of battle and that was what had to happen from March 1915. Soon after this came contingents from other imperial sources, from small beginnings flowed many valuable additions and reinforcements and to whom the memorials stand in France and Belgium alongside those for British regiments.

Then came the units of Kitchener's new armies, the volunteers who rushed to the colours in August and the autumn months of 1914, formed into battalions on numerous criteria the best known of which is certainly the 'Pals', friends who enlisted from the same town (Sheffield, Leeds, Accrington and numerous others), employer (Post Office Rifles for example), same schools (Public Schools Battalion) and common interest (Hull Sportsmen). Getting on for 300,000 volunteers appeared at the recruiting offices and were accepted for service by the end of September 1914. These new service battalions were organised around the established recruiting areas and took the names of regiments famous from the past. The Queen's Regiment (2nd Foot) took responsibility for thirty-one battalions, the Northumberland Fusiliers (5th Foot) fifty-two battalions, Royal Warwickshire Regiment (6th Foot) thirty battalions, and so on through the army list.

The arrangements for these volunteers' incorporation into the army, was and will remain, a prime example of the road to hell being paved with good intentions. The demands on the recruiting procedures for the new army were almost unsustainable in August and September 1914, the volunteers could not be properly equipped, clothed or accommodated. There were insufficient officers and NCOs to train the new units and morale had to be maintained against the odds. The solution was to keep together those who enlisted with a common association such as those listed above. The short term advantage was to maintain the enthusiasm and identity of this innovative type of soldier, the defect was found when the casualty lists were published. Small towns and some not so small, were faced with the loss of too many of their young men in one instalment. Emotionally the loss was too great; the loss to the communities too obvious. Though statistics do not confirm the folklore that a generation was lost to the trench warfare of the Great War, the belief is too strong in the vernacular history of the twentieth century. This opinion is reinforced by the war memorials that stand on public view, mute testimonies to the grief of the families whose names are inscribed and remembered annually with a single poppy leaf. To argue rationally that the losses were not as great as the beliefs established by the mourning of entire communities, is both offensive to the grief of those whose families lost sons, brothers, husbands; and non productive, the losses were the alternative to avoiding the conflict.

Casualties are one of the unpleasant outcomes of war; politicians forget this too easily, commentators never accepted the unpleasant truth that in Britain it is the politician who sends the army to war to fight as they must, not as they would.

Eventually volunteers ran out and after the half hearted Derby Scheme, full scale conscription was introduced in 1916 for adult males, who were medically acceptable, aged between seventeen years and six months and forty years old, with the limitation that active service in France or elsewhere would not be required until the recruit was aged over eighteen years.

In 1918 when the Armistice was declared the army had four distinct components who rubbed along together very well indeed despite their different origins, the remnants of the old regular army from 1914, the Territorial Forces, the volunteer new army and the post 1916 conscripts added to which there were the contingents from the Empire Canada, Australia and so on.

In the end Britain mobilised 8,375,000 from a population of 45,750,000 that is 18.3% (about 36.6% of the male population), France mobilised 8,500,000 (21.8%) of her population (43.6% of adult males) and Germany 13,250,000, 22.0% of the total and 44.0% of the males in the national population. Germany was for three years, until the autumn of 1917, fighting on both the Western Front and in alliance with Austro Hungarian forces in Russia; there are no easily available figures showing the proportion of the German Army on the Eastern Front. The alliance with Austria/Hungary has the corollary of increasing significantly the total numbers available to the German commanders. Equally the armies under British command included contingents from the Empire who are not accounted under the national population of Britain; that was the army that organised the manpower it received to defeat the outrageous ambitions of the Kaiser and his sycophantic, oligarchic government.

Note. The statistics quoted are taken from *Mud, Blood and Poppycock* by Gordon Corrigan who extracted his figures from official sources. The percentage calculation above of the male population mobilised by the combatant nations assumes a 50% male/female distribution between the two sexes; a condition that does not usually apply, females outnumbering males by a small proportion.

Equipment of War

To remind ourselves of the obvious, soldiers – both the individual and the soldier as a member of a unit of the armed force – engaged in fighting has the use of weapons to support his actions. The item concerned may be personal, bows and arrows, rifles etc. or provided by the controlling commander for larger scale effect on the enemy by launching missiles at the enemy. It is not necessary to split hairs about the means by which the enemy forces are damaged by offensive action. It is of no consequence that projectiles in 1914 could be launched over much greater distances than could be achieved by soldiers fighting for, or against, the Roman Army. The principles of weaponry had been around since the times of tribal warfare, personal weapons for the individual enabled soldiers to defend themselves as well as attack and dominate the enemy. At the beginning of organised war, clubs, axes and flint knives were the tools of the trade and in 1914, the rifle and the bayonet were the issue items for the soldier of the day, the purpose was the same. By the same process we have to accept that the boulder launched from a Roman ballista was in comparative terms just as awesome as a 4.5" mortar round in 1914.

Any attempt in this appreciation of the development of weaponry over the centuries is a diversion, others have done better than I and spent years of academic research in the accomplishment of their task. What we have to do is remind ourselves of the relative positions of the arms available to undertake the conflict in 1914.

In the sixty years since the Crimean War the development of weaponry

British gunners firing 18 lb field guns.
Probably in early weeks of the war, no helmets!

Shell dump 18 lb ammunition, Tommy in mixed dress.
Ammunition, meat and drink to a gunner.

ASC Sergeants and Warrant Officers take a break.

Pack horse loaded with trench stores for the front.
Pack horse, the MPV equivalent, 1914–1918.

Troops in a reserve trench, kit off but rifles handy.
Not for the first time, 'hurry up and wait!'

Troops of the Royal Irish Rifles in forward positions.
Mr. Atkins at the sharp end of action.

Tommy in winter quarters, rations up.
No rain, no mud, instead mind numbing cold.

8" howitzers of the Royal Garrison Artillery in action.
Artillery, the battlefield weapon of choice.

had been significant. The rifling of barrels and the breech loading of firearms, both personal and of the artillery, each was a milestone on the road to modern warfare. These changes when associated with the arrival of improved explosive materials such as nitro glycerine, cordite and TNT extended the range of the guns and eliminated the prodigious amount of smoke that resulted when weapons using 'black powder' were discharged. The first of several significant step changes was the introduction of the magazine fed rifle, replacing the musket. Then to put the icing on the cake, the recoil of artillery was tamed by the marriage of hydraulic cylinders to the barrel of the gun as a mechanism to absorb the power of the recoil. Numerous artillery pieces were produced before the Great War began but the French '75' was probably the best light field piece available in 1914. Unfortunately as the war progressed the call went out for bigger and better guns, the '75' with its flat trejectory was obsolescent almost before you could say 'bang'. Artillery in its many manifestations was to become the dominant consideration of the war and account for more British casualties than any other cause.

However in the imagery of those who condemn the manner in which the war was waged, the invention of the automatic machine gun by Hiram Maxim looms overall, creating a shadow, so distorted by legend that almost no sensible discussion can take place on the use, deployment and limitations of the machine gun as a weapon. This invention is seen by many who ought to know better as the dominating factor in the so called 'waste' of the Great War

The concept of Hiram was, as are most good ideas, simple. He invented a system which combined the weapon's own recoil to activate an automatic reloading process to eject the spent cartridge case and feed a new round of ammunition picked from a belt that fed to the breech, the fresh round being pushed into the firing chamber as the mechanism returned to the firing position. Providing that the thumb button trigger was in the depressed firing position, the firing pin would be released and the percussion cap in the base of the new cartridge detonated, the round discharged, and the cycle repeated.

The cyclical rate of fire could be as high as 500 rounds a minute and that is a lot of fire power when added to the rifles of a formation of infantry. In practice the normal rate of fire was usually about half the maximum. Two of Hiram's automatic weapons amounting to a full platoon of infantry, concentrated though in one place. Also the trajectory of the bullets in flight allowed the infantry to advance with the machine gun rounds passing overhead until the advancing soldiers came close to their objective, then the supporting machine gun must either stop firing or shift to an alternative target. The Maxim gun and its worthy successor the Vickers was a direct fire weapon, the target had to be in sight, an enemy soldier or soldiers nicely positioned in their trench head down, had little to fear from the machine gun. Until that is bright sparks at the front devised ways of elevating the gun, sending the bullets in a high arc to fall steeply into defensive trenches.

Part of the mythology of the Great War surrounds the alleged superiority of German Army resources of machine guns. The proposition of many critics is that the German Army was equipped in 1914 with four times the number of the MMGs provided for the British Army. This is misleading. The British Army was established for two MMGs per battalion of infantry which for a brigade provided a total of eight weapons. The German Army did not include a formation that matched the brigade of the British Army; the nearest German equivalent was the 'regiment' of four battalions; the British and German battalion being essentially equivalent in numerical terms. The German 'regiments' organisation included a machine gun company of eight weapons, nominally two per battalion. These eight guns could be deployed as a complete fire section of eight weapons or allocated to support battalion operations in numbers to suit the tactical situation. It was a difference of organisation and philosophy, the one in Willie's paper campaigns, the other the outcome of soldiering in the far corners of the Empire. Later the British established the Machine Gun Corps (MGC) and consolidated their Vickers MMGs into one command function. The infantry received the lighter man portable 28 lbs (12.5kg) Lewis gun for battalion service deployed at company/platoon level, as compensation.

To sustain the very high rate of fire of the MMG, the barrel was provided with a cooling water jacket. If the gun was fired continuously water evaporated at the rate of one and a half pints for every thousand rounds fired, another little chore for the soldier to deal with. No, don't believe the stories about refilling the water jacket with urine, the smell that results when the gun is fired and the coolant heated to boiling point or thereabouts is vile, to say nothing of the corrosive effect of such a mixture.

When the Machine Gun Corps (MGC) was formed in 1915, a six man team was established as the basic unit for operations, a team were responsible for each gun and tripod assembly weighing 73 lbs (32.5kg) and up to thirty boxes of ammunition each weighing 21lbs (9.4kg). Ammunition alone weighed more than 600 lbs (270 kg), plus ancillary items such as ranging equipment, tools, spares and cleaning equipment for the weapon, entrenching tools etc., plus the personal kit of the individual members of the crew with rifles, bayonet and so on, meant mobility needed careful planning.

As was the case with the losses suffered by the 'Pals Battalions' of Kitchener's New Armies, the reputation of the machine gun is pervasive in the dispute as to scale of the losses sustained during the Great War. There is absolute certainty about the impact of the fire from well deployed weapons firing in 'enfilade', that is into the flanks of the advancing enemy, the casualties were substantial. These casualties were to a very great extent amongst the same portion of the army who lost out when there was fighting to be undertaken. Once again it was the PBI (poor bloody infantry) who bore the brunt. Rightly they and their commanders emphasised the effect of this weapon. In modern terms we would call the gun, a force multiplier. The army of the day knew it as the scourge of their tours of duty, attacks and patrols. Nevertheless the analysis of the casualty returns of the Royal Army Medical Corps (RAMC) show that combined small arms fire, rifles, machine guns and other minor weapons, pistols, grenades and the like, accounted for 42% of casualties. Artillery fire accounted for over 50% of all British casualties. The perception of the machine gun as the reason for exceptional casualties is because the losses were concentrated in the front line fighting soldiery. It is unfair to denigrate the losses, they were real and no amount of statistical detail can restore those killed to life.

Nastier by far, so far as the opposition was concerned, was mortar fire, when just as the kettle was boiling a 3" mortar bomb lands at your feet from its high arcing trajectory, life becomes difficult. Shrapnel and high explosive in a confined space is a very unpleasant experience, if you live to tell the tale. The British developed the use of the mortar as weapon with great skill and enthusiasm eventually developing several varieties none of which were liked by the German soldiers and their officers.

We are forced back on the question posed several times already, what was the alternative? The tank was only in its infancy and there was no way to 'uninvent' the machine gun. Also we have to put on record that in 1914 Vickers produced 266 MMGs, in 1915–2405, 1916–7429 1917–21782 and 1918–39473; or was it 41699 guns in 1918; one book on the subject quotes two different figures in different chapters of the same book. (What hope is there of understanding a subject of such sensitivity if those who make a business of studying the history are unable to be consistent with their own statistics.) It seems not unreasonable to point out that the enemy were on the receiving end of a very large number of these effective guns, to their detriment no doubt. In addition to the Vickers MMG the army had introduced for front line infantry the Lewis Gun* a lighter, man portable automatic gun that could be easily moved and provide immediate tactical support to platoons and companies in their trenches. Production of these grew as the war progressed on the same pattern as the heavier weapon, 1914–8, 1915–2405, 1916–21615, 1917–45528, 1918–62303.

The point made in an earlier section, that the time required to create a manufacturing operation out of thin air to produce the weapons needed to wage a full blown modern high intensity war is very significant. If the political emphasis in one country has ignored the threat of a second nation with soldiers on every street corner with nothing much to do, then the army of the first country will be on the back foot when the shooting begins. So it was proved to be, yet again in August 1914.

Before we leave this portion of this citizen's review of the weapons available for use, two additional features of the means by which the

---

* The Lewis gun; an American invention made under licence in the UK by the Birmingham Small Arms Co (BSA). It was originally the weapon of choice for the nascent Royal Flying Corps.

armies fought the war need to be mentioned to demonstrate the range of 'man's inhumanity to man'. First the success of the enormous explosive tunnel mines dug under enemy, German, lines by the British filled with high explosive and detonated to great effect on the defenders. Nowhere was this more successful than the Messines Ridge attack of 1917. The problem with this procedure was it was quite literally a one shot weapon. The time and specialised effort needed to prepare each mine was prolonged and substantial, the geology of the proposed area of excavation had to be suitable and above all when the mine was detonated, the immediate follow up by the forces above ground had to be swiftly and competently exercised to capture a significant military objective. The mine in this form was far from being a weapon for universal application.

The second device that has past into legend from the Great War is 'the wire', barbed wire, invented originally to confine cattle and other animals on the open spaces on the plains of the mid west in the United States; it became on the Western Front an object of loathing. Those who now comment on the failure of 'generals' to destroy this obstacle to Allied offensives in advance of an attack, reveal all too frequently that they have reached their conclusions on the subject and do not wish to be confused by inconvenient facts. There are two features to be dealt with to assess the problems created for the Allies by wired defences. First, the Germans themselves are a methodical and astute nation who had created their army as a mirror of their national character, hence when the Germans incorporated barbed wire into their defences this was not an odd strand or coil laid out in no man's land, the wire was a major obstacle to progress. Often as much as thirty feet in depth, sometimes more, in front of the trenches, even more as part of the defences of the elaborate 'Hindenberg line'. The wire arranged to deflect any attacking force into the machine guns' fields of fire, parts of the wire or support posts often wired to flares, bombs or grenades primed to go off if disturbed. The whole array calculated with Teutonic thoroughness to make life difficult for the opposition. That is the nature of war; consideration for the welfare of the enemy is not an agenda item. Secondly, and closely allied to the earlier point, is that any operation to destroy the wire barrier is bound to be at best only partially successful; a new 'grazing' fuse for artillery shells was eventually introduced and did improve the outcome of British shell fire on German wire defences. Wire by its very nature does not suffer great damage by blast from an artillery shell, the blast passes over and round the strands, the supports may be damaged and driven into a shell hole taking the attached wire with it, but some of the wire itself remains intact, remaining a barrier to progress. Anyone who has had the misfortune to catch their ankle in a stray strand of wire, barbed or otherwise, during a walk in the countryside will confirm the tripping factor of wire in a hedgerow. Barbed wire was a wonderful weapon for both sides, soldiers hated it, it was a cheap, low maintenance part of the defensive framework and as described above difficult to remove or overcome.

Was enough done to find ways of dealing with the menace of 'the wire'? I don't know, there seems to be a total gap in the history of the Great War on the issue of ways and means of overcoming the problems created by the sophisticated use of this form of barrier on the Western Front. That is until the tank arrived on the scene and warfare began another of its redefining changes of form.

Almost the last aspect of this consideration is the introduction of gas as a weapon, the Germans did it first at second Ypres in April 1915 with chlorine released from cylinders. The effect was dramatic, tactical surprise was achieved. More importantly there was no readily available protection or response. The effect on morale was quite as important as the gains on the ground, surprisingly though the use of this new form of attack on an enemy did not result in the anticipated success. Gas in its early stages was localised in its effect and could not easily be brought forward to continue use as an advance progressed. It was also a double edged sword. Troops sent forward to follow up a gas attack often found themselves in danger of succumbing to the effects themselves. The Brits saw a good propaganda opportunity and exploited to the full the image of the lousy Hun. Then as so often in the past picked up the idea and brought new thinking to the issue, developed other versions of poison gas and alternative delivery systems, such as gas shells.

Finally the weapon that marked a revolution in modern warfare deserves its own chapter and the development and scope of military aviation is given some attention in Chapter 11, devoted to the Royal Flying Corps. Air power was almost a dream in 1914, by 1918 aerial warfare was properly the concern of all senior commanders.

Footnote.

J. M. Bourne in his contribution to a collection of essays that is a contemporary reappraisal of Field Marshal Haig (edited by Bond and Cave) quotes the following statistics for strength increases of the British Army between 1914 and 18: Infantry 469%, Artillery 520%, Engineers 1,429% and the Army Service Corps 2,212% (Chap 1, pg 4)

CHAPTER 8

The Business of Battle; Engagement

Wherever the interested and curious bystander looks and listens when the Great War is debated or explained there is an overwhelming sense that by some inversion of fact the responsibility for the commencement, destructive battles and losses were the responsibility of the Allied powers. On the Western Front this really means Britain and France. The plausible impression is created by the commentators that had it not been for these two nations all would have been well. Somehow the German's aggressive invasion and occupation of Belgium and a substantial portion of North East France by an army equipped and under training for years to defeat the French Army, are never allowed to get in the way of castigating the Allied military leaders for their perceived, belligerence, shortcomings and consequent allied losses.

Let us be quite clear on one essential fact of this conflict. It was the German Army in all its manifestations, from the leadership of Kaiser Wilhelm II as 'Supreme War Lord', von Moltke, nephew of the eponymous victor of the Franco Prussian war of 1871, von Kluck, von Falkenhayn, Hindenburg and Ludendorff *et al,* to Corporal Adolf Hitler and his comrades in arms in the front line who organised and carried out the killing* and injury* of allied soldiers. British and French generals and

---

*The exception that needs to be recorded is the accidental death and injury of soldiers by 'friendly fire' an almost inevitable by product of modern high intensity warfare. There were also the 346 soldiers executed in France (291 were of the British Army, the remainder were from Canada, New Zealand, the West Indies and the Chinese Labour Corps), out of a total of over 3,080 sentenced for offences which carried a death sentence. This was a penalty not limited to desertion and cowardice, other crimes included mutiny, looting, sleeping on sentry duty and murder. The number killed or injured by friendly fire in the confused fighting of 1914-1918 will never be known, it is certain however that the number will be minimal by comparison with the casualties caused by enemy action.

subordinate commanders did not stand behind their troops with machine guns and open fire. The war itself, the losses and casualties suffered, were and remain to this day the responsibility of the German nation; a responsibility that can never be avoided, ever.

This reminder brings us neatly to look at the first precept of conflict, summarised neatly by Brigadier General Nathan Forrest in the American Civil War, you have to be "firstest with the mostest," he said. The Staff College of the British Army reduced this homely language to more elegant terms; "The proper application of overwhelming force". Education is a wonderful thing, don't you think?

That was the precept applied by the Germans in August 1914: eighty divisions, more than a million soldiers on the Western Front alone. The problem for the Germans was the reluctance of the Allied forces to know when they are beaten. 'No hoper' Belgium defending her fortresses with grim determination against the odds. Not a thought given to the effect of the delays on the German's immaculate Schifflein Plan, and, when this delay was being dealt with, another bunch of professional busy bodies arrived on the scene by cross channel ferry and got stuck into the scrap.

Delays to the meticulously programmed advance absorbed additional reserves of men and importantly supplies, time as well as the armies marched on and as a consequence 'the rest is history', as we now say. Murphy was of course lurking in the wings.

The second precept to be emphasised yet again is that the responsibility of commanders at all levels of the armed forces is to use their resources to secure the defeat of the enemy. Even if it was not the intention to get mixed up in the particular problem that leads to conflict, once committed, it is the absolute duty of commanders to deliver victory to the nation and its government. Second place will not do, ever. Only the Korean War (1950–52) can be counted as a drawn match and that particular piece of nastiness was overseen by the United Nations: say no more. As an example of the subordination of military commanders to the government of the day it is only necessary to recall the 1957 Suez Campaign. After the successful initial phase of assault and landing, the British combined forces were motoring off down the Suez Canal in fine style set to deliver the recapture of the canal from Egyptian control. Then, when the international political environment turned nasty for Britain, the army was stopped in its tracks and subsequently withdrawn in short order from Egyptian territory.

In the context of the second precept we have already noted a military defeat in the field does not of itself deliver a total victory to the enemy. Armies may retreat but if the government sets its face and continues the war, as did Belgium in 1914, clinging to a sliver of national territory or by using other resources, victory has not been gained, the nations remain at war. Act II, of the European tragedy which opened to rave reviews in September 1939, illustrates the point. Poland, Holland, Norway, Greece and other nations refused to accept that military defeat and the occupation of the country was justification for political surrender, '*de Jure*' governments in exile, many making a temporary home in Britain, used whatever forces they could muster as part of an allied war effort, to their eternal credit; the Great Powers owe them no small debt, the occupying army became the '*de facto*' government.

Clearing the air with the foregoing ramblings on what is to be done, now allows the discussion to move forward to review how the military go about their business. In the context of this tour this means the strategy and tactics of military life and how the circumstances of Flanders, northern France and the weapons of the day had to be applied to dominate the military ambitions of Germany.

If you analyse military textbooks, and with luck cut through the verbiage and portentous language, you will find it boils down very simply to this; 'strategy' is deciding which battles to fight and 'tactics' is how you fight the battles. This neat, glib statement invites the smart guy to pick holes in the proposition by reason of its generality. The counter to this is that by avoiding specifics it means the commanders can derive a variety of strategies and tactics and apply them on a mix and match basis. As a simple example after the initial tactical encounter battles of 1914 the Allies, France and Britain, had to develop an adequate defensive strategy to prevent further German incursions, including an invasion of Britain, whilst preparing offensive strategies that could be overlaid on the arrangements for defence. From this point the decisions could be made as to what battles should be fought and then, it follows, the tactics to be used in the individual engagements. There you are, I told you it would not be difficult to get to grips with the subject, let's keep going!

The Grand Strategy is to decide where and by what means the enemy is to be fought, how the nation is to be defended and what campaigns must be fought to bring the main body of the enemy's forces to battle and defeat them. Defeat them to such an extent that the political will of the enemy to continue the conflict is eliminated. Strategy is more cerebral than tactics, there is, in most circumstances, more time to weigh the arguments, consider the alternatives and measure the resources available. The down side is that once the die is cast the penalty for a bad decision can be defeat. Strategy is not limited to the physical arrangements to pursue the conflict, it is also a mind game, very much concerned with the need to dominate the thinking and attitudes of the enemy's commanders and the political leaders of the opposing nation.

At the highest level of command generals have to impose their will on the leadership of the opposing armies. To achieve this difficult situation the enemy has to be denied victories. Nothing it is said, 'succeeds like success', and so it is in warfare, a victorious commander attracts an aura of invincibility that is inimical to the efforts of opposing armies. Napoleon was one such commander, whilst he was victorious all sorts of people wanted to 'touch the hem of his robe'. Come the retreat from Moscow in 1812 and Nemesis was upon him. The first constituents of the task to deny success, is to be equipped mentally and materially, to exploit weakness, capitalise on the enemy's mistakes and reinforce success. Field Marshal Montgomery used the term 'balance' and included this requirement to the conduct of his operations. In the campaigns he waged from 1942 to 1945 he devoted a significant amount of his efforts to making sure he was never surprised by the actions of the Axis armies and therefore caught off balance, which is not to say he was always able to forecast the dangers he and his forces faced. In the same way, Wellington in the Peninsula looked to his unconventional and elite reconnaissance officers to bring him the information he needed to appraise the enemy's intentions. To Nosey, 'what was on the other side of the hill' was the essential knowledge he needed to keep his strategy and tactics balanced.

Field Marshal Haig knew all this; he had spent years in preparation for this challenge. Haig however failed in modern eyes for the simple reason he did not tell anyone that he knew what he was doing. He was a reluctant verbal communicator, belonging to a society that admired the reticence of the stiff upper lift. This style was probably reinforced by the habits of the wealthy portion of Scottish Presbyterian society to which he belonged. Only if you were Oscar Wilde were you allowed to be publicly self promoting and we all know what became of him. Montgomery, when he played out his role in Act II, told anyone and everyone how good he was at his job and how he would succeed. His reputation has not attracted the virulent criticism suffered by Field Marshal Haig. General (later Field Marshal and Viscount) Slim, again in Act II of the twentieth century tragedy, but fighting in the Far East, told the people who mattered most, his troops, and was admired for his honesty even by the Australians; a signal honour rarely awarded to whinging 'Poms'.

At this point it has to be acknowledged that the strategic deployment of the Royal Navy, the blockade of the external trade of the Central Powers from overseas sources of food and raw material, was fundamental to the outcome of the Great War, part of the Grand Strategy. The navy was also represented in the land forces of the Western Front by 63rd (Royal Navy) Division. Their main role however, was where it should have been on the high seas. The pattern begins to emerge of the means by which the Great War was fought by the Allies. Germany had invaded and overrun Belgium and made a significant incursion with its armies into the industrial area of North East France. From these conquered territories the German Army must be forced to withdraw. The strategy was therefore to meet and defeat the enemy on the Western Front whilst blockading the Central Powers at sea and denying them access to raw materials and supplies from the rest of the world.

The argument that took place about the strategy of outflanking the Central Powers by an attack through Turkey was not a shining example of military and political thinking, in fact it was a dreadful mistake for which Lloyd George (LG) and Winston Churchill were responsible. To the very end of the war LG looked for the indirect approach seemingly unable or unwilling to grasp that the threat of defeat for the Allies was in

France, nowhere else. Diverting attention and resources to a subsidiary campaign would invite a crushing response by the German Army on the Western Front with the possibility of at least a serious disruption of allied efforts in France or even a major defeat. But LG was a politician with an agenda all his own. Professor Norman Stone has good things to say about the indirect approach. But he like many others who make special pleadings, put a case with just too many 'ifs' plus the complication of a supply train of extraordinary length that would consume large resources just to keep it operating. The argument was not viable.

Churchill when the outcome of the Dardanelles was recognised, had the good grace to activate his reserve commission and command a Territorial battalion of the Royal Fusiliers in France for nearly a year before returning to political life. Winston knew precisely how to retrieve his reputation and had the physical courage to put himself in the firing line to do just that.

Now back to the business of battle and how commanders go about the task of winning. In the first place we need to recognise at an early stage that battles have variety, the encounter battle as two or more formations probe and manoeuvre to gain advantage, surprise the enemy, and capture important objectives; all the ingredients of the German invasion and allied response of 1914. To counter such an incursion, defenders have to move their forces to deflect progress, break lines of communication and supplies, defend essential tactical objectives such as railway junctions, bridges, river crossings, high ground. An essential axiom of an offensive battle is that when the fighting is completed, a military objective must have been secured or successfully defended. Ground, space by itself, is a liability to be occupied and controlled, both of which responsibilities consume resources.

The commander's task is to apply the resources of men and *materiel* to maximum effect to initiate a momentum which will have the impact needed to overcome the enemy. As the war developed on the Western Front the concepts that had developed over the centuries had to be modified to achieve the required result. Previously the mounted cavalry had been used to create the shock effect that would create momentum and turn a battle into a success, usually after effective infantry actions. In the situation of 1914–18 it was realised very quickly that the weapon of choice for maximum effect was artillery, guns, the more the merrier. The problem for the British Army was it did not have enough and, worse still, even the limited number available given their own way, could fire off ammunition faster than it could be replaced. Hence the shell scandal of 1915, four rounds per gun per day. Furthermore when the territorial divisions arrived in France in 1915 the kindest description that could be applied to their guns was, obsolescent. The army therefore had to make do, until industry could catch up with the demands of this new type of warfare for bigger and better guns in large quantities, at once if not sooner.

The development of a style of conflict that used artillery to overwhelm the enemy before releasing infantry to occupy the positions presented a dilemma on the Western Front. The enemy positions were well disguised, well constructed and often positioned on reverse slopes, only visible to aerial observation/photography. The Allied commanders therefore had to rely on assumptions of artillery damage when planning their attack, most of which proved too optimistic. The job of the commanders was not helped by the inconsiderate way that their German equivalents ignored the problem created for the Allies. Surely the occupiers of these desirable fortifications could have organised, for a modest fee, Sunday afternoon excursions through their defence works with schnapps and sandwiches at the end. By this means the British would have known the extent of their problem. The reality was the German defence works were superb. Only when there was massive interference with the structure, as at Messines Ridge in 1917, when nineteen large mines packed with explosives were detonated, was the disruption sufficient to allow a subsequent coherent infantry advance the success it deserved.

The German command was equally aware of the need to deploy overwhelming artillery fire as a prelude to infantry action. Their expert, Lt. Col. Bruchmuller, designed the savage artillery barrage that preceded the offensive against the British Army in March 1918. The infantry advanced and advanced. The difficulty arose when the infantry advanced beyond the cover provided by the guns. The task of bringing the guns and ammunition forward over the old Somme battlefield and then the ground pounded by the German's preparatory barrage, proved to be of such difficulty that resources needed to sustain the advance were drained, and a downward spiral of failure began. The attacks faltered and failed because the momentum could not be maintained, the force was dissipated and left exposed to the artillery of the British Army which by now had more guns than the Germans. So began the slide to defeat.

Moving on, there are defensive battles as the enemy tries to get the upper hand, deliberate 'set piece' battles, feints, withdrawals, rearguards. Then there is one of the oldest of warfare's encounters, the siege. Remember Joshua, he of the trumpets and the falling walls of Jericho, together with many others known from the accounts of campaigns through the ages to the bloody storming of Badajoz in 1812 and Delhi's 'Red Fort' following the Indian Mutiny in 1858. Sieges are demanding to maintain and in most cases bloody to overcome, whether it is breaking in, or breaking out. Is this a factor to consider in this appreciation?

Following the retreat of the German Army after the first Battle of the Marne, then the subsequent 'race for the sea', both the Allies and the German Armies faced a continuous line of defensive positions from the Swiss border in the south to the North Sea in occupied Belgium. In the retreat to the defensive line the Germans behaved very badly, they took up their positions and dug themselves their very splendid fortifications on the high ground, all the best bits of real estate were used for their defensive line. Their positions included excellent open views of the badly drained lower ground of Flanders, which locations the Germans assigned to the Allied armies. As the armies of Germany retreated in the autumn of 1914, neither Britain nor France had the resources to contest the enemy's choice of positions on the high ground. The German generals did their job with skill and determination and no amount of gainsaying or argument can deny their effectiveness.

The German High Command had achieved a notable advantage by this action which would force the French and British Armies to fight future battles on ground chosen by their enemy! The result however was not all good, for the Germans now faced a development never envisaged in the war plan. Germany was under siege, the biggest siege in history from which there was to be no escape. Practically as described above the

Western Front battle line prevented access to the remainder of France; Spain, the Atlantic and Mediterranean. Holland, Switzerland and the Scandinavian countries were neutral but the Royal Navy was blockading the sea passageways from and to the Baltic. In southern Europe, Austria Hungary was an ally but Italy and the Balkans were belligerent; Rumania was to be occupied but provided access only to the Black Sea and thence to the Mediterranean, a sea under the supervision of the British and French Navies. The Russian Bear was in possession of most of the rest of the boundary from the Black Sea to the Baltic.

In the appraisals and histories of the Great War that I have encountered I cannot recall any of the writers, military, historical or journalistic making this particular point. It seems improbable to me that more than ninety years after the event I should produce a dazzling original insight on this overwritten subject. The result was the very worst that could have occurred for both the Central Powers and the Allies. The cost of breaking a siege is always high, the chances for the success of the besieged in withstanding a determined besieger are poor.

There is a very worthwhile book written in the immediate aftermath of the war (1920), *Storm of Steel*, by Ernst Junger who served as a much decorated lieutenant and later captain in the 73rd (Hanoverian) Regiment, a German regiment that bore the battle honour 'Gibraltar', until the Armistice in November 1918. I cannot recall him using the term 'siege', but for certain he describes in detail the shortages, rationing and despair that is the outcome of a protracted blockade and the demands placed upon an army who know their enemy to be better supplied. The minds of the German commanders became dominated by the expedients to which they were forced to resort in order to maintain their operations! Junger was of course writing in the immediate aftermath of the conflict and has no problem of facing the huge losses sustained by the German nation. Even in defeat he gives no indication that the war was a monumental crime against humanity, he regrets only that Germany and her Allies were forced to concede defeat.

The practical effect of this development was that all the techniques and procedures developed over centuries to manoeuvre fighting units of any size into a favourable position for attack or defence were useless.

Suddenly, turning the enemies flank, encirclement, pincer movements and so on were issues for the textbook. The armies of both the Allies and the Central Powers were in fixed lines that could only be changed by frontal assault. The axioms commanders had absorbed during their experience that offensive action needs to take place: on ground, with the weapons selected to match the task in hand and at a time of the commander's choice, became severely limited in their application. The French Army had developed its military ethos on the Napoleonic concept of continuous offensive action. The requirements of trench warfare needed the French High Command to undertake a fundamental reappraisal of how the nation's army was to fight; if it was done at all, it was not done well. The casualties of the French Army in the early stages of the war had a serious effect on its offensive capability.

In the same way the general principles on which engagements are fought became equally constrained. These principles of: define the objective, concentrate the resources, surprise, timing, control, speed and simplicity suddenly took on a whole new and much more limited meaning when the enemy could see what you were doing and the front line was knee deep in mud and other unpleasant by products of modern warfare. The feature of this new form of battle that was not resolved during the Great War was, control. For the first time army commanders could not see the full extent of the battle and deploy troops accordingly. The set piece scraps of 1914–18 had to be put in motion and soldiers left to get on with it. Communication from the fighting line was to all intents and purposes none existent, field telephones were disrupted by shell and mortar fire and mobile radio sets were still to be invented. Information on the progress of battles relied on the success or otherwise of messages scribbled by front line unit commanders as they progressed with the assigned action and relayed to battalion – and even sometimes to brigade HQs – by messengers (runners) who with no protection made their way back from the battle scene to the destination. It was not unknown for several of these later day 'Mercuries' to be killed or wounded before the information eventually reached the destination. Pigeons and dogs were also tried as alternatives, not surprisingly the poor animals proved equally vulnerable to the sustained nastiness of the Western Front.

It was a situation made for confusion, the fog of war suddenly got thicker. Senior commanders knew this, but were impotent. If they left their command posts to see what was going on they became unreachable and were limited to dealing with the troops in the immediate vicinity. Remaining at HQ left them badly informed. In one encounter in 1917 when tanks were deployed the brigade commander decided to lead from the front and took passage in one of the leading tanks. He found the scope of his command role was then limited to kicking the shoulders of his steersman, left shoulder go left, right shoulder go right, he soon had to abandon the experiment and get to position where at least he had a field telephone available.

A subsequent and common criticism by the armchair pundits is that generals sat in safety whilst others took the risk. The diary of the Irish Guards records that three officers acting as brigadier generals were killed in action during the Great War; three brigadier generals from one regiment sounds pretty risky when added to all the other officer losses, allowing for eighty regiments of the pre war army that comes to over 200 brigadier generals as casualties. The sixty divisions of the army in France in 1918 needed just about that number for command responsibilities alone. Richard Holmes in his substantive account of the war cites a figure of 'more than 300 general officers' as casualties. (Three major generals were killed by enemy action at the Battle of Loos alone in the spring of 1915.) During the 1939-45 war, three major generals died as a result of enemy action in all theatres of war*, over the five and a half years of the conflict. One only died in North West Europe.) Gordon Corrigan's book *Mud, Blood and Poppycock*, quotes almost the same figure for casualties as general officers of all ranks in the Great War; a figure of fifty-seven killed in the Great War is the number commonly used by informed historians. Whilst in the great scheme of casualties from this war, numerically the loss does not seem too large, just recall for a moment, a brigade commander is responsible for a formation of more than 6,200 soldiers of all ranks.

(* There is some divergence of information, John Keegan cites a figure of 22 for Act II.)

The unpleasant issue that has to be faced is that senior officers should not become casualties. The more senior and experienced an officer the greater the damage to the command structure of the army concerned, British, French or any other nation. A front line soldier can be trained in about four months. A subaltern (second lieutenant) took about the same time to train under the conditions of 1914–18. Subalterns also became casualties in about the same time span, on average, as the men they led, six weeks. A senior officer has taken years to accumulate the knowledge needed by his appointment, the moment an officer of senior rank becomes a casualty the army's resources of experience, ability and originality are reduced. Given the very limited size of the army prior to 1914 the loss of more than fifty generals and additionally the injury of more than 200 others, would have been a significant blow.

The digression above is meant to remind readers that nothing is as it seems in consideration of the Great War. There are so many issues all with interwoven strands that it is possible for any commentator to make his case, for or against some aspect of the conflict and its conduct and for the argument to have the appearance of reason and logic. I appreciate that I am doing the same thing, so what is the difference; I know I have a partiality and I am admitting it. The acid test of all the opinions comes back to the origins and the outcome of the war. When all the critics have had their say, which nations were invaded and wronged and by whom, and which nations won the military conflict?

Now we can revisit the proposition that Germany was under siege, the condition in which the Allied nations and the Central Powers found themselves when the encounter battles were completed and the battle lines set in the trenches of the Western Front by Christmas 1914. How was the siege to be broken? The Central Powers had to overcome one of their enemies; the question of course is which one to deal with first. In comments earlier in this appreciation the reader probably gathered from the text that Kaiser Wilhelm II did not achieve star status as either a strategist or a notable intellectual. For reasons that we can imply from events Willy went East. Why? Well, put in the simple terms of the appreciation I am undertaking he made one of the most basic of military mistakes; and his commanders let him, His Imperial Majesty, Emperor of

Germany and Supreme War Lord, did not know what to do when Plan 'A' failed. He and his commanders seemed beguiled by the numerical losses inflicted on the Russian Army as well as the territorial advances achieved by the German and Austro Hungarian Armies. Perhaps also they were looking at the resources of the Ukraine on which they were casting envious eyes. Now the two things Russia had in abundance were territory and manpower, losses of land and manpower could be sustained without affecting either national sovereignty or the war effort. An advance of twenty miles in Russia was probably the equivalent of twenty yards on the Western Front. The maxim that offensive battles must have a worthwhile military objective has been stated elsewhere but it bears repetition as reinforcement of the error into which the German High Command was drawn. Put in simple terms it was the wrong battle. The armies capable of inflicting defeat on the Central Powers were those of Britain and France. Russia for all its size would not have the quality of resources needed to secure victory against the combined German and Austro/Hungarian Armies. The Eastern Front campaigns moreover, were not fought without cost to the armies of the Central Powers, an alliance under siege used valuable and increasingly scarce resources to no military advantage. By such mistakes were the seeds of eventual defeat sown with careless abandon.

The issue became in 1915, by what actions could the siege be broken. Now sieges have been recorded as the centrepiece of some campaigns for as long as armies have been going into battle. The previously mentioned siege by Joshua of the city of Jericho, you will remember, was one of the actions in a war fought to secure the 'promised land'. By dint of carrying out the instructions of the Almighty to the letter and sending a band of trumpeters to march round outside the city walls blowing the odd fanfare or two at specified intervals, the walls came tumbling down and Joshua conquered Jericho. In reality what was really happening was some crafty excavations going on under the walls of the city. The trumpet band was initially a diversion and then the signal to burn away the timber props in the tunnels, the walls above crumbled then lo and behold the Hebrews won a victory for themselves and their God. There was also a siege if you recall that was broken by the tricky use of a wooden horse. The point being that the walls of the fortress, city, whatever, had to be breached or the gates released for the away team to gain a victory. This was the crux of the problem, the Allies to break in, or, the enemy to break out!

In 1812, just over a century prior to the Great War, our old friend the 'Sepoy General', Arthur Wellesley, was taking on the French in Spain and he dealt with two sieges to open the road for his advance into Spain and secure the province of Extremadura. The siege of Badajoz is the one to which our attention should be turned to make a comparison with the task faced by the Allied armies on the Western Front to achieve victory. An exhaustive review of the circumstances is not appropriate; it is the various parallels with circumstances a hundred years later. The political situation in London was far from certain in 1812. Lord Liverpool's government had been ousted in 1811, the Whigs, parliamentary opposition of the day, did not like the war but liked Napoleon and his ambitions less, thus reluctantly agreeing to the continuation of the efforts of the army and navy to defeat Napoleon. Then to cap it all Lord Liverpool's successor as Prime Minister, Spencer Perceval, was assassinated in 1812 when he was shot in the lobby of the House of Commons by John Bellingham, a deranged and bankrupt business man from St. Neots in Cambridgeshire. Liverpool returned to power with Wellington's brother as a member of the Cabinet. So far as the campaign was concerned, Wellington had spent a couple of years gathering resources and materials of war, winning, with mixed success, the support of Portuguese and Spanish politicians, generals and the leaders of the irregular armed bands of 'guerrillas' and building up the reserves of the British Army on which he would rely during the winters spent protected by the fortifications of 'Torres Vedras' close to Lisbon. Time would not wait on Wellington forever, the pressure was on, results were required and in the spring of 1812 that was the outcome. To the Allied forces an advantage, to the French a bloody nose. Cuidad Rodrigo and Badajoz besieged and captured in seven weeks, the road to Madrid was open.

The action to take Badajoz is one to concentrate the mind, a classic of siege warfare and nastiness. A citadel strongly held by experienced troops well supplied and commanded, an essential tactical point in the defence of the French controlled hinterland of Spain, Wellington must capture the fortress. The siege train was deployed, some of it captured from the French, the earthworks advanced by frantic digging, the artillery brought forward and a barrage commenced to open a breach in the walls. Slowly the gap was made, the walls began to crumble, the attacking forces gathered in battle formation with their equipment, ammunition and powder and on 6 April 1812 at 10.00 pm the 'forlorn hope' assaulted the breach and fought a bloody, bloody battle. The defenders were well prepared and had exploded mines, thrown *'chevaux de frise'* and other improvised defence works into the breach whilst using musket and cannon to prevent the attackers advancing into the city. The action at the breach drew in reserves from both sides and the outcome was in the balance. The fortress was lost by the French forces as a consequence of the attacker's secondary effort. The attack on the walls of the city incorporated a further action into the overall plan. An 'escalade', the use of scaling ladders, was made on the defences, well removed from the main point of battle. This second and smaller action was hard fought, but successful, the besieged had committed all their reserves to defending the main point of action; the attackers gained access, brought in a few additional troops and stormed the defenders of the breached walls in their rear. The city fell to Wellington. The defenders were surprised, their deployment unbalanced, the attackers exploited a weakness when the French were without available reserves to use against the second assault, the defenders lost control of the battle, a classic action of its type.

Badajoz was the Great War as it developed, in microcosm. Haig became Commander in Chief in December 1915, succeeding Sir John French at a time when territorial units from Britain had reached France as reinforcements, new contingents were arriving from the Empire and units of Kitchener's 'New Army' were joining the BEF in increasing numbers. A parallel with Wellington's two winters in the defended lines of Torres Vedras. As the new units were integrated into Britain's Army in France with all the attendant complications of command and control, supplies and transport, the political situation in London was unsettled. The 'scandal' of the shell shortage of 1915 and the failure of the campaign in the Dardanelles brought uncertainty, a perilous condition during a major war. Asquith was elbowed aside; Lloyd George became

Prime Minister in 1916. Then the Germans attacked the French fortress of Verdun in February 1916. The Allied leadership was badly off balance in both political and military terms.

By this circuitous route we return to the actual battles and conflicts of the Great War. There has been much time, acres of paper and rivers of ink devoted by historians and commentators to the high points of action in the years 1914–18. Most select for their attention some action, time period or specialised aspect of warfare, such as artillery or tank developments and develop a case to support an explanation for success or failure on arguments of limited scope. This is another difference I make in my appreciation. The Western Front during the Great War should not be broken down into discreet elements as a means to advance a particular opinion. It is an event of such magnitude that it has to be treated as a whole. Every attack, battle, bombardment, patrol and raiding party, all the weapons, devices, machines and equipment, every plan, order, battle drill and training course, all the officers, soldiers, nurses and non combatants were part of an enormous continuum of action for the whole fifty-one months of the conflict. Consider if you will, even for a brief moment, the story told by the battle honours of the regiments who sustained the conflict, look at the details of the honours awarded with their locations and dates defining actions large and small throughout the conflict. Some form part of a larger action, others are 'stand alone' events. Essentially the British Army did not rest and as it fought it developed its skills to fight 'all arms', co-ordinated actions. For their perseverance and courage the prize of victory came in November 1918.

To illustrate the point made above the list below identifies some but by no means all the major actions fought on the Western Front, following the encounter battles of Mons, Le Cateau, Ypres and the Marne during the late summer and autumn of 1914.

Date.	Location.	Armies committed. (Attacker named first)	Comment.
March 1915	Neuve Chapelle.	Brit/Indian v Ger.	N.C.captured.
April/May 1915	2nd Ypres.	Ger v Brit.	Poison gas used for first time.
May 1915	2nd Artois.	Fr v Ger.	Small Fr. gains.
May 1915	Aubers Ridge.	Brit v Ger.	
May 1915	Festubert.	Brit/Can v Ger.	
Sept 1915	3rd Artois.	Fr v Ger.	Small Fr. gains.
Sept 1915	Loos.	Brit v Ger.	Town captured.
Feb 1915.	Verdun.	Ger v Fr.	Fortress retained by French. Six month battle.
July 1916.	Somme.	Brit & Imperial, and Fr v Ger.	Five month Battle. First use of tanks.
April 1917.	Aisne	Fr v Ger.	Attack failed Mutinies in 68 of 112 Fr Divisions.
June 1917.	Messines.	Brit v Ger.	19 mines detonated prior to attack.
July 1917.	3rd Ypres. Passchendale	Brit v Ger.	Five month battle.
March 1918.	Spring Offensive.	Ger v Brit/Imperial and French.	Significant advances into allied territory.
July/August 1918.	Summer Counter attack by allied armies.	Brit/Imperial, Fr, Bel US v Ger	Advance towards German border.
November 1918.	Central Powers sue for an Armistice.		

The list on Pg 154 deals only with the high and in some cases low points of the campaign on the Western Front. The British Army, including the contingents provided by the Empire, were never at a loss for something to do, by way of example a regiment such as the Northumberland Fusiliers (5th Foot) were awarded sixty-eight separate battle honours for the continuous commitment to battle on the Western Front during the months and years the war was fought, endured and eventually won.

There were two portions of the campaign in the list above that are crucial to a balanced conclusion on the conduct of the Great War. In 1916 the Germans attempted the capture of the iconic French fortress of Verdun. This attack pre empted the agreement of December 1915 by Britain and France, for an attack on the German lines in Flanders on the River Somme in a joint action where the armies of the two nations were adjacent in the summer of that year, 1916. The second crucial period was the months from April to November of 1917, dealing first with the actions at Verdun and on the Somme. The Germans went on the offensive on 21st February 1916 to capture Verdun. Some historians have put forward a case that von Falkenheim, recognising that the most dangerous component of the Allied forces in France was the British Army, decided that the way to deal with the situation was to use substantial portions of his armies and reserves to assault a French fortress, geographically well to the south of the British held section of the front line. Such a proposition breaks an essential precept of military planning, the one that abjures all soldiers to 'keep the plan simple'. The German generals were many things but they were not insane. This is a proposition that cannot be taken seriously, what was serious was the scale and weight of the offensive against the fortress. The defence of Verdun absorbed more and more of the efforts and reserves of the French Army and nation, the army was being eviscerated by its efforts. The politicians in London and the senior British commanders knew it and understood that it was essential to support France. Likewise the Germans kept reinforcing the desperate struggle. The combined total of casualties, French and German, in twenty-one weeks and five days, exceeded 750,000

The offensive on the Somme had to go ahead as planned to relieve the pressure on the French nation and its army. What is more, the battle must be of such weight, consequence and duration that the German Army would have to divide what reserve forces remained to support their defences on the Somme, thus preventing any secondary deployment against the weakened French. Additionally Haig as the the Commander in Chief and his generals had to demonstrate that the rebuilt British Army, Kitchener's new army, was a force to be taken seriously. The 'new boy on the block', had to be treated as an opponent of significance, the cost in casualties and material was high but the strategy succeeded. The French continued the war; the Germans were seriously damaged as a professional army by the simultaneous battles and their own policy of 'no withdrawal'.

The second of the make or break periods in 1917 was, if anything, even more dangerous to the war aim of the Allies. The French campaign in April under General Nivelle not only failed it was bungled, French casualties, allowing for the extent and duration of the fighting were grievous, the morale of the *'poliu'** the French equivalent of Tommy Atkins, went into freefall and there were large scale mutinies in the army of France. Whole battalions and divisions ceased to be effective fighting units, overnight. How much the Germans knew of this is far from clear, eventually of course the Brits had to be let in on the secret and Haig needed to recast his strategic thinking to protect the Allied position on the Western Front. The planned battles by the British Army against tactical objectives had to be intensified and prolonged to occupy the attention of the Germans and so Passchendaele (3rd Ypres) was written into the history of the British Army and the myth of unnecessary slaughter reinforced.

Given the difficulties described above the inevitable question arises, how did the Western Allies secure victory; to this commentator the answer appears to have four components:

1. The German Army was able to transfer a substantial infantry force from the Eastern (Russian) Front during the winter of 1917/18 following the October revolution that overthrew the interim administration of Kerensky, who became head of the Russian

---

*Poliu, the French equivalent of a Private in the British army, literally translated it becomes 'the hairy one'.

government following the spring revolt that deposed the Tsar. The new government formed around the leadership of Lenin's Communist Party and the associated Soviets withdrew from the war and this was formalised in the treaty of Brest Litovisk in February 1918.

2. The German Army now had significant reserves (the German Army fielded 208 divisions on the Western Front in March 1918 immediately prior to the opening attack on 21st March of '*Kaiserschlacht*' which proved to be the last German effort to secure victory. (British and French forces amounted to 156 divisions.) The preparations were meticulous, morale was high in the front line and commanders were confident that with the newly devised tactics, using fire and movement tactics with concentrated artillery support, victory was within the grasp of Germany. It needed to be, German resources were by now seriously depleted. The outcome was the launching of the spring offensive on March 1918 aimed principally against the British Third and Fifth Armies positions. The British fell back in the face of the attack, withdrawing in all about forty miles. It was, though, a withdrawal, the defence line maintained its continuity, the enemy did not break through, no major communications centre was captured. It was a close run thing, forcing even Lloyd George to stop politicking and give serious attention to reinforcing the army in France with units that had been retained in Britain in case of invasion.

3. There were two significant military consequences for the German Army as a direct consequence of the failure to win a victory. First the German Army had relinquished some very strong defensive positions and now occupied some very ordinary trenches, just the sort of accommodation to which the British and French Allies had become accustomed from October 1914 onwards. The second issue was the extension of the supply line to the new German line with increasingly scarce supplies to be brought forward over the difficult terrain of the former Somme battlefields.

4. The artillery deployed by the British Army in 1918 was a thing of 'wonderous' power for its day. During the preceding months of fighting the Royal Artillery had mastered innovations and expansion for which scant credit is given. The regiment had expanded from the

regular army's 34,073 all ranks to 607,627 in 1918, almost an eighteen fold increase. Artillery pieces per division, of which there were six in 1914, was sixty-eight guns per division, a total of 410 guns; in 1918 the figure had risen to 100 guns per division a total of 6406 guns an increase of more than fifteen times the figure for 1914: infantry formations increased by a factor of twelve from five in 1914 to sixty-one divisions in March 1918. The gunners now understood and used new techniques of indirect fire; counter battery fire, defensive fire tasks, sound ranging and much more. The fire systems now used included creeping barrages, lifting barrages, box barrages, 'Chinese' barrages as well as good old fashioned area bombardment; the ammunition was improved and the fuses were reliable. The most significant advance was however that the infantry and the gunners had devised ways and means to coordinate their actions to act as a single battering ram against the siege wall created by the German trench system. The German advance of April and May had brought the enemy forward into a vulnerable position, a 'killing ground'. Just as the German tactics in the spring had changed under the imperatives of war so the British took the offensive in August 1918 advancing under intense artillery covering fire, against the weakened trench system of the Germans, advancing only as far as the covering fire allowed. Reinforcements passed through as the guns came forward to cover the next stage of the advance and so it continued until the enemy conceded defeat on 11th November 1918.

The combination in the German Army of 'battle fatigue' and extended supply lines created a weakness comparable with the 'escalade' of Badajoz in 1812; there were no German reserves left. Haig, soldier and commander, read the situation and acted.

The attack launched by the British in August 1918 was the culmination of all the effort, learning, adaptation, reorganisation and experience of four years of war. The British launched an all arms, coordinated offensive at the unintentionally created breech in the German defensive wall. Effectively the German spring campaign had opened the breech in the defences for the Allies to exploit. The August offensive by the armies of

Britain, France and the United States combined all the best aspects of military doctrin: surprise, timing, concentration of effort, coordination, reinforcement of success and 'fighting through' as the enemy retreated from their positions. The walls of the citadel came tumbling down; the opportunity for victory was seized.

For a moment consider how things might have been; what would have been the outcome if the Germans had prevailed against the French at Verdun in 1916 or after the mutinies in the French Army in 1917 and in either circumstance, France had sued for peace as in 1871. The British, at war with Germany could not continue the war on French territory, Germany had not invaded a scrap of British territory, other allies such as Belgium would fall like autumn leaves. Only a withdrawal to the embattled offshore island on whatever terms could be obtained was feasible. All the effort, casualties, expended wealth and grief would have been in vain. The next time anyone talks of 'Butcher Haig' ask the speaker to justify the alternative outcome and listen to the silence.

There certainly were mistakes of tactics; in fifty-one months of fighting it would have been miraculous if none had been made. The strategy pursued by Britain, whatever the dissenting opinions, delivered victory. This is the only perspective from which the decisions and events of the Great War have to be judged.

There are no prizes for noticing that the Allies, French and British, were more often on the attack than the Germans and that calls for some comment. First as a matter of record following the failure of the Schlieffen plan in 1914 the German commander, von Moltke, was replaced by General Erich von Falkenhayn. He regrouped the German Army following the reversals of the initial campaign, then when the spring offensives of 1915 went nowhere he resorted to a policy of attrition in an attempt to dislocate the build up of armies by the Allies that could meet and defeat the German Army in battle. Sounds to me like 'Plan B3', 'don't do anything and perhaps the problem will go away'. Falkenhayn himself was in due course replaced by the well known double act, Hindenberg and Ludendorff, they, it was soon apparent, did not 'do comedy' or it seems to me, original thinking, their recipe was more of the same, again and again.

On a more serious note there are two issues revealed by this policy, first 'von F' recognised a siege when he saw one and knew Germany was on the back foot; second, on the positive side, German forces were in occupation of almost all of Belgium and a sizable slice of northern France, with the German Army largely intact, that was about the best negotiating position possible, following the initial failure to accomplish the objectives of 'Plan Schlieffen'. The Allied nations had to break the siege to win and that would be a formidable task, a costly process both in terms of casualties and *material*. Alternatively the Allies would have to sue for peace from a position of weakness. The inherent defect of this policy is that the initiative was lost, the German High Command did not dictate the conduct of Allied affairs, they responded to Allied initiatives, large and small. Represented best by the instruction to all German formation commanders that ground must be held to the last man against any attack and should any ground be lost it must be immediately recovered by counter attack. John Terraine, who is a leading authority on the whole war, has recorded that during the Battle of the Somme in 1916, the German forces were committed to more than 320 counter attacks on former front line positions captured by the British attacks. The totals of casualties for the British and German armies for the Somme campaign were very similar.

The policy adopted by the German Army produces double casualties; the first when attacked, the second when the counter attack is made. The effect of this policy was to provide for the Allies a major tactical advantage. The advantage is generated in the following way. When a commander plans an action he manipulates his forces to place his enemy between the 'hammer' of his attack and an 'anvil' which the enemy is unable to avoid. Conventionally this will be at the level of platoon and company actions and will usually be a barrier formed by machine gun fire from unit resources or obstacles such as trenches or barbed wire. At higher levels of operation, brigade and above, the barriers will be such things as sustained artillery fire, a secondary attack or fortification, a minefield, river, sea or mountainous terrain. The objective is to force the enemy to conform to your plans and dispositions. The policy of 'no retreat' adopted by the German High Command from 1915 onwards effectively created the anvil against which their armies in many circumstances took a double dose of casualties for the same action.

The issue for the Allies was that by undertaking the siege of the Central Powers they too had to conform to the dispositions made by the enemy. Their advantage was that there was no overt doctrine that ensured double casualties, commanders were expected to make judgements based on situational needs.

The Great War was, above all, fought by the infantry, a war with artillery dominating the battlefield as support for both attack and defence. The human cost was concentrated in the battalions of the regular army, then the volunteers who made up Kitchener's armies and later the conscripts, reinforcements enlisted by the state that together combined to deliver final victory. The British Army never again faced such losses and casualties; other nations were not as diligent in the protection of their citizen soldiers, Russia, China and Japan used human life without compunction in the pursuit of victory in years to come. These countries were not democracies though, there was no public reckoning to bring them to account.

One of the enduring 'myths' of the Great War is the comment attributed to a member of the German command, perhaps von Falkenhayn, that the British were an army of 'lions lead by donkeys'. So far as I have been able to establish during my reading no verifiable attribution for this accusation can be been found. There was significant press correspondence on the actual quotation following the publication of Alan Clarke's historical account of the 1914–18 war. In a letter to the *Daily Telegraph* of 16 July 1963 a Mr. J. C. Clarke of Birmingham wrote that "despite enlisting the aid of the Librarian of the Imperial War Museum, London and the Library for Contemporary World War Literature in Stuttgart", he had to report that no trace could be found in these extensive archives of the origins and more significantly the attribution for this prejudiced comment. The author, Alan Clark, failed to reveal his source! No one in their right mind denies that British generals did not make mistakes; equally it is a false premise to suggest that the generals of other armies, allied and enemy, were not capable of error and on the balance of the information adduced were even more culpable.

Inevitably at the conclusion of this section we need to recall Wellington's maxim, 'we make war as we must not as we would'.

Remember if you will that on the Western Front all the armies took to trench warfare, the British did not invent this method of waging war. At the end of 1914 the Germans had about eighty divisions in the field, the French fifty-five or thereabouts and the British eight, mainly under strength. The French and German armies were not going to imitate the BEF, it was the British who conformed to both the defensive policies and the tactics adopted by the larger armies.

The question for the critics to answer remains as before, remembering that historically God exhibits a predisposition to favour the big battalions, what was the alternative?

Machine Guns and the Great War

A valuable analysis of numerous aspects of the introduction, deployment and tactical development of the machine gun was published in 2009. Paul Cornish, a senior curator at the Imperial War Museum specialising in firearms, does much in a volume of modest dimensions to explain without the use of purple prose the way allied armies used this weapon to significant and increasing effect in their own defence and eventual defeat of the German Army.

(*Machine Guns and the Great War*, Paul Cornish, Pen and Sword, ISBN 184884047-0)

Dedications

Albert Lucas, MM.

This dedication to Albert Lucas MM includes his companions, officers and men, who mobilised on 4th August 1914 as soldiers of 7th (City of Coventry) Battalion, Royal Warwickshire Regiment (6th Foot); a Territorial battalion forming part of 48th (South Midland) Division. Albert and the division went to France in March 1915, he survived the war, was wounded in 1916, returned to his unit fighting in various actions, was wounded again in October 1917 at 3rd Ypres (Passchendaele) and was awarded the Military Medal. When he was discharged from hospital he did not return to the Western Front and completed his service repairing boots in

Newcastle. During the war of 1939 -45 he served in the Home Guard and became lieutenant (QM) of his battalion, part of the war time organisation of the Royal Warwickshire Regiment.

Albert was father of the author's wife; he died in his eighty-fourth year at our home in Dorridge, Warwickshire in 1976.

Frank Aldington

Frank Aldington enlisted first into the Army Service Corps as a driver (m/t) and at some point in his service he was re-mustered and joined the Rifle Corps. His death is recorded as occurring between 17th and 19th November 1917 as the battle of Passchendaele was drawing to its close. He has no known grave. His name though appears on the Tyne Cot memorial, Ypres, Belgium, his parents grave in the churchyard of Knowle, Warwickshire and the memorial in the village church of Packwood a couple of miles away in the countryside he knew so well.

Frank would have been Great Uncle to the author's wife.

CHAPTER 9

Casualties; Cause and Effect

Note. This difficult subject is dealt with in two sections of one chapter, the first part more descriptive and the second part an attempt at a statistical comparison. Beware, the figures used in the two sections are not directly comparable, the first section uses information quoted by other writers whose sources if provided are cited. The analysis section is a comparison of the statistics quoted in the tabulation; the two sets of figures do not match in detail.

No one who has ambitions to argue a case about the Great War can avoid the necessity of considering the implications of the human cost of the losses incurred by the combatant armies during the fifty-one months of conflict. Before offering for consideration my comments, there are some very basic aspects of the conflict that need to be evaluated, they form a constant background to any discussion of this aspect of the war.

1. War and war like operations will cause casualties; they are the natural outcome of fighting. Once Europe set course for war in summer 1914, men and some women would be killed and injured, both as military and civilian casualties. That was the only certainty offered by events from August 1914.

2. This eruption of violence, beginning in 1914, was the most ferocious and widespread European war ever, unique in numerous ways for which there was no prior experience, militarily, technologically or politically within the social structures of the nations who became embroiled in the war.

3. The technology of weapons had advanced dramatically in a fifty-year period and had moved in favour of the defender. Improvements to artillery including the ammunition used, infantry equipped with breech

loading rifles and automatic machine guns dominated the battlefield. Airpower was a wholly new factor to be added to the equation of war. Remember if you will that the first manned flight using an internal combustion engine was made by the Wright Brothers only eleven years before the war began. Radio and telecommunications were rudimentary; Marconi's first transatlantic signal was made in 1900. Add to the list as you will.

4. British society and its leadership had no conception of the scope and influence that 'all out' total war would require of the emotional stamina of the nation. Why should the nation understand? It had never happened before to the British nation; Napoleon's war a hundred years previously had only used Britain's professional soldiers. There had been no '*levee en masse*' taking conscripts from their home to fight a foreign war.

5. There were no established tactical doctrines to which commanders could refer when facing an action. Indeed the opening phases of the campaign caused high casualties for both the German and French Armies. The various authorities available to the amateur researcher are surprisingly coy about the losses sustained, the nearest I have come across refers vaguely to the French suffering more than 306,000 casualties and officer losses of 20% of the regular establishment, in the opening weeks of the conflict. The figure for the German forces was 241,000. The British losses were numerically much lower, a direct consequences of the much smaller number of soldiers who fought in the first five months of the war.

Once the light of 1914 is substituted for the undiminished glare of hindsight the statistics of casualties can be approached in a less scornful frame of mind. Before any critic now condemns the decisions of military professionals who undertook command responsibilities it is essential that they offer proof that an alternative could have achieved an equivalent or better result. Better in so far as, the conflict was shortened, the material cost reduced, the casualties fewer, the grief of the population relieved and the outcome, so far as the achievement of a military and political solution at least would be, was satisfactory for the injured nations, as the eventual Versailles treaty of 1919. That is the frame into which the counter arguments must fit. The difficulty faced by both critics and protagonists is that there can be no rerun of events to prove a point, all is conjecture.

There are yet further complications to dealing with this most difficult aspect of the Great War. The world has become used to statements such as, 'more than 55,000 casualties on the first day of the Somme'. Later we shall look in more detail at the casual way in which figures such as this have been used to support a partisan assumption of failure with no attempt to fit the action to the demands and the outcome. Perhaps it was a disaster; the mere repetition of a statistic, however, it is not of itself, an argument.

The discussion of overall casualty numbers including killed, wounded and captured presents two immediate problems. The casualty reporting procedure for the three main players on the Western Front were not directly comparable. This means that if an attempt is made to compare the quality of command based on casualties the prime measure does not translate between the armies. On the face of it a dispassionate commentator would expect there to be little or no issue on the number of combatants killed or wounded in the armies of Britain, France or Germany, such is not the case apparently. John Terraine in his work *The Smoke and the Fire* Chap III, sets out information from official and academic sources from which the inference has to be that there is uncertainty as to the total number of casualties in the numbers quoted. The French information varies between 4.38 million and 6.0 million* including a total of dead that suggest that 1.385 million soldiers in the French Army were killed, but injured were somewhere between 3.0 million and 4.615 million. It is also far from clear if the total for the French Army includes the number of soldiers from the overseas territories such as Algeria.

The numbers for British casualties, also have some uncertainty, the official history quotes a total of 996,000 killed, including troops of the imperial contingents. These totals are though for all losses throughout the world where the British Armies fought. Two established historians of

---

*Comparing several sources gives some veracity to the figure for the number killed of 1.385 million, in a casualty total quoted by C.R.M.F Cruttwell of 4.385 million killed and wounded. The tidy total of 3.0 million injured should probably be treated with some caution; real life does not produce results such as this.

the Great War, John Terraine and Richard Holmes, use with confidence a figure of 750,000 for British soldiers killed on the Western Front. Soldiers from imperial contingents killed on the Western Front totalled 135,000, a total for the armies under British command of 885,000. Additionally there are those who died through disease, accidents and in the case of the Chinese labour corps, those murdered by their fellows for one reason or another. The official statistics for British dead, published by HMSO in 1919, give the following totals for the Western Front; officers 41,846, other ranks 661,960, a total of 703,806 to which must be added the soldiers from the imperial contingents, see above. This later figure seems too low, and it is more respectable to argue the case for the British Army based on the figure of Terraine and Holmes. The German information is more difficult to appraise. The original information was that the German dead totalled 1.8 million, official German sources now quote a figure of 2.037 million some of which occurred on the Russian Front, leaving a mysterious classification 'Missing and Prisoners' of more than a million.

Adjusting this figure to allow for the increase in the numbers killed still leave a total of more than 800,000. Britain returns fewer than 200,000 under this heading.

The paragraphs above are there to illustrate the argument that casualties were not unique to the forces under British command. It is therefore remarkable to the amateur that an author, Robin Cox, publishing in association with the Imperial War Museum, should in writing of Field Marshal Haig, make the unqualified comment that the British forces under his command suffered 750,000 'casualties' in 1916/17. The argument is tendentious; no counterbalancing information is given for other forces on the Western Front. For example the French and German forces together incurred 750,000 casualties in the battle for Verdun.

There is an apparent anxiety amongst those who write the populist version of these historic events to ignore not only the essentials of balanced analysis, the omissions unfortunately seem to have become the accepted version, reinforcing the errors and distorting what ought to be a matter of historical accuracy.

The second issue that arises is counting the wounded. As a starting point how did the reporting procedure operate in the British Army, and the imperial contingents. To recapitulate for a moment, once the lessons of the Crimean War were assessed and the necessary reforms introduced it was realised that the recovery of a trained soldier from injury was a much more economical way to secure replacements troops. The British Army reformed the Army Medical Corps, Royal (RAMC) from 1898, and its medical services with a network of treatment stations with doctors and trained medical orderlies. The Regimental Aid Post (RAP) was the first treatment station, from which soldiers were passed on through Advanced Dressing Stations to Casualty Clearing Stations, the injured then moved on to Field Hospitals or Base Hospitals; there were various categories, according to the treatment needed. The most seriously wounded were evacuated to hospitals in the Britain, a wound needing treatment at such an establishment was known as a 'Blighty One'. To complement the medical services there was an ambulance service using dedicated vehicles, trains, ships and even barges on inland waterways; all under the protection of the 'Red Cross'.

As is common in the British Army, if Tommy Atkins is to receive a benefit such as improved treatment for wounds, there is a price to pay. Once the new improved medical facilities were installed it became a military offence not to report an injury, however slight. This was done as a precaution to avoid the contamination of wounds which could lead to blood poisoning and gangrene, well before the days of antibiotics. Following the 'law of unexpected consequences' this meant that for the British Army and the imperial contingents numbers of wounded on the Western Front reported by the British included those whose injuries were minor, perhaps requiring little more than cleaning and stitches. Also there were soldiers, officers and men, who had been wounded previously and after recovery returned to duty, sometimes within a few days of the injury, under the abbreviated label, D&D – dressing and duties. The effect of this system of counting all wounds, however slight, was to emphasise the total without discrimination. As an example Bernard Freyberg who won his VC in France and commanded the New Zealand forces in the 1939-45 had numerous wounds as a consequence of his service in the Great

War. He was required to strip naked by Winston Churchill during one meeting when he was a general to allow the nosey Prime Minister to count more than a dozen scars. So far as I can find in the accounts I have read there is no way by which double counting can be separated from the total numbers reported. It is a fact that a soldier wounded in one encounter, returned to duty and wounded a second time in another battle is a casualty in each event but it is the same person injured within the army's mobilised strength each time it happens. This means that whilst the deduction of the killed and missing from the total casualty figures provides a figure for the wounded, there is no means of separating the minor injuries from the dangerous and crippling ones or the effect of including soldiers receiving multiple wounds but able to return to duty on two or more occasions. Also it also worth remembering that many soldiers were wounded more than once, but returned to their homes and re-established their lives when the hostilities ended in November 1918.

Note: As a statistic of the casualties suffered by the British Army to set another perspective on the issue; an analysis by the RAMC of the returns of injured treated revealed that 58% of the casualties treated suffered as a result of artillery fire, 39% as a consequence of rifle and machine gun bullets with the balance of 3% due to causes such as grenades, bayonet and gas. The problem again is that the perception of events is influenced by the concentration of circumstances in an entrenched front line, the infantry soldiers bore the brunt of small arms fire, artillery casualties occurred throughout the entire combat zone and sometimes further afield.

The procedure adopted for the British forces is therefore difficult or impossible to compare with German returns. The German system it seems did not include amongst the final reported total of casualties those soldiers "whose recovery was to be expected in a reasonable time". The numbers quoted as 'casualties' for a battle or in total for the war, are not a like for like comparison.

The numbers for the French Army are even more questionable. At the commencement of hostilities in 1914 and for some time thereafter, wounded French soldiers had to be returned to the locality where enlistment took place; surely a system certain to lead to mistakes.

From the above brief comments if casualties are to be used as a measure of the performance on the battlefield of an army and its commanders the inconsistency of information is a serious problem. Another aspect of a comparison of casualties has to make reference to the numbers of mobilised soldiers and if there is to be strict accuracy only the members of units in the combat zone should be counted. The 'non combs' serving in their home country or base area away from the action should be discounted, such a sophisticated analysis is beyond my resources and generalisations will have to suffice. The conclusion reached is that for the purposes of this account the most reliable indicator for effectiveness of the armies concerned should confine itself to the numbers of combatants killed on the Western Front. It is a crude measure at best, but now the dust has settled the official figures as given below are one way to illustrate the human cost to the three major combatant nations of Western Europe and their armies.

Apparent from the foregoing once again must be that when looking at the subject of the Great War, 1914–1918, nothing is as it seems, and there are rich seams of controversy to be mined wherever one looks. That said, some crude comparisons are available and are quoted. A statistical section follows with even more confusing details.

Country	Population in 1914	No mobilised.	No killed.	% killed.
Britain	45,750,000	8,900,000	750,000*	8.4
France	39,000,000	8,410,000	1,357,800	16.1
Germany	60,300,000	11,000,000	2,037,000**	18.5

---

* British totals for the Western Front (France and Belgium). Excludes those from imperial contingents, these details are for comparison of the effect on national populations.
** German total for all European commitments, see paras below for further discussion.

The base information for this comparison is taken from Gordon Corrigan's publication, *Mud, Blood and Poppycock*. In this book he quotes a figure for British killed of 702,410. This is close to the official return published in 1919, which as noted above is lower than the totals now commonly used by historians of note. The army fielded by Britain during the Great War had contingents from the Empire: Australia, Canada, New Zealand, South Africa and most notably India. To attempt to relate the casualties, killed or wounded, to the national populations of these countries is a task I cannot contemplate. In the tabular presentation I have used only the figures for Britain. If the numbers of those killed is expressed as a percentage of the total population of the countries the figures become, Britain 1.58%, France 3.7% and Germany 3.38%. I appreciate that these figures are playing with numbers; it is however a comparison of Allied and enemy losses which is, to say the least, startling.

Having advanced an argument above to explain the realities for numbers reported as wounded, figures available on the 'Wikipedia' website provide other interesting comparisons. The numbers cited for wounded are as follows: Britain, excluding imperial forces, 1,663,435; France 4,266,000, Russia 4,950,000, Germany 4,247,143. Taking into account the difference created because the German Army fought a war on two fronts, if 70% of the German casualties are allocated to the Western Front (see para below) that would give a figure for the number of wounded of 2,973,000, 44% more than the equivalent figure for British wounded! The number killed for the German Army on the Western Front would be 1,425,900, 90% more than British losses. The figures are at best rough estimates, they do reveal however a major discrepancy between the received wisdom of the 'Butchers and Bunglers' school of historical comment and the reality of my shaky estimates.

The implications of these figures have to be treated with caution, Britain fielded five infantry divisions and a cavalry division in August 1914, the French fifty-five and the German Army more than eighty divisions; more men in the field, more men get killed. The German assault on Verdun cost the French and German Armies dearly. In 1917 after the French spring offensive and the subsequent mutinies there was a period of hibernation by the French Army on the Western Front. Arras,

Messines Ridge and Passchendaele were all British operations and bloody they were, compensating in some way for the small numbers who were available for commitment by Britain in 1914.

This is by no means all the story or anything like it, when considering the casualty statistics it is essential to bear the following in mind:

1. The number of men mobilised by Britain will include those who were deployed to other theatres of war such as Gallipoli, Egypt and Palestine, Mesopotamia (modern day Iraq), Serbia, Italy and East Africa. To set against these deployments, British forces in France included contingents from Australia, Canada including Newfoundland, India, New Zealand and South Africa.

2. The German Army was fighting on two fronts, Russia in the East in conjunction with the armies of Austria Hungary as well as the Western Front in Belgium and France. The best information I have found indicates that the German Armies' *maximum* deployment of troops to the Eastern Front was 30%. The commitment to the Western Front would have been 70%. Adjusting this figure of the number mobilised to this ratio results in a deployment of approx 7.5 million in the German Armies confronting combined British and French manpower resources of 16,875,000. A ratio of 2.25:1 in favour of the Western Allies. Conventional military doctrine is that the ratio of attackers to defenders should be 3:1. That though does not allow for the Allies concentrating forces at the point of attack to achieve temporary numerical superiority.

3. Applying the same ratios to the German casualty figure the numbers killed in German Armies in France and Belgium during the fighting would be approximately 1,222,200 (15.3% of mobilised strength).

These crude adjustments of figures put another perspective on the arguments; French casualties would have been 11.4% more than the projected figure for the German Army, British casualties 18.5% less than the German figure. Another measure is to index the casualty totals, using the British figure as 100, the German casualties, based on the above estimated Western Front strengths and losses, would be 122 and for the French, 139.

Just as a reminder, the Germans were defending their gains in Belgium and France, the Western Allies were fighting to restore the *'status quo ante'*, for this to be achieved the biggest siege in history had to be broken.

Somewhere in the generalised myths of this war I seem to recall it is the British commanders, Haig in particular, who stand accused of careless commitment of troops to battle with a consequent excess of casualties. All is not as it seems, yet again.

A noticeable aspect of the texts of many of the accounts of the Great War is the liberal use of emotional or pejorative adjectives when the issue of battle actions, casualties and achievements are considered. A writer/commentator whose text relies on such words as; fiasco, needless, extravagant, prodigal, squander, fritter, slaughter and so on gives a clear indication of prejudice. The words are a clear warning to any reader to treat the opinions with caution. Any half way decent manager will admit that many decisions and plans made in business are based on information as appreciated at the time, with some allowance for the unforeseen, but success is never guaranteed. Many times a manager takes a chance, only when the effect on performance is seen in the accounts is the quality of their decisions revealed, managers though deal with accounts reckoned in cash, not human life.

Having expressed reservations about the value of unqualified casualty figures there are some published details which express the scale of the fighting by the armies on the Western Front and these are summarised below, not to point to failures, but to offer some information to enable the scale of the undertaking and the extent of the human endeavour consumed by the war of 1914–1918 to be remembered.

Engagement. (year)	Total casualties. (all forces)	British.	French.	German.
Neuve Chappel (1915)	23,500	10,500	n/c*	13,000
2nd Ypres (1915)	95,000	60,000	n/c*	35,000
Champagne (1915)	205,000	n/c*	145,000	60,000
Verdun (1916)	720,000	n/c*	380,200	339,800
Somme (1916)	1,070,000	450,500	200,000	419,500
Chemin des Dames (1917 Spring offensive)	160,000	n/c*	120,000	40,000
Passchendaele (1917 3rd Ypres)	470,000	245,000**	n/c*	200,000
Spring Offensive (1918)	270,000	150,000	allied total	120,000
Final offensive	350,000			

If the daily casualty rates of some of the battles are considered the details again help to define the scale of the endeavours. For the Somme in 1916 which lasted 141 days the daily rate of British casualties was 3195, Arras in 1917 lasting thirty-nine days was 4076 per day, 3rd Ypres was 2323 per day and the advance to victory beginning in August 1918, lasting ninety-six days was 3645 per day.

These details all reinforce the opinion already expressed that with a subject so vast, almost any argument can be sustained by using well selected information favourable to your personal point of view. A situation

*n/c. No formations committed from armies under national command.
** Number quoted at Versailles Conference, 1919.

which should serve as a caution to many is summed up in the well worn adage "I've made up my mind please don't confuse me with the facts".

In a conclusion for this portion, attention has to be turned to two of the most persistent myths that sustain prejudice on the issue of the Great War, firstly, that the losses amounted to the death of a generation. A generation is generally regarded as twenty-five years and, allowing for an even spread of soldiers in the age group eighteen to forty-three years, almost one million British Army soldiers are buried as a result of enemy action, 2.18% of the total population, approx 6.5% of the relevant age group of the population in 1914, a grievous but not unsustainable loss. It is not a generation, however you reconstruct the arithmetic. Secondly, the more difficult issue raised by the losses to 'Pals' Battalions' such as Accrington, Bradford and Leeds. Some writers put aside the folklore that surrounds the effect of the day in early July when numerous homes received the dreadful telegram that opened with the words 'The War Office regrets to inform you that Private Thomas Atkins no 88465 is reported killed in action' or one of the awful alternatives. To suggest as some do that the pain was equally spread through the nation and was therefore not special to one place is to misunderstand the communities of places such as Accrington, a northern mill town. More than 200 dead in one day, there would not be a family unaffected by the loss of a husband, son, brother, cousin, fiancé or nephew. The extended families that formed the basis of the close communities of such towns were both the strength and the weakness of the 'Pals' Battalions'; the grief of these communities must have been overwhelming. Small wonder there is folklore. Do not believe all that is written on the subject, but do use your own observations and mark the lengthy list of the names on the war memorials of our towns and villages. Beware at all times the professional media personalities and grief mongers with their crocodile tears.

To return finally in this portion of the account to the extent of the casualties, killed and wounded, and avoiding adjectives it needs to be repeated that all of the casualties – every single one of them – was unnecessary, this was a war that should never have taken place and Kaiser Wilhelm II, his army staff and the German nation all must accept responsibility. That said, when reading Ernst Younger's *Storm of Steel* there is no recognisable acknowledgement by him in the text that the occupation of another nation's territory was in anyway wrong; quite remarkable.

The 'Thankful Villages'

This term originated to describe the few communities, villages throughout the land, whose young men, needed for the armed forces of the Crown, were thankful; for all their men returned alive to their homes on completion of their service at the end of hostilities. Remarkable as such an event may seem.

The originator of this term was a writer and journalist, Arthur Mee, who wrote a series of guides to the counties of England and Wales titled *King's England* published during the 1930s. He expressed the view that there were at most thirty-two such communities, although he could only be positive about twenty-four. Later research has identified forty-one parishes who have the distinction of a 'Thankful Village' from the 16,000 such communities there were reckoned to be, when hostilities ceased in 1918.

The distribution of the parishes is quite random, twenty-one of the counties of England and Wales have villages that qualify. Somerset for example has seven of the total, Lincolnshire and Nottinghamshire four each, Gloucestershire three, Lancashire and Northamptonshire two each. The remainder, thirteen counties, each had one of these fortunate communities. Notable amongst this last group was the village of Arkholme in Lancashire which saw fifty-nine of its men go to war and all returned to tell their stories, or like so many 'keep their peace'. The experiences were so often shared only with those who had lived the experiences of the fighting man.

COUNTRY.	TOTAL MOBILISED. (millions)	KILLED & DIED. (millions)	% of mob'sed	WOUNDED. (millions)	PRISONERS & MISSING. (millions)	TOTAL CASUALTIES. (millions)	CASUALTIES as % of MOBILISED
Austria/Hungary. (cp)	7.8	1.2	15.4	3.62	2.2	7.02	90
Britain incl. Imperial troops. (ap)	8.904	0.908	10.8	2.0902	0.1916	3.1902	35.8
Belgium. (ap)	0.267	0.01376	5.1	0.0447	0.0347	0.9306	34.9
Bulgaria. (cp)	1.2	0.087	7.3	0.15239	0.02703	0.2669	22.2
France. (ap)	8.41	1.3578	16.1(5)	4.266	0.537	6.161	76.3
Germany. (cp)	11.0	1.7737*	16.1*	4.216	1.153*	7.1426	64.9
Greece. (ap)	0.23	0.005	2.2	0.021	0.001	0.017	11.7
Italy.(ap)	5.615	0.65	11.6	0.947	0.6	2.197	39.1
Japan. (ap)	0.8	0.0003	0.4	0.0009	0.00003	0.00121	0.2
Montenegro. (ap)	0.05	0.003	6	0.01	0.007	0.02	40
Portugal. (ap)	0.1	0.007222	7.2	0.013751	0.01232	0.03329	33.3
Romania. (ap)	0.75	0.3357	44.8	0.12	0.08	0.5357	71.4
Russia. (ap)	12.0	1.7	14.2	4.95	2.5	9.15	76.3
Serbia. (ap)	0.7073	0.045	6.4	0.1332	0.153	0.3311	46.8
Turkey. (cp)	2.85	0.325	11.4	0.4	0.25	0.975	34.2

COUNTRY.	TOTAL MOBILISED. (millions)	KILLED & DIED. (millions)	% of mob'sed	WOUNDED. (millions)	PRISONERS & MISSING. (millions)	TOTAL CASUALTIES. (millions)	CASUALTIES as % of MOBILISED
United States. (ap)	4.355	0.126	2.9	0.2343	0.0045	0.3648	8.2
Total, Allied Powers.	42.1888	5.1521	12.2	12.831	4.121	22.104	52.3
Total, Central Powers	22.85	3.386	14.8	8.388	3.629	15.4045	67.4
Total, all Combatant Nations.	65.038	8.538	13.12	21219.45	7.7501	37.5087	57.6
*German totals have been revised.		2.037	18.15	4.216	0,890	7.1426	64.9
(ap) Allied Powers.		(cp) Central Powers.		101			

178

Casualty Statistics; Commentary

1. Source
The compilers of the table of casualties qualify the information with the warning that the figures quoted are estimates compiled from reliable sources, all of which vary.

2. Commentary
2.1 The table of casualties is the most comprehensive summary found in the readily accessible sources of information, books and websites. The detailed figures vary, as is common, between sources and this issue is referred to in the main body of the text. The variation of detail between the individual sources does not upset the general pattern of losses sustained.

2.2 The figures from Table I demonstrate clearly that the war was essentially between seven combatant nations, Austria/Hungary, Britain, France, Germany, Russia, Italy and Turkey; the last two nations fighting in their own theatres of war and outside the Western Front battles.

2.3 The number of troops mobilised by nations is a reflection of several factors such as the population total, geography, national resources etc. The contribution of Japan was confined to the Pacific and maritime actions, Montenegro and Greece, the Balkans; America her late entry (April 1917) to the war and the long lead time needed to put the first battle equipped division into the field (ten months). British forces committed to the war included troops from the Empire. Any attempt to calculate the proportion of the male population of the Empire has to reconcile the huge population numbers of India such a factor will distort the credibility of the argument.

2.4 The term casualty/casualties has been discussed in the main text, the figures contained within the table illustrate well the anomalies that have arisen through the various practices adopted by different armies and one suspects in some cases the appalling standard of administration. For example; Austria/Hungary is reported as having 2.2 million 'prisoners and missing', 28% of the mobilised force; Russia 2.0 million, 20%; Germany 0.89 million, 8.09%; France 0.537 million 6.4%; Britain 0.1916 million, 2.15%. In the case of both Austria/Hungary and Russia there

179

must be the suspicion that the numbers killed is seriously under reported.

3. Statistical Information

"There are," said the sage; "Lies, damned lies and statistics"*. Venture here at your peril! (* attributed variously to Mark Twain, Henry Labouchere, Abraham Hewitt and Cdr. Holloway R. Frost)

3.1. Percentage calculations, carried out in the time honoured way we all experienced during our education. Beware though, percentages are stand alone figures, the 'averaging' of a series of percentages is a big statistical no no. And yes I did come across one author who tried to argue a point based on such a trick.

3.2. Average (preferred statistical term is mean), the measure of central tendency. We are all used to the common expressions; average temperature, speed, weight, etc. The arithmetical mean which is the one in use here is calculated in the conventional way. This is a straightforward arrangement and calculation, not difficult to undertake with modern electronic aids. The weakness is that the outcome of the calculations can be distorted if the figures used are heavily 'skewed' that is if there are too many results at one of the extremes of the range. This weights the average and can distort conclusions, unless the user has his wits about him or her. Also as with percentages, averaging averages is not an option unless provision is made for the different population sizes.

There is a second version of the 'mean' which in the context of the type of information contained within the casualty table has much to commend it; the median. This is a value of central tendency specifically related to the range of values to which it refers. It is calculated as the midpoint figure between the highest and lowest in the series without reference to the actual value of results in the range. Also unlike the mean referred to above, because the values remain unchanged the median for a range of percentages is a valid statistical comparison between the median of other relevant data.

When the mean and the median are used in conjunction with each other a clearer idea can result of the meaning of the figures. That is why politicians don't use them together.

4. Statistical Review

4.1 The tabulations that follow compare the casualties of the seven major combatant using the criteria of numbers mobilised. Four of the nations fought exclusively in their own theatres of war. In the East, Russia and Austria/Hungary, Asia Minor and the Middle East, Turkey and Southern Europe, Italy. The armies of these countries mobilised 87% of the combatants engaged in the Great War. The United States has been excluded, though it mobilised 4.35million men (6.7% of mobilised forces) the number deployed and the limited time during which they were committed to the conflict was thought to be insufficient for inclusion of their data, in this comparison.

The three tables that follow overleaf compare the effect of casualties for national armies with the median for this group of combatant forces.

Table II; Numbers killed and died as % of numbers mobilised

NATION	KILLED as % of MOBILISED
Britain	10.8
Turkey	11.4
Italy	11.6
Median	*13.45*
Russia	14.2
Austria/Hungary	15.4
France	16.1
Germany	16.1 later revised to 18.5

Table III; Number of casualties as % of numbers mobilised

NATION	CASUALTIES as % of MOBILISED
Turkey	34.2
Britain	35.8
Italy	39.1
Median	*62.1*
Germany	64.9
France	76.3
Russia	76.3
Austria/Hungary	90.0

Table IV; Total of Casualties

NATION	NUMBER of CASUALTIES (millions)
Turkey	0.975
Italy	2.2
Britain	3.19
Median	*5.06*
France	6.16
Austria/Hungary	7.02
Germany	7.14
Russia	9.15

NB. The casualties incurred by the German Army is a total, the proportion of those which resulted from action with the Austro/Hungarian Armies on the Eastern (Russian) Front is not shown in the sources consulted. Taking the division of resources as 70/30, Western to Eastern, the figure for % killed as a proportion of those mobilised of 18.5% has some credence. It seems unlikely that Germany would have committed less than 70% of its effort to its principal theatre of operations.

5. Death of a Generation?

The intention of this section is to use a model to look at the implications of the numbers killed for the society when hostilities ended and the actuality of war was removed from the social, political and economic equation of the day. Populations had been severely depleted by the death of significant numbers of men, concentrated as these losses were in a generational age span of twenty-five to thirty years: was it though the 'death of a generation'?

This change needed serious social and economic adjustments affecting, as it did, mainly the age group eighteen to forty-five years or thereabouts and there would be a disproportionate number in the affected cohort below the age of thirty-five years. Why? Because high intensity conflict is for young and fit men. Older soldiers have their place as leaders and trainers, but as front line footsloggers their contribution diminishes as age increases, the task is too physically demanding. Capt. J. C. Dunn, RAMC, Medical Officer, 2nd Bn, The Royal Welch Fusiliers makes the point a second time in his diaries published as, *The War the Infantry Knew*, Chap II and he should know!

The dead of the combatant armies we have to assume would have been of the same age group. This is not to say that older soldiers were not killed, artillery has a long reach. Also as the war lengthened all the combatant nations were forced to find soldiers from age groups which in 1914 would not have been considered.

The model has been constructed using various assumptions which are set out below. It is an attempt, no more, to provide an analysis by comparison of between three of the combatant nations of the effect of depleting national populations in the 'breeding' cohort of the social structure.

The assumptions made in the preparation of the model were as follows:

- National populations are divided equally male and female; there is in reality a slight imbalance with more females than males both by numbers and longevity.
- A generation span has been assumed to be twenty-five to thirty years. Casualties were concentrated in the age range eighteen to forty-five years, but a notional 5% adjustment has been introduced for those outside this age range.
- The national population assuming no distortion was divided into cohorts by age. The cohorts would reduce numerically by reason of natural causes over the years. The largest group would be the youngest and with equal age ranges each cohort would be smaller than its predecessor by reason of: the increase in national birth rates, illness, accident and emigration.
- The rate at which the cohorts diminish and the size of each, are assumptions for the purposes of this model.

Taking the information and the breakdown into age cohorts, the effects of the losses can be looked at in detail. The three combatant nations considered in alphabetical order are; Britain, France and Germany.

Britain
Population, 45,750,000. Males, 22,875,000. No. mobilised, 8,500,000. No. killed 775,000

Population cohorts by age range, percentage and number (millions).

Age	0-5	6-15	16-25	26-35	36-45	46-55	56-65	66-75	76+
%	6	16	15.5	14.5	13	12	10	8	5
No.	1.373	3.66	3.546	3.317	2.974	2.745	2.288	1.83	1.144

Crucial population age group, ages sixteen to forty-five: 9,837.
43% of male population.

No. killed, adjusted to 95% for out of age range casualties, 0.735, ie 7.5% of crucial age range.

France

Population, 39,000,000. Males, 19,500,000. No mobilised 8,410,000. No. killed 1,391,000

Population cohorts by age range, percentage and number (millions).

Age	0-5	6-15	16-25	26-35	36-45	46-55	56-65	66-75	76+
%	6	16	15.5	14.5	13	12	10	8	5
No.	1.17	3.120	3.023	2.878	2.535	2.340	1.950	1.560	0.975

Crucial population age group, ages sixteen to forty-five: 8,436. 43% of male population.
No. killed, adjusted to 95% for out of age range casualties, 1.391, ie 16.5% of crucial age range.

Germany

Population, 60,300,000. Males, 30,150,000. No mobilised, 13,250,000. No. killed, 2,037,000

Population cohorts by age range, percentage and number (millions) .

Age	0-5	6-15	16-25	26-35	36-45	46-55	56-65	66-75	76+
%	6	16	15.5	14.5	13	12	10	8	5
No.	1.809	4.824	4.673	4.372	3.920	3.618	3.015	2.412	1.508

Crucial population age group, ages sixteen to forty-five: 2.965. 43% of male population.
No. killed, adjusted to 95% for out of age range casualties, 2.037, ie 14.9% of crucial age range.

The question therefore is did the losses amount to the death of a generation? The answer has to be a qualified no. There were towns and communities that suffered disproportionate losses and to which attention was naturally drawn. The British nation lost 7.5% of its young men a significant but not devastating proportion, had it been evenly spread which it was not. It followed from this that in an age when the social morality of the day frowned on extra marital activities a young married man would not 'play away' and have children outside a regular family. In such circumstances, things being as they were, young women went unmarried and essentially childless. One estimate puts the figure at one million; that though seems likely to be an overstatement. They were not though lost to the nation and the years between the wars saw women taking employment and gaining seniority and respect for their contribution, often against strong male opposition in professions such as medicine, teaching, journalism and politics.

German losses of this crucial generation were double those of Britain; France suffered losses to an even greater extent. The British legend, as is all good folklore before it, is founded in fact, but accuracy is lost in translation.

6. Summary

6.1 The data included in the tables should be interpreted, as should all statistics, as confirmation of general circumstances and perspective, trends rather than proof positive of any exact number or specific proposition. The issues of significance that can be summarised from the information are as follows.

6.1.1 The figures of 'Prisoners and Missing' in the returns of Austria/Hungary and Russia are of such magnitude when compared to the numbers of 'killed' and 'wounded' that serious doubt arises as to whether the numbers for any of the categories are an adequate reflection of the extent of the damage done to the armies and nations involved in the conflict.

6.1.2 The number of 'Prisoners and Missing' reported for the German Army is also too great for such a well disciplined fighting organisation. This may account in part for the upward revision of numbers killed for the German Army from the figure quoted above of 1.7737 million (16.1% of mobilised strength) to a more recent higher total of 2.037 million

(18.5% of mobilised strength). This increased figure for Germans killed should lead to a reduction of the 'Prisoners and Missing' figure from the original 1.153 million to 890,000 which remains an astonishingly high figure for the thorough Teutonic state of Germany.

6.1.3 The arrangement of the figures for the seven major combatant nations in rank order with the 'median' for comparison is as near as we are likely to come to identifying the true position of armies in the casualty league. The armies under British command suffered less by way of numbers killed, wounded, prisoners and missing than any of the other combatant armies on the Western Front and in terms of the war fought in Europe, Asia Minor and the Middle East did not sustain disproportionate casualties in pursuit of victory.

6.1.4 As casualties have a causal connection with the quality of command the evidence of these statistics supports a conclusion that although not perfect, the achievements of British generals was at least as good as that of other combatants and better than those whose national armies casualties exceed the median for the category; France, Germany, Russia and Austria/Hungary. Despite the losses the British Army made a better job of conserving its manpower than the other major combatant nations.

QUOD ERAT DEMONSTRANDUM.

Dedication.

Miss Edna Snell*.
(an unremarked casualty of the conflict)

This section is dedicated to Miss Snell who died aged 105 in the millennium year 2000. At the age of twenty years in 1915 her fiancée, Billie Smith, a Kitchener soldier aged twenty-two years, was killed in France. She never forgot her young love and died in her sleep holding her only remaining memento, a photograph on the back of which he had inscribed his last message of affection.

(*source, *Daily Telegraph* report)

CHAPTER 10

The Royal Navy

The Royal Navy went to war in 1914 as the darling of the nation. Capital investment had been lavished on the senior service since the wooden walls of England were replaced first by the 'iron-clad', then by armoured steel, steam driven monsters. Money had been poured into the navy to protect imperial trade. The overseas possessions provided harbours, coaling stations and dockyards. The concept of *'Pax Brittanica'* and freedom to navigate the seven seas was the justification for the unusually generous treatment the navy received from governments and the treasury. Ship type followed ship type; guns of any calibre you like were manufactured to replace muzzle loading cannon and then installed in the floating fortresses. Steam was mixed with sail, for a time propellers could be raised and lowered at the captain's whim. For the guns, sponsons, barbettes and turrets were all given a trial. Power, speed and tonnage were increased, electrical systems were introduced, steam turbines replaced the inefficient double and triple expansion, reciprocating engines. After trial and error at last the naval architects determined a ship design to make the most of the new technology. Single calibre main armament fore and aft*, mounted in rotating turrets located on the centre line, command centre, bridge that is, forward of the midpoint of the hull, immediately aft of the forward guns, secondary weapons of common calibre aft of the bridge to port and starboard sides of the hull; engines and fuel deep in the hull, together with ammunition.

---

* For a time there was an additional big gun turret located on the centre line just aft of mid ships, of necessity the guns of this turret could only fire to port or starboard in broadside fire and was therefore of limited utility

The 'iron-clad' with auxiliary steam engines, successor to the wooden walls ship of the line, became transformed into a recognisable, armoured steel, battle wagon, or cruiser, or destroyer, or frigate; the principals were the same it was the size that varied, until that is one looked at the new fangled submarine armed with the Whitehead torpedo.

The key to the whole edifice was coal. Warships of the day consumed prodigious quantities of the best Welsh steaming coal. To sustain the supply of this fuel the trade routes had to be kept open for all, this was a task, so the argument ran, which only the fair minded British, who already had worldwide coaling stations in the harbours of numerous colonies, could be trusted to undertake. Do you detect the self sustaining nature of the proposition? The Germans, post 1871, and in particular Kaiser Wilhelm II took serious exception to this assumption of supremacy. Willy's Germany convinced itself that the new nation had a right to a 'Place in the Sun'. And so another section of the road to Armageddon slotted into place.

The outline of the naval arms race from the time of Edward VII's accession to the throne is described in an earlier portion of this expedition through history and is not to be repeated here. The aspect of the British response to the German policy of naval expansion not included in the previous ramblings is the issue of personalities. At this critical juncture in history, the Royal Navy came under the influence of a professional naval officer of intellectual genius and maverick personality, John 'Jackie' Fisher, later Admiral of the Fleet and Peer of the Realm. Admiral Fisher by himself would have been a handful for the political establishment, but it never rains etc. Who else was making a name and building a career as a politician, none other than Winston Spencer Churchill. The two together were dynamite looking for an explosion.

Admiral Fisher was the man who envisaged the full development of the twentieth century ship of the line and the outcome of his inspiration was a 'capital ship', a battleship which took the class name of the first ship built, HMS Dreadnought. The new ship consolidated all the experience acquired of steam powered warships and produced, for the time, a leviathan, 18,110 tons, 527 ft (176m) long, 10 x 12" main guns in five turrets plus secondary armament plus torpedo tubes, the armoured hull driven by direct drive steam turbines to provide a design maximum speed of twenty-one knots. Later ships were "bigger and better" and called super Dreadnoughts. The ships for which he was responsible were Fisher's masterpiece, all other capital ships worldwide were immediately obsolescent, Wilhelm II of Germany was mortified. So, incidentally, were all the other governments worldwide who had bought ships from British yards before the advent of Dreadnought. Nice big earner for Vickers and all the other shipbuilders replacing the obsolescent battle wagons so recently built and paid for; Oh Perfidious (and profitable) Albion!

The race was on, between 1905, when Dreadnought was launched, and 1914; Britain built thirty-two battleships and ten, more lightly armoured, higher speed, battle cruisers; the Germans nineteen and six respectively. There was a major difficulty for the German construction programme. The factor that determined the number of capital ships which could be completed was not, as many suppose, the number of hulls laid down or even the manufacture and installation of the engines. The limitation was, for the Germans, the inability of Herr Krupp to make the turrets and guns for the new ships in sufficient numbers. In the ten year period leading to the Great War Britain's capital ship production exceeded Germany by almost 60%. Amongst the significant innovations of the Dreadnought design specification was the introduction of steam turbine engines. This innovative design had been pioneered by the British engineer Charles Parsons who publicised the advantage of his invention by setting his experimental craft 'Turbinia' on a daring high speed trial through the Fleet review for Queen Victoria's Diamond Jubilee in 1897.

The advantage of the turbine is that because of the limited number of moving parts, essentially a single shaft on which rotors and stators are positioned, practically a series of shaped blades that catch the force of high pressure steam injected into the casing in which the turbine is contained. The simplicity of design allows sustained high performance for long periods. A great advantage when the demands of a fleet action are needed on call. The Royal Navy's 'Queen Elizabeth' Class of oil fired 'super' Dreadnoughts proved to a very reliable combination of fuel, boilers and engines. The alternative used previously, triple expansion, reciprocating engines were of a different order of complication. Each engine has three sets of cylinders, pistons with glands that leak, cranks, bearings and other sundry gee gaws that need constant lubrication and even then can and usually do malfunction at the crucial moment. Operate engines of this sort to the limit for any length of time and it all ends in tears. Not what you need when you are committed to high speed action against a determined enemy who can stay the course. The German fleet at Jutland included six pre Dreadnought capital ships in the 'battle order', there were no such ships in the larger British 'Grand Fleet' when battle was joined.

The problem encountered in the transition of naval warfare from the established procedures of the wooden fleets dependant on sail and wind to the techniques and concepts needed to make the most of the Dreadnought class of ship, is that from the time the Napoleonic wars were completed the navy did not fight a single fleet action. It, the 'navy', appeared on the scene in 1827 to reinforce the Greeks in their fight to obtain independence from the Ottoman Empire and huffed and puffed during the Crimean War. Nowhere though were battle tactics given a trial in the cauldron of warfare. It was a grave disadvantage; the issues of command and control, gunnery direction, signalling and manoeuvre of the innovative self propelled, modern steel warship in the confusion of battle were in the Royal Navy all a matter of theory. Well almost, in June 1893 Admiral Sir George Tyron, C in C Mediterranean Fleet was commanding an exercise in the Eastern Med during daylight in calm conditions, he took matters further, with two columns of six battleships in each. His intention appears to have been to reverse the course of his ships. He gave orders and the ships turned towards each other, there was insufficient sea room. The flag ship, HMS Victoria had a serious coming together with the leading ship of the second column, HMS Camperdown. Victoria sank and with her the admiral, taking with him his reputation as an irascible martinet who entertained the belief that a subordinate, even one of flag rank, who received the time of day from Sir George should be grateful.

The only practical example of what could and could not be done was the experiences of the respective navies in the Russo Japanese War when the Japanese won two resounding victories and effectively destroyed the Russian Navy.

The Battle of Tsushima in May 1905 was not a battle of equals. The Japanese had launched a pre-emptive naval attack on the Russian Pacific fleet in their base at Port Arthur in February 1904. Over the next few weeks more actions between the fleets inflicted further damage to the Russian ships that survived the initial raid. In December 1904 Port Arthur itself was captured by Japanese ground forces. The Russian Naval forces on the east coast of the nation had to all intents and purposes been eliminated. The few remaining ships were forced to withdraw to Vladivostock, further north. Russia was in naval terms at an enormous disadvantage. Given the distances between the navigable seaboards of the nation, the northern seaboard with the Arctic Ocean was not an option, the concept of mutual support was no more than so many words and quite unachievable. She was also short of shipbuilding capacity and the ability to manufacture heavy armaments.

Russia was drawn into the war by the aggressive incursions of the Japanese and a response had to be made to defend the eastern seaboard of the Tsar's empire. The Russian Baltic Fleet was dispatched, to sail half way round the world and confront the enemy. For any navy without a single dedicated coaling station or dockyard between the port of departure and destination such a voyage, via the Cape of Good Hope for the capital ships and the Suez Canal for the smaller ones, was a monumental undertaking. Every type of support vessel had to be found. Colliers, repair ships, hospital ships, stores ships and probably others as well were essential to the enterprise. In all probability the Royal Navy of Britain would have given any suggestion of such an enterprise no chance of success at all, for the Russians it was an action born of desperation. So it proved to be.

The Russian fleet made its way from the Baltic into the Atlantic, sinking a British fishing boat in the North Sea, having mistaken the trawler for a Japanese torpedo boat! (An event that does not speak well of the nautical competence of the Russian Naval command.) The ships of the Russian Baltic Fleet finally reached the Straits of Korea on 27 May 1905 with the objective of sailing on to the harbour and dockyard of Vladivostock to make good the wear and tear of a six month voyage from the Baltic. The Japanese, commanded by Admiral Heihachiro Togo, had other ideas. Bright eyed, fresh and close to home ports, Togo's ships met the Russians off the Island of Tsushima to do battle. The Russian battle line advanced at a stately nine knots, probably the maximum possible. The Japanese went in at full tilt, crossed the 'T' of the advancing Russians and devastated their enemy. In just a few hours and a quick bit of clearing up the following morning the Russians were routed. Two fleets lost in just a few months, Oscar Wilde's Lady Bracknell would certainly have had something to say about such carelessness.

In the space of a year the vulnerability of battleships to the devastation of high explosives was made plain for all to see. What happened? The major navies and their governments went on building bigger and better battleships. Who was in the forefront of the building programme, none other than Britain's Admiral 'Jackie' Fisher, hotly pursued by Germany and Willie.

The point of these digressions from the events of the Great War is to realise that the actual experience of using the power of the twentieth century battle fleet had only been tested in practice on a very limited scale. Even the manoeuvring was largely a matter of adaptation of the techniques of the line of battle of the wooden sailing men o' war. In the absence of war conditions, fighting the enemy was not available to influence the tactical or strategic philosophy of the Royal Navy. Instead the Lords of the Admiralty transformed appearance into a measure of fighting qualities. Even the quality of the gunfire was compromised as the heat from the big shells was so intense the paint on the gun barrels blistered. This spoilt the appearance and often required the ship's captain to purchase high grade enamel paint, at his own expense, to smarten things up again. For too long the navy did not take gunnery seriously, only the determination of Fisher and another admiral of very different qualities, Sir Percy Scott, brought the voice of reason to the subject, imposing improvements in the performance of HM ships in their prime task of sinking the enemy. If they had not done so the achievements of the Allied armies who were to fight tooth and nail every day from August 1914 to November 1918 were in danger of being thrown away.

To level such serious accusations against a national institution calls for justification. Consider the following.

1. The newly commissioned battleship, HMS Audacious, sank in the Irish Sea on 27 October 1914, after hitting a single mine.

2. Three cruisers, admittedly not new, HMSs Aboukir, Crecy and Houge sank as a result of torpedo action by the submarine U9 in the North Sea, when undertaking close blockade duty. There was heavy loss of life.

3. The German battle cruiser Goeben and the light cruiser Breslau escaped the surveillance of the Royal Navy and the French Navy off the coast of Morocco, sailed through the Mediterranean to Constantinople, modern Istanbul, and joined the fleet of Germany's ally, Turkey.

4. The Royal Navy in its wisdom, knowing full well that the Germans had deployed a small but powerful squadron in the Pacific, provided no reinforcement to the command of Sir Christopher Craddock whose main constituents were the HMSs, Canopus a pre Dreadnought battleship, Monmouth and Good Hope armoured cruisers, the light cruiser, Glasgow and a converted liner Otranto. Murphy was of course lurking in the wings and sure enough action was joined off the coast of southern Chile at Coronel. Admiral Craddock and his command were obliterated. Glasgow escaped though hit by gun fire five times. Otranto had been ordered to escape. The position was only recovered by the hasty dispatch of the battle cruisers Inflexible and Invincible under Sir Doveton Sturdee. He was coaling his ships in the Falklands Islands when the German squadron showed up, the outcome evened the score.

5. The German heavy ships were not deterred from nuisance raids on English east coast ports and towns such as Hartlepool and Scarborough.

6. The introduction of submarine warfare by the Germans found the Admiralty with no plans for the protection of merchant shipping; shipping that sustained the war effort on the Western Front. The convoy system was introduced only when losses reached a point of national crisis and was forced on a reluctant navy. The shipping losses were then brought down to an acceptable tonnage.

7. German commerce raiders went on the loose in the Indian Ocean

and only a lot of effort dealt with the problem including sinking the notorious Emden. There were no plans or ships in place to cut off the raiders' source of supply until damage had been done.

8. The Royal Navy's engagement in January 1915 off the Dogger Bank in the North Sea was inconclusive, the British were present in superior numbers of capital ships, five to three, gunfire seriously damaged two of the three German ships. Then, would you believe it, the navy got its signals mixed up and instead of going after the withdrawing enemy ships, concentrated on one that was already badly damaged. It was a precursor of Jutland.

9. The navy deployed older ships, pre Dreadnought, that failed to force the passage of the Dardanelles as part of the joint offensive with France against Germany's ally Turkey and lost several ships to mines and shell fire.

10. Then there was Jutland on 31st May and 1st June 1916. The controversy surrounding the clash of the titans has been recounted times without number and has provided a rich source of material for any point of view you like to take. The bald facts of the event are that the British capital ship forces outnumbered the opposition in a ratio of 1.5/1.0. The Royal Navy gained the tactical advantage of crossing the enemies 'T' not once but twice. The German High Seas Fleet though paid some attention to the perils of dealing with a battle scene if their fleet were to be at a disadvantage. The outcome of their planning was to conceive and introduce to their battle plans a manoeuvre referred to as a 'battle turn away'. This allowed for all the ships of a formation to turn away simultaneously from a point of danger. This tactic it seems had not been considered by the Royal Navy who expected their opposition to turn in sequence and take their punishment. The British Grand Fleet lost more capital ships than the German High Seas Fleet and the Germans returned to their home port. However never again did the German ships venture battle with the Royal Navy. It was a tactical draw but a strategic victory.

11. Then as if this sorry litany was insufficient, there was the 'battle' of May Island. The setting for this event was the Firth of Forth on the afternoon and evening of 31st January 1918. The Isle of May is a

rocky outcrop, big enough for a lighthouse and a couple of cottages five miles from the northern shore of the estuary on a line running south from Crail on the northern shore to Dunbar on the southern shore of the Firth. The occasion, a fleet exercise. From the Rosyth base the Royal Navy's 5th Battle squadron (three battleships) with 2nd Battle cruiser squadron (four battle cruisers) with their attendant escorts in company with 12th and 13th Submarine Flotillas (all 'K' class vessels) were to put to sea and join the Grand Fleet which had earlier sailed from Scapa Flow, together they would look for trouble. As the capital ships progressed towards the open sea with their escorts, trouble loomed in the murk of a Scottish winter's day for the submarines of the 13th Flotilla that were central to the disorder to follow. The 'K' boats were, to say the least, of unusual design. Steam driven and capable of twenty-one knots for surface operations, when submerged the boilers were put out and electric power took over. They were poor sea boats in anything but flat calm as well as being unhandy for navigation and manoeuvre. Their role was to go to sea with the fleet, submerge when the enemy was sighted and launch torpedo attacks on the opposing forces. Quite how a submerged submarine able to operate at a maximum of six knots was meant to catch up with target moving at least three times that speed has never been clearly explained. However, the two flotillas were part of the 'order of battle' so off they went cruising on the surface at nineteen knots. Murphy was not going to miss such a wonderful opportunity to interfere, two small vessels, nothing to do with the exercise, got in the way as the ships passed the Isle of May, one of the 'K' boats, K14, took avoiding action, her helm jammed, K14 collided with her sister K22. Confusion reigned, signals took hours to reach the commanders concerned, navigation lights were misread, course alterations unrecognised for their inherent danger. In all there were five collisions, two of the 'K' boats were sunk, nine officers and ninety-five ratings lost their lives; all without a shot being fired.

The responsibility for the poor achievement appears to be a matter of strategic philosophy and intellectual preconceptions. There was a rigidity of command that relieved big ship commanders of initiative. The Admiralty fighting instructions for the Grand Fleet at Jutland was a volume of several hundred pages. Admiral Jellico was one of those responsible for the preparation of this manual, so cannot escape responsibility for any shortcomings. Reading of the events of that day, 31st May 1916, the impression is gained that both the captains of the capital ships and the admirals in command of sub divisions of the fleet took the approach that, if the situation encountered was not covered by the 'Fighting Instructions' then the event was of no consequence. A reasonable proposition for consideration is that the atmosphere of the command structure of admirals such as Hood, Jeram, Evan Thomas *et al* reporting to the Fleet Commander Jellico were in a stifling and introspective society. This was a closed community where all discussion began from an assumption of British superiority. I may be wrong but it seems incomprehensible to me that a naval force of the quality of the Grand Fleet could fail to defeat their enemy comprehensively when presented with the supreme tactical advantage, not once but twice within a few hours.

Communications and signals between ships, squadrons, flag ships and of all things the Fleet Commander, Jellicoe, were badly handled. Vice Admiral Beatty allowed at least ten minutes to elapse before replying to one signal from Jellicoe! My contention is that whilst the use of signals by flag was appropriate for slow moving sailing ships, insufficient attention had been given to the arrangements to pass orders and information between fast moving units spread over several dozen square miles of ocean. It seems unrealistic to expect all ships of a sub unit to see command signals with equal clarity given the variations of light and the confusion created by smoke from coal burning furnaces, however big the flag. The traditional signalling procedure with flags was initiated from the commander's ship, who hoisted the flag signal which then had to be acknowledged by the other ships of the unit, when the flag was hauled down the order was executed. An arduous and time consuming arrangement and what about the regular occurrence of night, flags are not much use then or am I missing something?

Then there was the loss of the battle cruisers by catastrophic explosions. Subsequent exploration of wrecks of the battle cruisers lost during the action has identified a possible cause. In the 'mind set' of the navy, rate of fire was all: the storage and handling of ammunition secondary. One explanation of the damage suffered by the ships lost was that the handling of the cordite charges was defective. Cordite charges were apparently stored outside the magazines built for their protection, during the battle! The reason, the arrangement allowed for faster handling. Someone blundered.

The issue of signals had become a serious presence in naval actions. The 'powers that be' on shore were now in a position to second guess the commander at sea with the ships and issue orders for the conduct of affairs; unlike the army during the Great War when generals in France were unable to make contact with formations in battle. Admirals went to sea and expected to take control of the battle as it progressed. Conflict of command is, as any half decent manager will tell you, a prime way to create confusion, the commander/manager responsible must be allowed to fight his battles as he will, if he fails he is dismissed. If however someone peers over his shoulder and gives new instructions half way through an action then who made the wrong decision, the buck has nowhere to rest, has it? Take if you will the confusion caused in Act II at the Battle of the Barents Sea and the handling of orders for convoy PQ 17. The lessons took too long to learn.

It is of course easy, as I have tried to explain in other sections of this consideration, to read into the accounts of past events, defects that to the men responsible at the time were the opposite, the right thing to do. At best the outcomes of the encounters are only evidence of problems not an understanding of all the contributing factors, particularly the human contribution. Can we be certain that it was the admirals and captains who made the mistakes? May it not have been the yeoman of signals who, in the smoke and fog of battle, saw what he expected to see and so gave misleading information? No one can be certain, unless it is yourself you wish to convince.

What then are the achievements that stand to the credit of the Royal Navy in the Great War? First, foremost for seagoing operations and essential to the final outcome of defeating Germany must be, the credit for running the cross channel supply route from the coastal ports of south east England to France. This vital sea lane remained open all the time the army needed its supplies. The German Navy was unable to cause any significant interruption or loss. Boring, wet, cold, routine small ship escort duty, minesweeping and anti submarine patrols, a task that goes almost without comment and is given little or no credit. Second in the list is the eventual success of the convoy system to bring supplies from overseas. Not only was it essential to the outcome of the Great War it also prepared the navy for the convoy operations of Act II from 1939-45. The submarine service found its feet and gave a good account of itself, particularly in the Baltic and the Black Sea. As also did the concept of anti submarine warfare, meaning that in the nick of time for Act II, supplementing the convoy system, there was equipment, first hydrophones, that was developed subsequently into the ASDIC system, later there was radar, and a tactical philosophy which could take the war to the enemy.

The most dashing operation the navy undertook during the Great War must be the events of St. George's Day, 23rd April 1918 and the raid on Zeebrugge. The Germans during their occupation of Belgium had used the ports of Zeebrugge and Ostend and the inland waterways leading to the city of Bruges to develop a naval base for submarines, coastal warships, motor launches and the like with an overlay of destroyers. These forces were deployed against coastal shipping in the Thames Estuary and the coast of Kent. The submarine base was used by boats making for the Atlantic approaches to Britain. These submarines reportedly took passage through the Straits of Dover! The presence of these facilities and the interference with British coastal shipping was an unwanted complication. Something had to be done. Now here was a job about which the navy knew a great deal. The Royal Navy had been raiding enemy ports for generations, since Drake singed the King of Spain's beard at Cadiz in 1587. The words of Drake's instructions included the following "…*to impeach the joining together of the King of Spain's fleet out of its many parts…*" (great stuff). A scheme was prepared, Vice Admiral Sir Roger Keyes took command, sailors and marines, officers and men volunteered and trained for the party and off they went. Keyes in command sailed in the modern destroyer HMS Warwick, leading the rest of the flotilla headed by the obsolete light cruiser HMS Vindictive, two Mersey ferries, Iris and Daffodil, a couple of scrap submarines C1 and C3 that could, if you had a vivid imagination, be described as seaworthy; these two vessels were bomb ships; plus a gaggle of motor launches and three block ships. They sailed on the evening of 22nd April 1918 for Zeebrugge and Ostend. In the early hours of St George's Day battle commenced. The flotilla stormed the port of Zeebrugge, destroyed a significant portion of the causeway leading to the 'Mole' of the harbour with one of the exploding submarines, sank the block ships in the main navigation channel, seriously damaged the port installations and then went home in time for lunch. The raid on Ostend was not completed; the crafty enemy had moved a navigation buoy and interfered with one portion of the plan. 'Vindictive' went back on to Ostend on 9th May and in a follow up action blocked the navigation channel from Bruges.

The achievements of the navy at sea during the Great War have to reflect the fact that unless the enemy puts to sea, given modern sea defences, battle cannot be joined. The Grand Fleet defended the nation but did not defeat the enemy. Supplies from around the world reached Britain to feed the nation and supply the war effort but the threat of submarines and mines to shipping remained until the last shot was fired. It was not that the Royal Navy did things wrong, it is more that what it did was not quite what was needed; ships were in the wrong place at the wrong time, as at Coronel in 1914, then, emergency action was required to recover the balance of events.

For this situation to have developed the Admiralty, its senior commanders and its political masters for two generations have to answer and they are not now available to explain how the rot set in. Some references above are as far as it is reasonable to venture within the scope of this consideration. We can however turn to the commanders and admirals of the day and ask knowing what we do, what were the shortcomings? Sir John Jellicoe, Commander at Jutland was absolute in his strategy that the Grand Fleet must be available in such force on demand that the German Fleet would be unable to secure a victory. Force had to be concentrated and this doctrine dominated naval strategy and tactical thinking, the 'what' aspect of the equation was understood the 'how' factor was much less clearly understood. He did not "lose the war in an afternoon" as Winston Churchill suggested was a possibility. What he did lose was the initiative. Sir John became C in C of the Grand Fleet in 1914 under Jackie Fisher and succeeded him as First Sea Lord the professional head of the navy in 1916. (The first Lord of the Admiralty was a politician and member of the government of the day.) Jellicoe handed over his command to Sir David Beatty. Admiral Beatty had an outstanding early career in the Royal Navy, being made 'post' that is, promoted to captain, at the age of twenty-nine. His contemporaries would be lucky to reach the same rank by the age of forty. He had charisma, charm and a rich wife. As a commander with independence he had flair and ability which marked him for high office. His achievement as vice admiral commanding the Grand Fleet's battle cruisers was disappointing. Just enough doubt is raised by reading of events to suggest he was not a good team player and that he lacked that last degree of intellect needed to make the contribution he and his ships should have delivered when action against the Germans was joined. The one name that readers of the naval aspects of the Great War are unable to avoid is that of Commodore Tyrwhitt, later admiral, this officer was from 1914 to 1918 in commanded of the 'light forces' out of Harwich. He took the war to the enemy at any opportunity. When the signals went out advising of the encounter of the fleets off Jutland, Tyrwhitt's light forces had to be peremptorily ordered back to harbour, their fire eating commodore having taken his forces to sea on his own initiative. I am sure that if he could have found the means he would have taken his ships up the River Spree and bombarded the Brandenburg Gate in Berlin. He was truly in the mould of one of Nelson's band of brothers.

Then there was the Royal Naval Air Service (RNAS) the equivalent of the army's RFC. This service also had to find a role to fulfill from sea level as it were. No one knew what the new service could achieve. Initially all the aircraft and airships of the service had to be land based. A disadvantage for a force committed to the support of the navy. Reconnaissance work was the first and obvious role and indeed much effort was applied to the task operating both fixed wing aircraft and airships. There is however a real difference between searching a wide area of empty sea and patrolling over a landscape as did the RFC. An empty landscape can be just what the commander needs to insert his forces into a position to exploit enemy weakness. An empty seascape is just that, empty. It tells you nothing of the enemy or his activity.

If you do put your ships in the empty slot there is no certainty that the enemy will turn up for a game.

The RNAS trialed various options including launching aircraft by catapult from ships and introducing ships able to launch and retrieve seaplanes. HMS Engadine was one such and had a 'walk-on role' at Jutland. Then just when ideas were getting a bit thin on the ground the Germans saved the day. The enemy started using their aircraft and airships to attack England and London in particular. Air defence became essential and so, the sailors turned aeronauts were given an opportunity to make a name for themselves. The RNAS was on the same footing as the RFC when it came to experience and equipment for aerial combat, they made it up as they went along, adapted and invented where they could. That any of the enemy were shot down given the limitations just mentioned is a tribute to tenacity and courage of a very high order. The intruders were challenged and did suffer losses. On 1st April 1918 the RNAS joined the RFC, to form the RAF, but you knew that already.

It is best not to leave the brief mention of the RNAS without a tribute to one of its members who represents the spirit of the original service, by describing in part the way things had to be done if airships were to remain serviceable. Archie Binding was thirty when the war started in 1914; he had worked in the family cartage firm after leaving school. His father, who must have been an enterprising man, quickly saw the advantages of motor transport and changed from horse drawn carts to motor vehicles in advance of most other businesses. Archie was therefore in pole position to learn the skills of the new mechanical contraptions. He turned himself into a more than competent mechanic, after an engineering apprenticeship. On enlistment into the navy his skills ensured rapid promotion to petty officer and then chief petty officer. The duties and postings that followed led to some hair raising experiences as the engineering petty officer was responsible for the performance of the twin 150hp 'Sunbeam' engines which powered an airship, a responsibility which included flying on operations. The ignition systems of these engines incorporated an unreliable 'magneto' system, prone to failure at inconvenient moments, as in the middle of a sortie. This would mean the CPO Binding plus tools and spares, would climb out of the relative safety of the open gondola which passed for crew accommodation, swarm across the unprotected framework of the airship whilst in flight, remove the faulty component, replace it with the spare, go through the procedure to restart the engine, make sure all was well, then climb back to the crew gondola. Often to provide extra excitement this routine had to be undertaken in the dark. Of such adventurous men was the RNAS founded. Archie logged over 3000 hrs of flying time in airships, was awarded the Air Force Cross (AFC) in 1919, and served as an engineer officer in the Fire Service between 1940 and 1945, he died in 1991 aged 105.

The most spectacular achievement of the navy has to be however the work of Captain, later Rear Admiral, Reginald 'Blinker' Hall and his small team of analysts who, working from the anonymous Room 40 of the Admiralty building, broke the German Naval codes and for most of the war British Intelligence staff read the secret radio and cable traffic not only of the German Navy, but additionally the diplomatic messages including the 'Zimmerman telegram' of which more later. It was the contents of this disastrous signal and the handling of the knowledge that brought the United States into the war and hastened the defeat of Germany.

The outstanding success of this dedicated team of specialists was to lead to the creation of specialist radio listening services in cooperation with code and cipher analysts that enabled the British armed services to prepare for Act II and through the Bletchley Park establishment, attack and win a serious and more complicated game of electronic cat and mouse.

The Armistice in November 1918 brought an end to the war and the German High Seas Fleet sailed across the North Sea to Scapa Flow for internment, escorted by ships of the Grand Fleet now commanded by Admiral Sir David Beatty. The High Seas Fleet came to anchor in the principal war station of the Royal Navy as evidence of their surrender, flying only a black flag. Each ship retained on board a small crew of German Naval personnel as 'caretakers' in case of emergency. In June

1919 this small contingent scuttled the entire High Seas Fleet under the noses of the Royal Navy. From this inglorious and watery finale of naval activity the German ships were salvaged by a firm of Wolverhampton scrap metal merchants, Cox and Danks, who even as late as 1970 had on display outside their offices and yard in Oldbury, a pair of large calibre shells from the German battle fleet.

The conduct of the wartime operations of the Royal Navy was like the Curate's egg, good in parts and certainly was not of the quality expected of a service in which so much money, emotional capital and political effort had been invested; but the criticism is muted. Is it because the navy's casualties for the four years of war was less than 40,000 lives? An issue for future debate perhaps?

CHAPTER 11

The Royal Flying Corps; (Royal Air Force).

As a reminder of the time scale in which we are dealing, the brothers Wright made their first successful flight of a manned, powered aircraft at Kittiwake, Maine, U.S.A. in December 1903. Colonel 'Bill' Cody (originally Cowdery) launched his first successful flight of an aircraft on behalf of the British Army at Farnborough in Hampshire in 1908. In 1914, ten years plus a few months after the first flight and only six years after Cody's first aircraft had taken to the air; forty-eight planes set out in August 1914 with the BEF to make their contribution to the army's commitment to support the French against the German offensive. To fly one of these early machines was in itself an act of great courage, confidence or lunacy; reliable they were not, either mechanically or aeronautically, but fly they did and to war they went. The combined strength of aircraft of all types in service with the British and French Armies was 273, the Germans had 246

The task allocated, in August 1914, to these early airmen, was reconnaissance to act in a role which traditionally had been undertaken by the cavalry. So that is what they did, scout for enemy activity and did their best using none to accurate maps to find and identify the movement of enemy troops. Then, because in the first hectic days the fog of war was causing uncertainty, the role of the airmen was extended to include finding and reporting on the position of British and French troops whose position was not known to commanders and headquarters. To the surprise of nobody the opposing forces each took a dim view of this first version of a 'spy in the sky' but certainly at the beginning had no realistic way to deal with the incursions. It was left, despite pre war experiments, to the air crew to improvise a solution. This they did by firing rifles and revolvers at each other. Thus was the second role of flying, aerial combat was initiated. There is no record of any damage to men or machines by these early encounters. Considering all the variables of this 'miss and miss' technique we should not be surprised*.

The development of adequate guns for defensive and offensive aerial warfare was a serious technical challenge to the inexperienced builders of aircraft and the armaments industry. The forward firing automatic machine gun was the obvious candidate for use in the air, but where to mount said gun? There was no electric firing mechanism, the gun had to be operated using a firing trigger or button. To put guns immediately in front of the pilot meant the bullets had to be synchronised with the revolutions of the propeller or disaster would ensue. The provision of a practical interrupter gear proved to be a serious technical challenge. A gun capable of firing through the boss of the propeller was the dream of the airborne cavalry; it was not to be realised for the Allied air forces. It would also have been only one gun and as the war in the air progressed it became clear to all sides that to cripple another plane by aerial gun fire required a lot of ammunition. The easy solution would have been to use several guns as was eventually arranged on fighters for the 1939 episode. Then we find more problems, snag number eight or is it nine? Using the guns available required the manual replacement of spent ammunition feeds, belts or drums. Now how was that to be achieved? If the aircraft were a single seat fighter, the pilot in addition to keeping his 'plane in the air had to take time out to unclip and replace the drum or belt then rearm the firing mechanism and return to find the enemy. This task would have been bad enough in favorable conditions but at several thousand feet above ground, travelling at some speed in the consequent slip stream with gloved, frozen fingers in a temperature degrees colder than at ground level the challenge presented was monumental. If the 'plane was a two man job with an observer/gunner added, then at least

---

* Trials had been undertaken prior to the outbreak of war in 1914 to evaluate weapons suitable for aircraft use. The 'Lewis' light machine gun was specified for use by the RFC in 1914, availability was another issue though and the manufacturing and delivery of these guns in worthwhile numbers for service use was a lengthy and, for the airman, frustrating process.

the pilot could bend his mind to flying the machine whilst the second crewman dealt with the air warfare and armaments aspects of their excursion. To the credit of all the aircrew this was what they undertook and brought confusion to the enemies of the King.

The RFC attracted the adventurer to their ranks and very often such personalities have ideas that escape the attention of more conformist minds. As the value of aerial reconnaissance quickly became established, someone, somewhere, said, just as Toad would have done; "I say you chaps why don't we take a camera with us and take some pictures of the troops on the ground? Then there would be no more bally argument about what we have seen and where." Photo-reconnaissance was up and running. Now here the British were on the back foot again in technical terms. The nation with the most advanced camera and in particular lens industry was Germany. Carl Zeiss of Jena was the leading supplier of optical lenses when August 1914's events broke upon the world. Murphy appearing from the sidelines again! British industry using firms such as Ross of London had to up their game dramatically.

Very quickly, considering the starting point, the Allies were producing good photo images of enemy positions and the location of 'lines of communication', forward supply dumps, gun positions and much else besides. Commanders were now in a position to see a record of positions beyond the front line and look at areas of which the enemy would rather the opposition knew nothing. There is only one way to prevent this happening, the spy in the sky has to be destroyed, shot down. As the technique of aerial photography developed the task of flying the planes to precise patterns and coordinates became the order of the day. Straight level, flying whilst the camera records the image below might be the needed for the job in hand, for the pilot the inherent dangers were increased dramatically. The German airmen could have a pop at these new sitting ducks and did. The Red Baron (Richthofen) had a field day.

That brings us back to the dilemmas posed by aerial combat in this new form of warfare. Clearly the force that had the best machines in sufficient numbers ought to prevail. The Germans deployed for three of the four years of the war better 'planes. The British quickly began producing sufficient of their less effective machines to outnumber the

Germans; stalemate, perhaps? In July 1916 there were twenty-seven RFC squadrons with 421 aircraft. Their commander was a man of steel who understood the 'Military Imperative' that winning is all! The formations and 'planes were deployed and flown very aggressively, to their human and technical limits and beyond, gaining air parity and sometimes air superiority.

The third major task undertaken by the RFC was artillery spotting. In an earlier section the difficulties of controlling indirect fire were described. The pilots of the RFC were in a unique position and for the first time in warfare it was possible to see the effect of the indirect fire of shot and shell, whether the target was receiving its intended punishment. The problem was that whilst the airmen could see the result there was no means to tell the gunners on the ground what they should do to improve the accuracy of the shooting. Improvisation was the order of the day systems of visual signals were devised to correct the target registration of the gunners until it became possible to install a rudimentary radio transmitter in the spotting planes. Then messages could be sent using Morse code to ground stations who would relay the corrections to the artillery and the gunfire would hit the target. Whereupon the enemy would up and off to another location and the whole procedure began again. This tactic was a continual problem, if the target was mobile the enemy quickly recognised the corrections being made to the gun fire and because this was a professional army, jumped about a bit and lived to fight another day.

As war in the air developed the opportunity to use aircraft to interfere with the activities of troops on the ground, independently of such resources as artillery, came into the reckoning. Such an idea was fine, but there were two problems: weapons and delivery. The idea of a 'bomb' launched at the enemy from the ground by a mortar was not new, but from an aircraft, that, as we now say, was 'a whole new ball game'. Off to the drawing board and fused aerial bombs were devised. Wonderful, we have aircraft, bombs and targets, all we now have to do is drop the missiles onto the targets and we can all go home for tea; not so. The need for accuracy creeps into the equation. The bombs we are considering at this point in the development of aerial warfare were not the Barnes Wallis five ton 'Tallboys', these were fifty pounders (twenty-four kg) just about enough to give the local rodents a headache. The accurate delivery of air born bombs was then and continues to be a problem. A parallel idea was to use aircraft armed with machine guns to attack enemy ground forces, the 'plane as an adjunct to operations on the ground had staked its claim for inclusion in the considerations of the generals. Later larger planes with twin engines were developed, capable of flying to distant targets and bombing strategic locations, not just the poor bloody infantry in the front line.

The casualties suffered by the RFC are disguised from general appreciation by the imbalance of aircrew to ground staff in a squadron establishment. A squadron of a dozen planes with four extra aircrews would have a ratio of aircrew, pilots and observers, to ground staff of approximately one to fifteen. Although there were casualties on the ground the aircrew bore the brunt. At critical times some units lost the equivalent of the entire aircrew establishment in one month. Thirty-two killed and injured is a loss rate of 1200% (384) per annum for the combatant element of the unit. The comparison with infantry battalions now becomes more obvious. The PBI could take casualties of 380 in one day, but that was the exception. More common were the losses experienced by the 1st Bn. King's Royal Rifle Corps who lost twenty-eight dead during January 1915 which included thirteen days of front line trench service. Using this figure to calculate an annual loss, which is a pretty dubious procedure but makes a point, the battalion's annual casualty total would be 335, approx 50% of the combatant strength. The drain on aircrew resources caused great anxiety and proved to be a dilemma not just in this conflict but also in Act II that opened in 1939.

When the RFC went to war in August 1914 nobody actually knew how to use or command the resources put at the disposal of the army. From the very beginning the new born air arm had to improvise, invent and innovate to achieve recognition. This was one of those circumstances where it was literally true that you 'made things up as you went along'. This was true also of the French and German air components. In circumstances such as this the quality of command is often the key to results. Britain by some happenstance in August 1915 had available for appointment Colonel (later Major General) Hugh Trenchard to command the growing aerial resources. ("Cometh the hour, cometh the man" apologies to Sir Walter Scott for the popular misquotation.) General Trenchard had joined the British Army in 1893, transferred to the RFC in 1913 at the age of forty and prior to mobilisation in August 1914 was Assistant Commandant of the Central Flying School. As war loomed and the army deployed in France he took command of 1 Wing of the RFC. Events moved on, the first field commander of the RFC returned to Britain to resume the appointment of Director of Military Aeronautics in August 1915; Trenchard was appointed to the vacancy in the rank of brigadier general. Here was a thinking man in command, one who had the intellect, vision, military experience and power of leadership to forge a new weapon of war. There are not many of whom that can be said. Hannibal and his elephants was Trenchard's predecessor for that wreath of laurels.

The new commander had qualified as a pilot, he had a keen personal and professional interest in flying and he was a trained soldier who could read the military situation on the ground and apply the increasing resources of the RFC to the achievement of winning the war. Despite the increasing importance of air power he was not comfortable with the cult of 'air aces'. The likes of such airmen as Bishop, Ball and McCudden were appreciated for their success against their German equivalents and appropriately recognised with awards. More importantly their success was used to bolster morale, the Germans are not invulnerable was the point made. Such success was also good for recruitment and that was vital. Trenchard was a pragmatist and knew that to fulfil his dictum 'no empty chairs at breakfast' there must be a continual replacement of the daily casualty losses.

The achievements of the Royal Flying Corps (RFC) and the Royal Naval Air Service (RNAS) were recognised by the combination of the two organisations on 1st April 1918 to form the Royal Air Force (RAF). The RFC/RAF was not responsible for winning the war: that decision had to be achieved on the ground. But without the contribution of the newly established aerial cavalry the war on the ground could have been lost. A second and, at the time, unappreciated outcome of the success of the

RFC/RAF was that the foundations had been well and truly laid for the air defence of Britain when the curtain went up in 1939 on Act II of this awful brawl.

The Royal Flying Corps, the Royal Naval Air Service and the successor Royal Air Force, fought the war with determination and imagination and deserve the recognition given for their achievements. The Royal Air Force was off to a flying start concluding their war of only seven months with the courage and skills learned by the pioneers and founders of their success.

Dedication

F. E. B. Jones.

This chapter of my summary of the Great War is dedicated to Colonel F. E. B. Jones, late RFC/RAF and Royal Signals. 'Feeby' was commissioned as a pilot in the RFC, and flew with both the RFC and the RAF after its formation on 1st April 1918. Leaving the service after the war he returned to the family business in Birmingham. He maintained a military connection by joining the Territorial Army 48th (SM) Signal Regiment. In 1939 he went to France with the Regiment when it was sent with 48th Division of the BEF, he returned to Britain during the evacuation through Dunkirk. In 1941 he was released from army service to rejoin the family business and manage the reorganisation of essential production for the war effort, following serious damage to the factory premises by German bombing. He retained his commitment to the Territorial Army and both commanded and later was appointed Honorary Colonel of 48th Signal Regiment (subsequently renumbered 35th (V) Signal Regiment).

A gentleman and soldier held in much affection by those who had the privilege of his friendship.

CHAPTER 12

AMERICA; The United States

The entry of the United States to the Great War was an event much desired by the Allied governments of Britain and France. As the war wasted resources of men and *materiel*, exhaustion before victory seemed a real possibility for the Allies. Additionally, by the spring of 1917 Russia had become a very uncertain partner on the military scene. The provisional government of Kerensky that followed the abdication of Tsar Nicholas II had declared an intention to the continuation of hostilities, the value of the military effort however was an unknown quantity. October 1917 saw the Bolsheviks and Lenin seize power with the declared intention of making peace for Russia independently of Britain and France. The Germans, ever ready to oblige, imposed the Treaty of Brest Litovsk in February 1918.

The extent of American resources, money, *materiel* and above all manpower was the counterweight to the Russian withdrawal; America though had no standing army of significance and was completely without experience of the intensity of industrial scale warfare as it had developed from August 1914. To compensate, time was essential to assemble a force of sufficient strength to deal with the additional German forces that would become available from the east, time was what the Allies did not have. American reinforcement of the Allied war effort was feared by the German High Command who also knew time was at a premium. There was a circle to be squared here.

There are various questions raised concerning the attitudes and contributions of America, its government, its newspapers and its people. For the moment two of these issues can be addressed as it is my opinion that they together explain all the other considerations. We have to remember that in 1914 the United States of America had been a nation state for less than 150 years, at which time the majority of the landmass was unexplored. Texas joined the union in 1845 and after the war against Mexico in 1848 and the subsequent Treaty of Guadalupe Hidalgo that ceded California, other states were incorporated into the new nation; the process though was not completed for the forty-eight State nation of 1914 until Arizona and New Mexico were included in 1912. Communications across the sprawling country, despite Wells Fargo, was slow and uncertain. Even the arrival of the railways only scratched the surface of rural communications. These acquisitions followed earlier settlements with Spain and France to absorb Florida in 1818 and in 1819 by the 'Louisiana Purchase' the territory that forms the mid western states from the Gulf of Mexico to the Canadian border.

America was a very young country, by comparison with the nations of Europe, it had put in place the framework of government, administration, business and commerce then went and put the whole structure at risk with the Civil War that was not resolved until 1865. As a nation the United States was unsure of its international role, unlike European nations whose borders and institutions had been taking shape for more than 2,000 years. It is from this uncertainty I believe that the almost forgotten 'Monroe doctrine' derived. This was the shield and shelter of American foreign policy well after the Great War and the 1919 Treaty of Versailles had become history.

To summarise, the doctrine of Monroe, which takes its name from the President of that name, was established in 1823 and it amounted to this; America would look after the security of the Americas and not expect interference by, or from, European countries. In consideration of this obligation America would not take sides or commit military or naval resources to European affairs. The intent was actually to warn off the Spanish who were looking for opportunities to regain colonies in South America, lost through wars of independence. As a policy this was always one with a very suspicious validity. The presence of Canada, at that date a British colony, on the entire northern border of the United States, British, French and Dutch interests in the Caribbean, as well as central and South America were, it seems, to be of no account. In practice when

213

the Emperor Napoleon III of France established a puppet government in Mexico under the rule of his cousin Maximilian, the United States could do nothing about it; internally the Civil War was underway! Leave it to Uncle Sam was the underlying message, we know what is best for the Americas; isolationist in concept it appears now to me as 'arms length' colonialism.

What the policy did provide was a 'one size fits all' political axe that 'Congress' could wield against the President to proscribe or support military activities. Hence in 1914, quite properly, the American government took the view that events in Europe should not involve intervention by the United States. That was a defensible foreign policy, provided the conflict amounted to a limited positional war, as for example 1871. No more than a few weeks were needed before the true scale of the war and the extent of German ambition became apparent. Two and a half years were to elapse however before America declared war. The 'No Foreign War' lobby was very powerful.

The second issue affecting the judgment of the American government was the military resources available. The American Army was tiny, about 70,000 men, 400 obsolete artillery pieces, 1,500 machine guns of four different calibres and only enough war emergency ammunition in store to sustain a three battalion attack. There was not a single divisional formation with a headquarters and supporting troops, equipped for operations; ten months was needed before the first one became available, a full year to organise two field ready divisions. The command structure was such that there were only seven major generals on the active list and the concept of 'staff work' as practised by European armies was unknown. America was militarily unfit to go to war; that was the second constraint on a declaration of war against, well, anybody!

To reach a political position at which point a declaration of war would became acceptable to the establishment and the people of the nation; something, other than purely political considerations, had to become part of the American awareness of German ambitions as well as the consequences of an Allied defeat in Europe. Who better to provide this impetus than the German government? No one!

Reference has been made earlier, pg 203, to the activities of the

British Admiralty's intercept and decoding achievements and the 'Zimmerman telegram'. This was the event that changed American minds, the facts of which are in bare detail, as follows. The German Foreign Minister, Arthur Zimmerman, hatched a cunning plan. The aim was to ensure the continued neutrality of the U.S.A., this was to be achieved by diverting American attention to events in their own backyard. Zimmerman sent a diplomatic cable to the German Minister (Ambassador) in Mexico who was thus authorised to offer in secret negotiation with the President of Mexico, an alliance between the two countries in which Mexico would go to war, with German support, against the United States to recover the territories including Califonia, ceded in the 1848 treaty. The plan went further and suggested that when war between America and Mexico was certain, the Japanese could then be invited to join the fun to further their ambitions in the Philippines.

Unfortunately for the Germans, Room 40 at the British Admiralty intercepted the message, broke the code and read the details of the plan. The American President, Woodrow Wilson, was provided with access to the text by means which did not compromise the security of the intercept service. He decided to use the information to put an end to a debate in Congress on the arming of merchant ships. In this he was unsuccessful. Opinion was generally that British Intelligence had planted a clever fake. That is until Arthur Zimmerman himself stood up in class, a press conference actually, and said, "Yes, that's my message." The fat, as they say, was well and truly in the fire.

The President, his government and Congress could not tolerate such interference in the affairs of the United States. The telegram was the equivalent of marching a division of the German Army along Pennsylvania Avenue. On 6th April 1917 the United States of America went to war with Germany, the rest is history.

There is in the Zimmerman folly an uncanny foreshadowing of events in 1941 in the ineptitude of the German actions. In 1917 the uncertainties introduced by the commissioning of such a plan had so many possibilities for failure it should never have been given any credence in diplomatic or political terms. As a parallel, when Japan bombed Pearl Harbour in December 1941, precipitating war with America in the Pacific. Adolf

Hitler, casually it appears, declared war on the United States when it was by no means certain that Congress would sanction a war against Germany. American participation in both wars was a direct result of German hubris and institutional insanity.

As to the military contribution of America to the eventual victory of the Allies in 1918, that is for others to tell. The US army took a long time to organise, train and equip but was in on the last act in 1918 and fought well alongside the French, albeit using a lot of borrowed equipment, in the final offensive actions in the Argonne and Champagne regions.

There is a small ingredient to add as preparation, as it were, for further thought on the contribution of the US Army. Paul Cornish of the Imperial War Museum provides the following on the preparation of the expanding American Army for the fighting. "The American Expeditionary Force arrived in France with a tactical mindset which was strongly at variance with that which three years of industrial warfare had imposed upon the armies of the Allies. The US Army was wedded to the concept of the supremacy of the infantryman, armed with rifle and bayonet. Their commander, General John Pershing, believed that the American soldier taught how to shoot, how to take advantage of terrain, and how to rely upon hasty entrenchment, retain the ability to drive the enemy from his trenches and by the same tactics, defeat him in the open". Trench warfare he considered was a tactical aberration into which the Allies had been drawn and he looked to restore open warfare. The essential of US military doctrine was to look to self-reliant infantry, effective use of the rifle and bayonet, unlimited objectives and aggression at all levels of the combat forces.

What, I wonder, did General Pershing think each of the armies on the Western Front had been trying to achieve?

Such a military mindset does not reflect well on the responsible commanders at the stage when the Americans were preparing for battle. It might even allow a modicum of credit to the British and French commanders for the efforts they made to break the deadlock.

CHAPTER 13

German Perspectives

The objective and intention of this long appraisal of the Great War was to focus on the success of British effort; success that enabled the six division army that went to war in Europe in August 1914 to become an organisation of sixty divisions and lead the Allies to victory in the final campaign during the autumn of 1918. The Germans however were the enemy and it is impractical to exclude from the sources consulted opinions and information of the professional soldiers who were sent to war on behalf of Kaiser Wilhelm II. Some semblance of impartiality can be provided with a selective summary of the German assessment of the effectiveness of the British Army as it expanded relentlessly to wage war on equal terms. It seems reasonable to bring forward some of the published comments from German sources on their British enemy. This is not exhaustive, rather is it summarised as a counterpoint to the myths that have become ingrained as received wisdom of the bungling British generals; a calumny born of malign prejudice, or is there a whiff of Marxist rectitude as well?

To restate details of the German situation already made in other parts of the text as a focus for the main points at issue. The German Army that went to war in 1914 was an army that had never fought a war. The unification of Germany had enabled the constituent states of the new nation to organise a new land force using the resources of the semi autonomous princely states of Bavaria, Brandenburg, Hanover, Prussia, Saxony *et al* to combine them and their armies with Teutonic efficiency, into a mighty force. Dominated by the Prussian's General Staff with their military ethos, the German Army looked to be thing of beauty and a joy forever.

There were the two snags to which earlier reference has been made, first not all of the other German states admired the Prussian style and took exception to the assumption of superiority. There is even reference in one account of the tension that arose when officers of the armies of constituent states of the new Germany, such as Bavaria, found that they were to serve in a lower rank in the German Army than their rank as an officer in the army of their own state. The second snag was simply this, the new all purpose army had never fought a war. In all its martial glory never once had its plans been confused by the enemy pulling a fast one, the weather turning foul, the reinforcements getting lost, the communications going awry; events all too familiar to soldiers of all ranks in the British Army. Never once had the new German Army had to order the rear ranks of a field force to face about and fight as disciplined demons, when the enemy appeared from both front and rear. The compensation was the German General Staff, an elite officer corps of grandeur that had planned all things to such perfection that uncertainty had been eliminated; such faith, such folly!

At the commencement of hostilities in August 1914 there are accounts that record the surprise of the German commanders when they found the opposition included a significant British presence. The speed of mobilisation and the deployment of the BEF in France as a fighting force took them unawares, a major tactical mistake by the Germans in the first days of the war. The skill at arms, musketry, to the old regular army also taught the Germans some nasty lessons, fast. It is well attested that the soldiers of the German Army were convinced the British were using machine guns in significant numbers to create the weight of fire faced by their advancing infantry. For certain the classic stopping action by II Corps of the BEF at Le Cateau commanded by Lt. Gen. Smith Dorrian, was unexpected and very unwelcome.

Quite one of the most intriguing accounts of war on the Western Front is *Storm of Steel* by the previously mentioned Ernst Junger of the 73rd Hanoverian Regt. for many months of the Great War, fighting as a junior infantry commander against both the British and French. The account he wrote has the authentic tone of immediate recall, his memory is untainted by the weight of historical reconsideration. Christopher Duffy has also prepared a valuable summary of German opinions in his book *Through German Eyes*. He has used diary extracts and contemporaneous official material from German sources to build a word picture of how British operations influenced enemy ideas and attitudes.

From both these sources it immediately becomes clear that the front line German soldiers loathed and detested the barbed wire defences of the British positions at the front and were of the opinion that the Brits were too damned good with their machine guns. Matters got worse, so far as machine guns were concerned when the Vickers MMG was consolidated into the Machine Gun Corps and the front line infantry were issued with the portable Lewis gun. By the time the Battle of the Somme took place each platoon of a British infantry regiment had a Lewis gun as part of its weaponry, with the Vickers providing additional fire power. The German Army could not match the Lewis gun, imperfect as it was; another small ingredient to add to the cake of alternative conclusions.

The German equivalent of Tommy Atkins, 'Fritz Schmidt'?, also found other close quarter trench weapons, the 2" spigot mortar, the 3" tube mortar and the larger 4" and 6" versions to be thoroughly nasty; both the weapons and the way they were used by Tommy. Then there were the unofficial items used to make a point in close quarter fighting, pick helves for example with half a yard of barbed wire wrapped around the business end, knuckle dusters and entrenching tools with the spade end ground to razor sharpness, all these, when wielded by a determined enemy, can make quite an impression on the resistance of those under attack. Before considering other aspects of the fighting as the Germans saw things, we should pay our respects to one other item of trench fighting: the British hand grenade, the Mills bomb. A success from the day it came into use, replacing the improvised devices such as jam tins packed with scrap nails and other crude inventions. The Mills bomb, designed by a manufacturer of golf balls, was a classic device easy to use and deadly in effect, 2lbs (0.8 kg) of iron in the shape of an olive, filled with explosives which shattered the casing on detonation and spread a shower of hot metal at significant velocity within a radius of ten yards. The real advantage was that the national game of cricket had taught many of the young soldiers to throw a cricket ball with great accuracy up to sixty yards. This was a skill the Germans could not replicate for two reasons, throwing skills and the long wooden handle of the German 'potato masher' grenade. The grenade was another hated device. What was that rumble from the myth mill? Some critics complaining that the playing fields of the nation are not appropriate places for training to win wars, tosh!

And what of Thomas Atkins, how was he regarded by the enemy? As previously commented the German Army had no experience of the British soldier in action, diary excerpts do offer some guide to the attitudes of the front line German troops. Tommy was regarded as a doughty fighter, particularly in defence, he was seen as tough, well organised and well supplied. In attack the opinion seems to have been that the British showed insufficient imagination and as such failed to make the most of opportunities both during local actions and in larger battles. Tommy was much admired for being a prodigious 'digger'; several accounts refer to the speed at which a British detachment could convert a few shell holes into a defensible strong point. The Germans were critical of the lack of information given to the front line soldiers, commenting that when junior leaders were lost or put out of action the ordinary soldier was at a loss to know what to do. Perhaps the British policy of 'need to know' went too far. This is how Lt. Junger saw things when his company surprised a party of British who had made their way by some means through German lines during an action. Unusually in his experience, the British party surrendered. At more senior levels the criticism that I have found is the willingness of British commanders to reinforce tactical failure. The counter argument needs to be made; the impetus of an action has to be maintained. For this reason extra troops are sent as reinforcements to keep the action moving. Now a decision within the context of any battle is always a matter of judgement. If you win, the right thing was done; fail and you are to blame for the losses. In so far as this criticism is valid I can only ask, what was done by the Germans during the Battle of Verdun? Failure was reinforced consistently. The policy of immediate 'counter attack' to recover lost ground is much the same. Two sides of the same coin, I wonder?

As the months passed, the Allied armies and the enemy strove to find a means to dominate the battlefield and impose their will on opposing forces. The increasing significance of the artillery was recognised. This was the 'Arm' of the combatant armies that protected the PBI in the front line trenches, interdicted enemy positions, the 'lines of communication' and rear areas. The guns also provided the infantry with much needed protection before and during attacks. Briefly in the section on the Royal Flying Corps, reference was made to the achievements of the Royal Regiment of Artillery and the RFC. Between them by 1916 they had devised and brought into operation systems and equipment which enabled indirect artillery fire to be directed with much greater accuracy than had previously been thought possible. The qualitative improvement in fire control with further refinements continued through to 1918 when a devastating barrage launched the British attack in August 1918, the eventual outcome being the defeat of the German Army and surrender on 11th November.

After the Battle of Cambrai at which tanks made their first appearance the German General, Erich von Ludendorff recorded that; *"the enemy [British] enhanced the power of their infantry to a comprehensive degree by [use] of the machine. Our efforts [German] depended too much on the men."* It is this change of emphasis which is notable in the context of diary entries. Consistently reference is made by diarists to the amount and quality of arms, ammunition, stores and equipment available to the British Army. The siege was having its effect on both the available supplies and the morale of the Germans who had to do the fighting. The climax of this situation was reached during the German spring campaign of 1918 when German soldiery abandoned the actions to which they were committed and went 'a looting', just as soldiers have done for centuries when there's booty for the taking.

As a comment on the way the Germans regarded the British response to the exigencies of war I plead in aid the following opinions of General von Kuhl, Chief of Staff, Army Group Crown Prince Rupprecht.

First, "What Britain actually achieved went a good deal further. *"It is impossible to have reckoned on that in advance."* Britain deployed forces in Macedonia, the Middle East, German colonies [in Africa], Europe, the Western Front, Serbia and Italy. *"The mighty reinforcement and reorganisation of the British Army in the course of this war amounted to an administrative achievement of the first order."* (my italics). This opinion confirms that at the highest level of operations within the German command, strategic surprise was achieved; a pearl beyond price in the war fought by the British commanders. Odd perhaps that such a favourable opinion of the British achievement never ranks for a mention when the latter day critics are offering their opinions.

Second, *"It would be quite wrong to deny the British credit for the way they fought and for the obstinate way they brushed aside the heaviest casualties and kept renewing their assaults. It would be equally wrong to suggest that there was any possibility that they may have broken through."* The fact that, despite this, they continued their offensive was justified by the British on the basis of the overall situation. After the total collapse of the Russian offensive in July 1917, the Russian Army as a fighting force had completely fallen out of the picture. The Italian front was in complete tatters in October. Above all the hitting power of the French, after the failure of the offensive on the Aisne and in Champagne, followed by the mutinies and internal disturbances was so greatly reduced that they were in urgently need of reorganisation and relief.

"The United States was still not in a position to do anything. *"The one and only army capable of offensive action was the British. If they had broken off their offensive, the German Army would* [could?] *have seized the initiative and attacked the Allies where they were weak.* To this end it would have been possible to have withdrawn strong forces from the east after the collapse of the Russians. *For these reasons the British had to go on attacking until the onset of winter ruled out a German counter attack. Today, now that we are fully aware about the critical situation in which the French Army found itself during the summer of 1917, there can be absolutely no doubt that through its tenacity, the British Army bridged the crisis in France.* The French Army gained time to recover its strength; the German reserves were drawn towards Flanders. The sacrifices that the British made for the 'Entente' were fully justified."(source; Der Weltkreig 1914–1918 Band II, Berlin 1929 (in translation) Kuhl v. General d. Inf.)

My point exactly, confirmed by a German general whose task it was to defeat the Allied armies.

Having made these points that the efforts of the force under British command had not gone unrecognised by senior German commanders, these comments need to be treated with some caution. One explanation could be that the favourable comments are intended to shift the focus of blame for the failure of the German nation and its army to win the war for which they were responsible; no more nor less than an example of the 'Macavity' beloved of modern politicos, an argument to exonerate themselves. The comments of Ernst Junger though have the authentic tone of the junior field commander. In particular when he writes of the surprise experienced by the advancing forces of the German Army including himself during the spring offensive of 1918 when the quality and extent of supplies available to the British forces was revealed.

Chapter 8 of the main text (pg. 155) makes reference to the German attack on Verdun with the strategic objective of breaking the French Army before dealing the British Army a decisive blow forcing their withdrawal from continental Europe. Richard Holmes in his book *Western Front* makes an interesting point. The policy described does appear in the post war memoirs of the Field Marshal von Falkenhayn, the snag is that there is no documentary evidence that the proposal was made to the German supreme command in 1915/16. The available state and military records for the relevant time do not include any reference to such a strategy or planning options to seek battle with the British Army, should Verdun fall to the German attack. This poses the question of authenticity, was the Field Marshal being constructively imaginative *post hoc?* Or was the old boy lying in his teeth? Haig gets a hard time for apparently amending his diaries, what about others?

A German Commentary; a domestic viewpoint

A book published in English translation in 2007 provides some insight into the opinions of an upper middle class German family from the late nineteenth century until the conclusion of the Second World War in 1945. The family archives and importantly the personal diaries of the Klamroth family have been researched and documented by Frau Wibke Bruhns (b. 1938), the daughter of Hans George Klamroth (b.1898) and his wife Else Podeus who was Danish. The family were wealthy, influential, manufacturers and merchants, land owners; the *'haute-bourgeoisie'* of the Imperial German class system, not though aristocratic 'Junkers'. They lived well and exercised a benevolent, paternalistic oversight of both their families and their employees; they were though committed to the ambitions of Bismarck and Wilhelm II to create a place in the sun for the new Germany.

Both Kurt, the father, and his son Hans Georg (HG) served in the army through the system that obliged all males to undertake service in the armed forces. Just as in Britain the social standing of the family ensured that their army service was as officers. Kurt commanded a reserve supply column, first in Belgium and then on the Eastern Front during the Great War. HG became involved with the 'Nazi party' during the 1930s and was for a short period a member of the SS. The majority of his service though was with sections of the army dealing with 'Intelligence' matters.

The atmosphere created by the reworking of the diaries and documentation is a curious mirror of 'Edwardian' England; self confident and assured. There are though undertones of envy and anxiety that the new Germany was not respected to the same extent as France and Britain. The progress of events in the summer of 1914 does not seem to cause the Klamroths of the day to have second thoughts. War declared, Belgium and France invaded and the BEF joining the battle, the edited diary entries concern the alleged use of soft nosed *'dum dum'* bullets by the British Army and the effrontery of unidentified Belgian *'francs-tireurs'* (guerrillas of the day) resisting the advance of the German Army. Later in the war the issue of shortages and the means by which HG as a young man could find an appointment in the cavalry and avoid the nasty reality of the infantry and in all probability the Western Front! Not once it seems does the family consider their nation's aggressive actions to be in any way unreasonable. The consequence of the Allied victory producing the Treaty of Versailles in 1919 also records the anger of the diarists at the 'War Guilt' clause and the 'unreasonable' terms of the reparations forced on Germany. Not a whisper about Brest Litovisk in 1918 when the unequal settlement between Germany and Russia enforced annexation of the Baltic States plus large portions of the Ukraine.

As events progress in Germany following the 1919 settlement the diarist finds the French tiresome and expects sympathy for their damaged dignity. After the 'Weimar Republic' and the catastrophic inflation; enter stage right Adolf Hitler and his National Socialist Party. HG is an early joiner, to protect his business interests you understand, reserve officer training at weekends and cultivating his party credentials. The atmosphere created by the accounts in the diary suggest that the Klamroths see Hitler and the Nazis as aliens running Germany until the old order is able to resume their proper place. History we know did not go with this hopeful version of events; the second act of the tragedy of total war consumes Germany, damages the free democracies almost beyond repair and provides a platform for the equally abhorrent Communism of Russia to force the world into a 'Cold War'.

HG pays with his life for his involvement in the plot to assassinate Adolf Hitler, not it appears to redress the effect of German aggression, but to protect German national interests from the advancing Russian Army and the political commissars included in the baggage train.

The interpretation that eventually developed was sceptical disbelief. The original diarists, their wives, relations and employees were guiltless in the events between 1914–18 and 1939–45; France, Britain (always referred to as England) were to blame for shortages, bombing raids and all the other nastiness that the family suffered. The culpability of Wilhelm II, Hindenberg, Ludendorff, Adolf Hitler and the National Socialist (Nazi) Party for the wars and their outcome was not the responsibility of the population of the German nation, or so the text provided by Frau Bruhns would have us believe.

The description of the lifestyle of the family over the years is fascinating reading; the treatment of the family's participation in the events of the thirty-one years between 1914 and 1945 is breathtaking in its complacency and denial. There seems no alternative but to conclude that 'contrition' is not within the scope of reactions of which the collective psyche of the German people is responsible.

There is more to consider for completion of this summary of the perspectives through which the Germans considered their commitment to the Great War in Europe from 1914 to 1918. It is not attractive now to look back and offer an account, however brief of the distortions that passed for national policies. There appears in retrospect to have been a malign style of reasoning that found an outlet in some disgraceful actions taken in pursuit of the victory Germany believed was its due. This appears to have been a cast of mind that was to find even more dreadful means of expression twenty-five years later in Act II of this European tragedy.

The events chosen for comparison in this portion of the account have been arranged deliberately to proceed from the general to the particular, leaving the sequence and the outcome to speak for itself, or otherwise.

First in the order of consideration is the issue to which allusion has already been made that the whole enterprise of Germany's war with Europe in 1914 was an enterprise of startling risk. Yes I know all wars are a matter of risk. Where, however, did the Kaiser, his General Staff and the government find the confidence to convert Belgium into a satrap province and look to the occupation of a significant portion of the Ukraine as an extension of the German Empire. On what authority were they to base their government? Were the residents of the newly colonised territories expected to welcome '*Pax Germanica*' as another phase of life? What reaction was anticipated from the Russian Orthodox Church and its priesthood? How were the Landowning aristocracy and indeed the peasants of mother Russia to be treated? The questions tumble out in a cascade once the issue is raised. I have never found any explanations. Has anyone else?

Having raised the question of the validity of the whole enterprise there are also issues to be put that reflect upon the attitude of the Germans in respect of how the war was to be conducted and the effect of the actions on world opinion. In this category of events first for consideration must rank the Zimmerman Telegram.* By what mental gymnastics did the government of Germany conclude that its interests would be advanced by promoting a war between the United States of America and its poverty stricken neighbour, Mexico? This was not just digging oneself deeper into a hole; it was a completely new excavation.

---

* Details of this adventure are described in Chapter 12, America.

Every neutral nation in the world now had to think it could be a target for German diplomatic or military adventures.

And so the sorry litany continued. The introduction of unrestricted submarine warfare began in 1916, not with the sinking of one or two cargo ships but the torpedoing of a 35,000 ton passenger liner, the Lusitania, on 7th May1915. 1,154 non combatants died, this, in the days when the general principle was observed 'women and children first'. The ship was a legitimate target. The consequence of the sinking and the loss of life was international opprobrium; for which apparently Germans had no concern. Their intention was to make a point to the whole world. The use of the submarine during the Great War was a vexed question but it was a legitimate weapon of war. The error was in the rules of engagement. Submarine commanders were clearly awaiting the order to apply the policy, the error was to authorise immediate attacks on ships which would have non combatant passengers on board as well as the crew. International opinion and in particular those of Americans was disgust. Another hole blown in the proposition that Germany was defending its legitimate rights.

Then there was the Wilson Peace Plan advanced to the nations at war by the President of the United States and rejected out of hand by the Germans. A rejection made when the German Army was in occupation of most of Belgium and a slice of northern France which included valuable coal and iron smelting resources. Probably the plan was not in the interests of Germany nearly two years into a costly war, Germany though did hold a good negotiating hand which it did not use. Once the chance for a negotiated peace passed there was no way out of the tangle other than the defeat for one side or the other.

As the scale of the comparisons reduces the fate of Belgium has to be considered. The nation was invaded when, as was its right in international law, it refused permission for the German Army and its supplies to transit the national territory to invade France. The Belgians and their army resisted the incursion by force of arms and were defeated to the extent that the majority of the country was occupied. King Albert and the remainder of his forces clung stubbornly to the small strip of Belgium between the North Sea and Ypres. Throughout the war the Belgians acted in concert with their Allies but retained an army independent of both the French and British commands, fighting on behalf of the occupied portion of their country. The Germans were not pleased with the way Belgium and her army reacted and set about demonstrating their perspective of events. At the time the more lurid press reports were awash with accounts of 'atrocities', the raping of nuns, bayoneting of babies, summary executions and deportation for forced labour. The press reports were not perhaps as concerned with accuracy as they should have been and the extent of the acts described needs to be treated with caution. There are however two serious pieces of evidence that cannot be ignored. Firstly, the American Minister (Ambassador) in Belgium made numerous reports to Washington of acts of repression that lend credence to the newspaper reports of atrocities* occurring if not the scale on which they were carried out. Figures of 200 civilian deaths in the town of Andenne and 400 in Tamines are quoted by Richard Holmes, another reliable source. Secondly there is Louvain, a Belgium city with one of the oldest universities in Europe, a centre of learning and scholarship recognised throughout the world, including one of the largest collections of medieval manuscripts and records in Europe. How did the Germans treat this centre of culture and learning? Louvain was put to the sword, ransacked, burnt to a significant extent, the library destroyed; an action of which the Visigoths who sacked Rome 1,500 years previously would have been proud; so much for German culture.

Finally there was an act which revolted Britain in particular but also set a bench mark against which German intentions were judged by the world at large for years to come. In August 1914 a middle aged British nurse was taking some holiday at home in England from her duties in a Belgian nursing school. She returned immediately to her work when the war commenced, by which time the school had become a Red Cross hospital. She nursed the patient casualties, British, Belgian, French and when they arrived German, without regard for their nationality. She remained in Brussels when the city was occupied by the Germans. As

---

*John Lewis-Stempel cites a figure of 6,500 executions of Belgian and French civilians in his book *Six Weeks*.

such her actions were unimpeachable. Then the lady concerned committed herself to hiding Allied soldiers from the Germans and helping them to escape to neutral Holland. In this act she was in clear breach of international laws on the role of civilians of any nationality within occupied territories, for such actions the penalties include death. Spies were executed, neither the British or the French hesitated to deal summarily with those caught up in espionage, which had an immediate military purpose. The humanitarian actions of the nurse were not of military significance, was the interpretation of the world at large. The Germans did not agree; at dawn on 12th October 1915, a firing squad on a rifle range outside Brussels executed Edith Cavell.

World opinion was outraged!

CHAPTER 14

Generals, Historians and Critics

One feature of the fallout from the Great War is the effect on the reputation of individuals and in particular the generals of the British Army. From a historical standpoint, conventionally, generals who were successful and won, received a good press, losers were soon forgotten. The different treatment meted out, retrospectively, for the military leaders of the 1914/18 conflict is quite exceptional. The leaders available for a particular war are a matter of chance, five years earlier or later and the personalities will be different for no other reason than the passage of time. Britain sent its army to war in 1914 with the senior officers available and in 1918 the army presented the government with a win: result! After a short period of euphoria, the reputation of senior officers went into decline to the point that a whole school of history grew up to excoriate the generals as 'Butchers and Bunglers', the opposite of the usual treatment.

It was not the intention of this account of the Great War's place in the history of the twentieth century to undertake a detailed review of individual personalities, others have done the original research in English, French and German with scholarship and diligence, which is both time consuming and beyond my abilities. In most cases, but by no means all, I am offering each as an example of how individual talents enabled a team to meet the threat the Allied nations faced. As for the Germans named, read for yourself.

The officers named in the following summary are just a few of those who contributed to the Allied victory, without their experience, determination and effort there would have been no victory. Flawless paragons of military endeavour they were not, they were though the best the nation had. Senior commanders cannot be plucked from some alternative occupation, shipbuilding say, and let loose with 100,000 soldiers when a determined enemy is knocking at the gates. On the job learning has to be kept to a minimum, which is not to allow all commanders the increase of experience that should accumulate by the success and failure of events as they unfold.

First for consideration has to be, Field Marshal Earl Kitchener of Khartoum, putting aside the technicality that by convention Field Marshals do not retire, they remain on the active list until death, Kitchener did not have command responsibility during the Great War, he was Minister of War. To him must go the credit for two achievements, firstly he was one of the very few who realised once war broke out in Europe on the scale of August 1914 that the conflict would be long and drawn out, three years was his estimate. Second he was able to deploy his knowledge and experience of military affairs to organise the 'Kitchener armies' of volunteers in such a way that the new formations became worthy reinforcements for the hard pressed remnants of the original forces of the BEF that went to France in August 1914. History does not allow us the judgment of any contribution he could have made to the second half of the Great War. HMS Hampshire on which he was sailing to Russia was sunk with heavy loss of life by a German mine of Orkney in June 1916. He it was though who created the foundations for eventual victory.

Second on the race card for a mention is Field Marshal Sir William Robertson who as CIGS became the professional head of the British Army in 1915. His career began as a trooper (private) and he made it to the very peak of his profession in the army 'crippled by class' odd that! Not only must 'Wully' have been an outstanding soldier with all that implies, he must have been a very shrewd* judge of men of which more later. It was not to be expected that his background and career would produce a sophisticated political general, such as Sir Henry Wilson. It follows then that when Lloyd George (LG) arrived on the scene as Prime Minister the sparks would fly, and they did. LG opening on one occasion

---

* Shrewd, a word now out of fashion but fitting exactly the character of Robertson: it means "keen witted in practical affairs, astute", would that more of our leaders today applied such a talent to their responsibilities.

by saying "I've heard di, da, di, da, di, da" and adding his opinion to conclude the issue; 'Wully' thought for a moment and responded "An' I've heard different" and went no further, subject closed. Politicians find such a style of discussion almost incomprehensible. There is no dissimulation, no explanation offered. I suspect LG was caught flat footed in some misrepresentation of a situation of which 'Wully' was fully informed. The emphatic contradiction told LG, 'you're walking on water and I know you are, so back off'.

Robertson's tenure as CIGS from 1915 to early 1918 was of enormous significance, he it was who controlled the relationship between government and commanders, moderated the demands for men and *materiel* by the soldiers and deflected politicians from over ambitious alternatives to war on the Western Front. Gordon Corrigan in his summation of events *Mud, Blood and Poppycock*, (Chap 11), quotes an example, verbatim, of the text of a memo from the CIGS (Robertson) to Lord Curzon (Foreign Secretary) which begins, "It would be valuable if you could explain to the Prime Minister (LG) – "; continuing with an explanation of the difficult terrain in Salonika and the sheer impossibility of undertaking the military action proposed by the PM in this theatre of war.

The influence wielded by Robertson was immense in numerous ways; in one particular though the decisions he took, more than any other, influenced the way the war was fought. As professional head of the army it was for him to agree recommendations to appoint the British Armys' senior commanders. He moulded the team to meet and defeat the enemy. He understood in the instinctive way of an 'old and bold' soldier, that the best available must be concentrated at the point of the greatest danger, the Western Front. The critics' view is the generals were not good enough, but they were the only ones available to the army and the nation. Robertson's employment of his commanders in ways that made the best of their strengths and characters was inspired, a talent which it seems has gone almost unrecognised.

Continuing the review now in the order of events, two of the most well known names of the Great War rank for consideration, with two of the lesser names; Field Marshal Sir John French, subsequently raised to the peerage as an Earl, and his successor Field Marshal Sir Douglas Haig, also raised to the peerage as an Earl. Sir John commanded the BEF when it mobilised and went to France in August 1914. He had command experience in South Africa and had held numerous staff appointments up to 1914 when he was CIGS. There occurred then the 'Curragh incident' and the threat by officers in Ireland to resign if required to take military action against protestant activists in Ulster. The government of the day did not meet undertakings given to the army and French resigned as CIGS. French was recalled in 1914 and commanded the BEF in France until December 1915. As C in C in 1914 he faced a situation for which he and all the other British generals had no experience. He was to command the British forces as an ally of the French in the minor role that by force of the comparative numerical strengths of the two armies was the only option available. Not since Waterloo had Britain fought in continental Europe when in 1815 Wellington led coalition forces with the Prussian Marshal, Blucher. Field Marshal French was not used to making war in consort with Allied armies and did not speak French. Nevertheless he faced the responsibility and with the troops of the two corps on which the BEF was initially based made life difficult for the German attackers; to the extent that with the assistance of poor German decisions the Schlieffen plan failed. Then as the campaign solidified into trench warfare he settled the BEF into its defensive lines, incorporated reinforcements into the organisation of the army, held the line against the enemy attack at second Ypres in the spring of 1915 and launched the unsuccessful attack at Loos in 1915. What he did not do, because it was beyond his power, was win the war. The politicians needed an explanation and he was a readymade fall guy, replaced by Douglas Haig in December 1915. The change was not welcomed by Sir John who then put pen to paper and in a book he wrote, *1914*, criticised the political direction of the war, oops!

There are aspects of Sir John's behavior, not least the authorship of the book mentioned above, which are distinctly odd for an army officer of the Victorian and Edwardian era. Society and in particular the closed community of the army had very different ideas on acceptable norms of lifestyle to be expected of those in the public eye to those current in society today. He married when a very junior officer, almost unheard of at that time, then divorced his wife. He kept a mistress, three black marks before we get serious. He used his friendship with Charles Repington, a former officer (Lt Col) required to resign his commission for paying too much attention to other officers' wives, then a correspondent for *The Times*, to plant stories attacking the government for the inadequate supply of shells in 1915; the shortage was a serious business but two wrongs don't make a right. He was also reputedly poor at personal finance, to the extent that he borrowed money, £2,500 is one suggested amount, a very large sum at the time, from a more junior officer; the officer who provided the loan, Douglas Haig. The breaches of army conventions of the day in that brief summary are astounding; a guardian angel somewhere was on overtime, most officers would not survive one or at the most two such misdeeds. More damaging for the army was the dislike he had for Lt. Gen. Horace Smith Dorrien, who took command of II Corps in August 1914 when the original commander, Grierson, died of a heart attack as the BEF mobilised in France. The origins of the antipathy arose from the changes made by Smith Dorrien to the training of cavalry formations when he succeeded French as C in C Aldershot. French was a cavalryman, Smith Dorrien an infantryman, the latter set in train changes to the training of cavalry units to use them as mounted infantry. French who was Inspector General of Cavalry was fiercely opposed and from then on there was a very unpleasant mutual antagonism.

Generals it has to be said by the nature of their responsibilities need to be determined and forceful personalities, 'shrinking violets' get no sympathy as senior commanders. If they are unable to develop ideas and put them into action in the face of opposition, they fail, that after all is the nature of warfare. Generals must, however, have allies amongst their peers, particularly amongst those of different opinion, teams are not built on 'yes men', controlled dissent is vital to the development of creative action. French it seems did not understand this need.

Nevertheless he saw the BEF through the first very difficult fifteen months of the war and left it better able to face the future than it was during the early weeks of the conflict.

Douglas Haig, who was successor to French, commanded I Corps of the BEF from August 1914, as the size of the BEF in France increased he became Commander 1st Army and then in December 1915 the BEF's

Commander in Chief. There were, it would seem, some times during the first weeks of the war when Haig was less than sure of himself or so it is said. My point is, which of the generals of the early weeks got ten out of ten, none. Haig, just as all the others had to, needed to learn how to handle this new high intensity warfare with the multiplicity of complications it brought with it. Kitchener and Robertson were needed for other things and contemporaries of Haig were clearly not judged suitable. Rightly or wrongly we will never know.

The task of C in C was complicated by the responsibilities of commanding the smaller component of the Allied armies in France. This was a task for which none of the commanders available had experience, there was no training manual, Wellington was the last Brit who had fought a major war as a coalition general. Haig grew into the responsibilities, he had to protect the BEF and larger British interests whilst supporting joint actions to bring about the defeat of the German Army, this was a tall order. Those concerned had to make things up as they went along. In this Haig did better than anyone anticipated.

The name Haig was not unknown in 1914 in Britain and its Empire, and it remains so now. A member of the family which made its money dosing the population with a medicine of many people's choice, his character took more from the Scottish Presbyterian tradition than it did from the geniality of a dram or three. Reserved and unsocial by repute, he found some difficulty in expressing himself verbally with clarity and conviction. His preference was for the written word. The feature of the man that ought to be recognised is his intellect, he was one with Kitchener recognising the implications of events in 1914 and planning for a long war. His task was to impose his will on the German Army and bring about its defeat. John Terraine has done much to address this problem and published in 1963, *Douglas Haig, 'The Educated Soldier'* as a well argued defence of the man and his actions.

I have argued elsewhere in these ramblings that the BEF had, from the commencement of the German offensive against Verdun in February 1916, to fight the war in such a manner that the French government and Army would continue the conflict until Germany was defeated. This was the prime responsibility of the C in C, without success in this aspect of affairs all other considerations and all the previous casualties were wasted. Field Marshal Haig should be recognised for the architecture of his strategy, not vilified because the German Army got in the way and killed and maimed Allied soldiers.

The Field Marshal may have foolishly offered himself to his critics as a hostage to fortune. Some researchers suggest that he rewrote his original diaries, not just necessary sub editing, the originals being destroyed. If that is so it was an open goal for all those who want to find fault, which is what happened. He should have known better or been better advised.

As the BEF mobilised it was a two corps army, Haig we know commanded I Corps and Horace Smith Dorrien took command of II Corps. The dispositions of the BEF were such that as the battle developed during the opening weeks, II Corps and Smith Dorrien were in the hot seat, fighting fiercely day after day, retreating from Mons and engaging the German Army in a classic stopping action at Le Cateau. In this action, II Corps faced six German divisions, held them when they attacked; inflicting severe casualties then disengaged from the battle and withdrew. Smith Dorrien had in fact been ordered by Sir John French to continue the retreat through Le Cateau, he decided that following earlier engagements this was impracticable given the fatigue of his soldiers and the dispersion of his units. He was able to call on the support of additional forces from Major General Snow's 4th Division and cavalry from Major General Allenby's division, who would fight dismounted when necessary. These troops were in the locality as they continued to withdraw under pressure from the Germans. French was advised of the action planned by the Commander of II Corps, his reply was not a model of clarity. The men of II Corps fought their action and withdrew successfully; Smith Dorrien was tagged as 'The General who disobeyed'. That was unfair; commanders on the spot have the responsibility of judging the validity of orders and acting in accordance with their own appreciation of conditions. That is why officers have 'original authority'. The Nelsonian blind eye is an important component of command. What the events did do though was to exacerbate further the ill feeling between the C in C and one of his corps commanders. From then on he was a marked man. In the spring of the following year he proposed a withdrawal at Ypres to a more easily defensible position, the right thing to do militarily but a 'no no' from a political perspective. Robertson, ever tactful, advised him that he had sealed his own fate with the immortal line " 'Orace your fer 'ome".

The proposition that is raised by these events has some unpleasant undercurrents; French disliked Smith Dorrien who had shown himself to be a competent commander in the field and very much his own man. The BEF was expanding rapidly as the Territorial Forces reinforced the original regular formations. Senior commanders of proven ability were very scarce, yet Smith Dorrien lost his command and returned to Britain. The events do not square with the demands of the moment. French we know had an obligation to Haig; Haig also had some influence at Court, his wife was a lady in waiting to the Queen. Was this something Sir John hoped he might turn to his advantage? Although by the middle of 1915 Haig had lost confidence in the generalship of French. What though would have been the outcome if Smith Dorrien had been preferred to Haig as replacement for French in December 1915?

There is though one suggestion of a dark cloud that has been raised to cast doubt on the true nature of Smith Dorrien and that concerns his temperament. Generals as noted above can be of fiery temperament, several writers though refer to the violence of Smith Dorrien's outbursts in terms that suggest more than the impatience of a man striving to achieve against the odds. I wonder if this was one of those circumstances in which 'Wully's' instinct saw a more dangerous condition in the outbursts and took the hard decision in the best interests of the British Army? Following his return to Britain Sir Horace fell victim to a serious illness and did not take up the appointment as Commander of the East African campaign. Later he became Governor of Gibraltar, retired in 1923 and was killed in a car accident in 1932. Whatever the answers, Horace Smith Dorrien has a memorial, a stone obelisk erected by his admirers on a lonely, windswept hilltop above the Derbyshire village of Crich.

If this portion of the review were to continue at the length of the above paragraphs, there would be no end in sight for weeks to come and that is not the purpose, the intent was again to demonstrate the complex conditions created by the demands of the Great War.

Before we leave the subject some of the other commanders should be acknowledged, Plummer and Maxse for their never ending efforts to train and care for their men, Trenchard who built the RFC, Allenby who was posted from the Western Front to the Middle East where he conducted a sparklingly successful campaign to defeat the Turks. Monash from Australia and Currie from Canada who built the troops of these nascent nations into such battle worthy units that they formed the spearhead on 8th August 1918, opening the attack at the battle of Amiens and initiating the Allied advance to victory; Pershing of the USA who managed somehow to reconcile the unrealistic constraints of Congress, President Wilson, his own preconceptions with the military demands of the Great War. Jan Smuts the former Boer Commander who became an admired soldier statesman in not one, but both acts, of the German war of the twentieth century. Then the other generals of British Armies, Horne 1st Army, Byng 3[rd,] and Rawlinson 4th, all committed by their duty to the defeat of the sovereign's enemies. Like it or not anyone who reviews the Great War has to recognise that the perceptions of responsibility within the army and nation that went to war in 1914 are utterly changed ninety years later.

There is an insider's account and commentary of events that is little reported but despite the *caveats* previously brought to the attention of the reader the account is well worth attention.

In 1953, Maj. Gen. Sir John (Tavish) Davidson, KCMG, CB, DSO, published in book form a critique and description of events and circumstances of Allied military operations in France in 1917 and 1918. The author during the period 1916–18 held the appointment of Director of Military Operation at General Headquarters of the British Army in France. He was an essential member of the inner circle, an officer from whom Haig would have required analysis, argument, alternatives, diligence and unflinching loyalty. In shorthand terms he was, with the Chief of Staff, Field Marshal Haig's right hand. This was the officer who saw everything and everyone, understood in full the strategy, purpose and constraints which the C in C, Haig, had to take account in his deployment and use of the British forces placed at his disposal; a uniquely privileged position.

The text provides descriptions, comments and alternatives to various aspects of events in the years in question which shed another light on aspect of events, personalities, circumstances and crucially the strategic philosophy adopted under Haig's leadership. The first example summarised below is cited to illustrate the alternative version of circumstances that preoccupied the C in C and his subordinates. Other examples are in the briefest form words will allow.

First: there is in the accounts of the French Army's campaign in 1917 recognition that after Nivelle's spring offensive failed, this lead to disillusionment and mutiny which affected significant portions of the French Army. This was too large an event to escape notice in relevant accounts of the time. Davidson though paints a much bleaker picture, his version of the situation as it developed was that to all intents and purposes the French Army lost all coherence as a fighting force at the height of the disorder in the summer of 1917. Two divisions only, were considered battle worthy and with the colonial troops for a crucial period, the only formations on which reliance could be placed. Not only was the army in confusion, there was also widespread political dissent and civil disturbance with strikes and riots, 'avowedly pacifist' politicians arrested, together with the appearance of a left wing dissident organisation *'Le Bonnet Rouge.'* Haig and his General Staff had to plan on the basis that the activities of the British Army including all the overseas components should attract the attention of the German High Command and the armies at its disposal. The Germans must at all costs be diverted from any ambition to attack the French held portions of the Western Front: the route to Third Ypres (Passchendaele) was the means to this end.

Second: the successful attack on and capture of the Broodseinde ridge on 4th October 1917 was regarded by the German High Command as a major setback and the official German History refers to the success of the British forces as 'a Black Day' and Ludendorff described that the outcome *"was extraordinarily severe and again we [Germans] only came through it with enormous losses."* A prime objective was, by the admission of the attacked, achieved.

Third: as would normally be expected the weather varied during the

Third Ypres, legend has it that there was continuous rainfall during the weeks of the battle. Not so apparently, wet in August when the offensive was launched, dry in September and early October. So much so that there was added to the usual perils of battle, the effect of bullets, shells and shrapnel ricocheting from the hard ground, compounding the perils of direct fire by this secondary hazard; wet again from the middle of October until the battle was drawn to a conclusion in the middle of November when the Canadians captured and consolidated their position on the high ground at Passchendaele.

Fourth: General Davidson draws on German commanders' diaries and reports to establish the concern, amounting almost to despair, of the enemy commanders as their divisions and formations were drawn into the maelstrom and returned damaged almost beyond recovery. The official British historian, Brig. Gen. Sir James Edmonds, CB, CMG is also quoted and reinforces the reports of the likes of Crown Prince Ruprecht, Ludendorff and von Kuhl.

Finally: the introduction to the book is provided by Viscount Trenchard, the Commander of the Royal Flying Corps and subsequently the Royal Air Force in France during this crucial period. In a few hundred words he sharpens the focus of present day perceptions and opinions by summarising the constraints, attitudes and actions of those who exercised the responsibilities of command for Britain and her forces in France as circumstances demanded to defeat the barbarians at the gates. This was the achievement of all those who served.

The most unsatisfactory aspect of the critics of Haig, his commanders, staff, campaigns, planning, direction and control of the war in France is that the myth of the 'Butchers and Bunglers' gained popular credence despite the accounts of events available which interpreted events in a more balanced and realistic way. That is the flaw in their argument, the information used was made to fit preconceptions; there is no greater sin for a serious study of history!

The names of two other generals are worthy of mention to illustrate the undying humour of Thomas Atkins, always able to make a joke at someone's expense. From the army of France, General Franchet D'Esperey known throughout the BEF as 'Desperate Frankie' and from the enemy,

General Alexander von Kluck, there are no prizes for guessing what Tommy did to this general's last name!

The generals have had their day, now what of the historians, some of whom were generals as well. They come in all shapes and sizes. Easiest by far to categorise are those who were there. The men who when the tumult and the shouting died wrote and in most cases published their accounts of events as they experienced them. Each time one of these histories is read some new aspect of experience is to be found. The accounts are the primary source of our knowledge and for the experienced researcher valuable material to cross reference the numerous accounts of events. Factually these versions of events are the most straightforward, in particular those completed within a decade of the war's end, prior to the onset of revisionism. Each of these accounts has to be treated with respect. That being said historians have to apply a dose of healthy scepticism even to vernacular accounts; details between accounts are often contradictory. In particular questions have to be raised when the details related are provided by those who served their country well but were not by profession military men. The communicators, C. Day Lewis, Robert Graves, Siegfried Sassoon, *et al*, were each able to summon up the images of despair faced by the fighting men, turning the emotions they experienced against their own leaders too often, neglecting the inconvenience of German participation. The extent of their experiences and the mourning that followed the death of friends allows them a place in the library of records written on the subject. They must though have equal credit with other narrators, the sharpness of their words does not promote their evaluation above that of others.

Then there are the writers who were soldiers and also by intent became historians, Capt. B. H. Liddell Hart and Lt. Col. J. F. C. Fuller are of this caste. Each is sharply critical of the conduct of the war on the Western Front and it has to be said made a respectable living from their writing and lectures. Lt. Col. Fuller remained in the army eventually achieving the rank of major general. Each had an understanding of how the tactical doctrine should be changed but do not appear to have appreciated the difficulties of putting such doctrines in place. When the men, equipment and opportunity occurred in August 1918, then the armies under British command used every resource available: air power, tanks, artillery, cavalry and infantry to launch the assault and stormed to victory in a hundred days; at no small cost in casualties, a precursor of the 'Blitzkreig' of Act II of the tragedy.

Later day soldier historians have done great service to counteract the 'Butchers and Bunglers' school of thinking, Gordon Corrigan, Richard Holmes, Alan Mallinson and John Terraine are outstanding for the quality of their analysis and clarity of their prose.

The academic historians, the likes of Correlli Barnett, Arthur Bryant and A. J. P. Taylor are each valuable sources of factual material, they have the time and access to resources denied to the amateur dabbler, all have done admirable work to trace the pattern and sequence of events. What they were not and had never been were commanders on the ground, facing problems calling for immediate decisions, knowing at best no more than half of the information needed. Historians of this calibre would be better received if their own ideas developed in retrospect were not substituted as the solution to complicated multi faceted situations. They should also be treated with suspicion when claiming second sight and favouring particular personalities whilst criticizing others, did they ever meet these men and understand their characters, if not, their credibility as judges of the outcome of events is compromised, hearsay evidence, as such, always has to be treated with great caution!

The list can go on, whatever has been written including this commentary can be criticised for partiality. The subject is so vast that the best that can be hoped for is the honest admission of intentions and realistic support from factual material of propositions and explanations. The accounts that have to be treated with suspicion are those that substitute the judgement of hindsight, battles cannot be replayed with a different script to prove a point; wars are immediate and the outcome of events settles the situation, to play the 'ah but if' game gets you nowhere, the past as they say is history.

Then there are the correspondents and diarists whose letters and written accounts of the time have in more recent years found life in the numerous books and programmes that have stimulated the national conscience. The words written are often poignant, affectionate, expressing pride in achievement, as well as longing for a peaceful end. Letters were censored, so rarely contain much by way of true detail of events, their value lies in the reaction of the men of all ranks to the task in hand, so often there is explicit concern to succeed and win against the Germans who were perceived by soldiers of all ranks as a real and potent enemy against whom victory was essential.

Mixed within all the available material on the Great War can be found comment and criticism which is both unfair and unrealistic. An example has been quoted of the idea of providing armour for soldiers on the Somme as protection against small arms fire; it is unrealistic in the extreme to advance such a proposition, given the state of technology of the day. Other examples include the complaint that the provision of reflecting metal triangles on the packs carried by soldiers during an advance to make it easier for men to follow each other, made them more vulnerable to marksmen. The same critic however passes over without comment the detail that Scottish units painted a white saltire (St. Andrews cross) on their packs. Either both were misguided or both were sensible aids. Pipers playing their comrades into battle were just as brave or misguided as the men who ran with footballs towards the enemy trenches. As a conclusion to this short paragraph of warning there is the ill informed criticism by one author who, on finding in the diary of a regular officer of the Great War an entry following the announcement of the Armistice in November 1918 that reads "Now we can return to some proper soldiering", castigates the diarist for the flippant treatment of the war just ended and the losses suffered. This critic clearly has no understanding at all of the 'low key' ethic of understatement that was the essential attribute of the British officer, officers who had just lead their army to victory.

Commentators of this group are in general terms unreliable, their inconsistent are too obvious.

CHAPTER 15

Conclusions; Fighting through

All expeditions have to come to an end, this journey has gone on as long as it should, and it follows therefore that I must put into perspective the numerous influences that bore upon the British participation in the Great War.

The first element to be revisited has to be the social structure of nineteenth century Britain. The nation had in the space of a hundred years transformed itself from an agrarian, land-dependent community, substantially governed by a political oligarchy, into a modern industrial and commercial society. A world leader in commercial and financial ventures, various aspects of manufacture, politically mature with a democratically elected government, even if this aspect was, by today's criteria, less than perfect. Furthermore through its imperial adventures it was responsible for the government of a quarter of the world's landmass. This success, and make no mistake it was an enormous achievement, equal to, if not greater than that of Imperial Rome. The changes and growth were undertaken with an army, including its militias and reserves never more than 1% of the population and never included conscription or the *'levee en masse'*. This was a stark contrast to the major powers in continental Europe, to whom large standing armies were a demonstration of nationhood.

The second consideration is the role undertaken by the army which acted as an expeditionary force, dispatched in small columns and formations to reinforce political action and act as an imperial police force. It, the army, did not think in European dimensions; the responsibility for this state of affairs is principally the responsibility of the governments of various complexions who held power from the time that the House of

Stuart was restored to the throne. The army has to accept responsibility for letting the various parliamentary regimes and the associated ministers get away with this blind eye policy for more than 200 years. The army conquered territory in the new worlds and fought numerous dynastic coalition wars in Europe at the behest of the nation's governments. The odd scrap of European territory fell under British rule as a consequence of some of the campaigns, and subsequent treaties in Europe: Gibraltar, Malta, Minorca, Corfu, Cyprus, Heligoland to name a few. None of Britain's wars in mainland Europe were wars of conquest or government, once Calais, the last vestige of continental possessions, was lost to French action in the reign of Queen Mary in 1556. The overall effect of this vicarious association with the quarrelsome states of mainland Europe amounted to experience without responsibility in the political arena. Militarily the nations of Europe defined their objectives in terms of either dynastic control or landmass conquest within the boundaries of their continent; imperial adventures took second place. That was a perception alien to the military mind of Britain. The attitude of Britain's soldiers was global, the nation could only be invaded by sea and the strength of the Royal Navy was such that any attempt to deliver an adequate invasion force was remote; for example Spain's Armada in 1588. The flaw was that until Wilhelm II was recognised as a serious threat, the need for Britain to support France with an army of significant size was not identified until it was too late, almost.

The outcome for the army of 1914 and its commanders, sent to France to support the French and Belgians, who overnight had become allies, was in military terms the worst of all worlds. The battle was to be fought on ground suited to the plan of the enemy, at a time of his choice, plus the option to dictate weapons and tactics, the British Army was on the back foot. The British Army though, despite the manifest disadvantages it faced in 1914, did bring something special to the party. Since Marlborough took the army to continental Europe in the early years of the eighteenth century it had been on campaign somewhere in the world almost continuously, every type of military action was woven into the fabric of its experience, the quality of the cloth was to be tested beyond imagination by the Great War, it was not found wanting.

Arising out of these considerations we arrive at the third aspect for consideration, derived from the details recorded in the main text. Which of the European powers initiated the conflict? This is the core question for which an answer has to be found. To draw a parallel, to establish a case to prosecute for murder it is necessary to show motive, means and opportunity. Britain, whilst deeply suspicious of Wilhelm II's intentions, had no motive, inadequate means and no opportunity to initiate a war in continental Europe. France had the motive, the defeat of 1871 and the loss of Alsace and Lorraine, the opportunity, a common border with Germany, but as a nation she was short suited on means, insufficient military clout. Russia had no immediately obvious motive for a 'set to' with Germany and certainly in the years prior to August 1914 had a preoccupation with the reconstruction of her armed forces following the Russo Japanese War. Austria/Hungary had no argument with either Britain or France, neither had she as a nation the opportunity by any practical means to have a go at either nation, her objective was to keep the uppity Serbs in their place. Germany on the other hand had an excess of means as well as her delusional motives, all she lacked was opportunity; this to be provided on cue, free, *gratis* and for nothing by Gavirilo Princip. This was a situation grasped with both hands by Willie and his high command; never it appears did it cross their minds that the campaign would not be a replay of the 1871 war.

Britain was wrong footed, politically and militarily by the events of the summer of 1914, of that there is no argument. British participation in the Great War became therefore the least unsatisfactory of a bag full of unpleasant options, is the fourth conclusion.

Once the lists were joined though the fifth conclusion reached is that there was no alternative but the defeat of Germany and her armed forces, nothing else would do. To this monumental task Britain, her Empire and her people set their minds, wealth and effort.

The conclusions on military issues, the method, follow from the preceding five. Paramount amongst them is the essential realisation that neither France nor Britain acting alone could defeat the German Army in the field. Neither nation could deploy an army of sufficient size to overcome the Germans. The war had to be fought as an alliance between the two nations. Field Marshal French seems to have been uncomfortable with the concept of fighting the campaign as one of two allied commanders. Douglas Haig was more astute. He soon realised after he took command, as the Germans attacked the French fortress of Verdun, that he needed to design his strategy in such a way that the French would continue the war until Germany was defeated.

The next conclusion has to address the methods by which the war was waged and won. The arguments go back and forth between protagonists, each claiming unique visions of success without loss, injury and death. To them all I must remind them of two features of war. Firstly, war produces casualties killed and wounded, second, battles and campaigns can never be re fought, the very fact that the personalities are different, by reason of the death of some of those who played out the action first time round, will compromise attempts to show one way or the other the advantages or defects of alternatives. Like it or not the acid test of the quality of military action is, who won? Britain, France and their Allies were the successful team. Almost one hundred years after the event it is difficult in the extreme to focus attention on the unbelievably harsh task and standard against which the British Army would be judged; that however was the requirement and expectation of the nation. The expectation was fulfilled, ask yourself now what would have been the effect on the Britain and its people if the result had been otherwise.

As a corollary to this conclusion is the constant debate about the poor quality of command, the waste of human resources by stupidity and 'bungling'. Of one thing I am sure, each of us who considers the subject of the Great War finds themselves in sympathy with the men of all ranks who served at the front. It was a perilous, grim, fearful, mind wrecking experience that killed many, wounded and maimed others and marked the consciousness of all who served there. When it comes to a judgement on success or failure, as an army commanded by men who despite their experience and efforts were fallible; the weight of information is that the armies under British command won their war at significantly lower human cost, both the actual numbers killed and wounded, than the French or German Armies who fought on the Western Front. Would the numbers have been lower still if alternative plans or methods had been used? No one can tell. One thing is certain however, the weather frequently marred operations, rain, rain and more rain, then just as a reminder of how unkind luck can be; on Easter Sunday in April 1917 when the British launched a successful attack at Messines Ridge, it snowed not just a few flakes but a full blown snow storm with matching temperatures.

There is one aspect of the approach of many writers and media personalities that has become prominent following the ascendancy of the 'Butchers and Bunglers' school of historians which also ranks for comment as this review draws to a conclusion. The emphasis has been placed for about twenty years on the personal accounts of the front line soldier, officers and other ranks. Their diaries, letters and memoirs have been analysed, reviewed and deconstructed for nuances of attitude and meaning. No opportunity has been lost to enlist our sympathy for the horrors to which the front line soldier was subjected. It is a very subtle way to continue the campaign that discredit's the generals who lead the army, did their duty and delivered victory to the sovereign and Parliament. The fighting man gets the credit, the generals the blame.

The German responsibility for the whole War was correctly included as the 'war guilt' clause of the 1919 Treaty of Versailles. It was a proper reflection of the sentiments of nations who had to bear the brunt of German aggression. No amount of revisionism, "piety nor wit/ shall lure it back to cancel half a line/ nor all your tears wash out a word of it". There and only there is the blame to be laid.

The personal difficulty I have experienced in completing this review of the Great War is that it is a subject of such complexity. It is in many respects similar to peeling an onion; each layer and portion of skin when removed uncovers more issues and complications for assessment. I have avoided detailed analysis of individual actions. I do not have the resources or experience to consider the implications of 2/7th Blankshires failing to join up with 4th Loamshires. The objective was to put British successes in the Great War into context and pose the issue to critics of providing an alternative to the achievements of the British Army on the Western Front.

The final aspect of these conclusions is one of personal tribute based only on my assessment of the quality, determination, hardihood and fearless resolution in the face of enormous odds that was needed, daily and hourly by the soldiers of the Great War, some not out of their teenage adolescence. An example now to demonstrate the gulf in the perceptions of responsibility to highlight my point: the official war photographer to the Australian forces for the last twelve months of the war, Frank Hurley, went to France to take up his duties within a few weeks of reaching England as one of the complement of crew who all survived the epic of Edward Shackleton's 1914 Antarctic expedition. Here was a man who in today's terms would have been feted and counselled, interviewed and analysed to 'allow' him to adjust to the 'trauma' of his experiences. How were things done then? "Pack your bags chum, get your kit together your off to France to photograph the action", which is what he did. I know this man was not technically in the firing line, the point of the example though is that no one saw anything untoward in his treatment. Much was asked and expected of the citizens of the day and the citizens expected much of themselves.

Lawrence Binyon wrote his tribute 'To the fallen' with the lines known to so many 'They shall grow not old…' Kipling wrote another poem, surely the epitaph for his son. Consider the power of the allegory in the first eight words of the poem that follows, if then there is a tear close to the surface as you appreciate the remainder of this epitaph with images, more poignant even than Binyon's, know well that you are as one with those whose determination made their place in history unique and is their 'Achievement'.

Gethsemane.

The Garden called Gethsemane
In Picardy it was,
And there the people came to see
The English soldiers pass,
We used to pass we used to pass
Or halt as it may be,
And ship our masks in case of gas
Beyond Gethsemane.

The Garden called Gethsemane,
It held a pretty lass,
But all the time she talked to me
I prayed my cup might pass.
The officer sat on the chair,
The men lay on the grass,
And all the time we halted there
I prayed might cup might pass.

It didn't pass – it didn't pass –
It didn't pass from me.
I drank of it when we met the gas
Beyond Gethsemane.

APPENDIX I

Army ranks, organisation and formations.

The text of *Achievement* includes references at various points to the rank structure used by the army to delegate responsibility and organise its affairs on and off the battlefield. The information below is no more than a bird's eye view of ranks and formations. It is a complicated subject and the best I can do is to provide an outline guide as a basis for the contents within the body of the text.

The information summarised below is based on the nomenclature used in an infantry unit. There are variations for units of the old cavalry regiments, foot guards, artillery, engineers and other technical formations. The base model of ranks for these variants of terminology remains comparable to the example below.

Non commissioned and warrant officers.

Rank.	Insignia.	Command responsibility.	Comment.
Private	none	none	Tommy Atkins.
Lance Corporal	Single chevron worn on sleeve at the elbow.	Sometimes 2 i/c of a section.	
Corporal.	Two chevrons worn as above.	Section command of 7 soldiers	first step in promotion.
Sergeant.	Three chevrons worn as above	2 i/c of a platoon of 4 sections.	

Rank.	Insignia.	Command responsibility.	Comment.
Staff Sergeant	Crown above 3 chevrons, worn on sleeve at the elbow.		Sometimes known as Colour Sgts.
Warrant Officer II Sergeant Major	Crown worn above cuff of jacket.	Senior NCO of a company of 150 all ranks	
Regimental Quarter Master Sergeant	Crown within laurel wreath	2 i/c to Regimental Quartermaster.	
Warrant Officer I	The Royal Arms, worn above the cuff of jacket.	Senior NCO of a battalion.	

Notes on the non commissioned ranks of the army.

- Lance corporal is technically not a rank, it is an appointment and as such can be attached to someone for a particular duty and when the duty is completed the stripe is relinquished. It is often used to give promising young soldiers a taste of responsibility and to measure their ability.
- Soldiers in a substantive rank which does not have a specific command responsibility, for example staff sergeants, will usually be deployed in specialist roles such as company quartermaster sergeant or an instructor in a training unit.

Commissioned (Officer) ranks

Rank.	Insignia.	Command responsibility.	Comment.
Second Lieutenant (subaltern)	Single star worn on cuff of jacket or shoulder epaulet as determined by regimental custom.	Platoon of up to 35 soldiers.	First command
Lieutenant	Two stars worn as above.	Platoon or specialist role eg. Intelligence Officer.	
Captain	Three stars worn as above.	2 i/c of a Company.	
Major	Crown worn as above.	Company Commander of up to 227 soldiers and officers.	
Lieutenant Colonel	Crown and star worn as above.	Battalion Commander.	
Colonel	Crown and two stars. as above. Plus red gorget patches on the collar of uniform and red cap band.		Usually undertakes a staff appointment or may be i/c a training establishment.
Brigadier General	Crown and three stars. Plus red gorget patches and red cap band.	Brigade Commander of up to 6,100 all ranks.	In 1922 the rank was reduced from General officer status.

Rank.	Insignia.	Command responsibility.	Comment.
Major General	Star over crossed sabre and baton with gorget patches and red cap band.	Divisional Commander of up to 19,600 all ranks, 3 brigades in 1915.	
Lieutenant General	Crown over crossed sabre and baton with gorget patches and red cap band.	Corps Commander, 2 or. more divisions plus Corps troops min. of 40,000 all ranks.	
General	Crown and star over crossed sabre and baton. Red gorget patches and	Army commander, minimum 2 Corps and army formations min 90,000 all ranks.	
Field Marshal	Crown over crossed sabre and baton within a laurel wreath.	Theatre commander eg France March 1918, 5 armies.	

As the main text of *Achievement* is concerned with the Great War the position in which the rank insignia appears conforms to the uniform conventions of the time. Subsequent changes to the dress regulations changed the position. The insignia for officers was standardised to be worn on shoulder epaulets of service and battle dress. In more recent times when in 'field' or 'battle' order rank insignia are worn on a fabric patch attached to the upper section of the uniform jacket.

• The progression through the ranks of the army is based on service, seniority in the rank, as well as competence. By this means ability and service are rewarded. In the army of 1914 there were private soldiers who had not progressed one step in the promotion stakes after twenty years of service.

- Permanent employment in a rank requires the soldier to have achieved 'substantive' status. The units of the army from the highest to the lowest are organised around their 'establishment' strength. The total for all the army's units from private to general gives each battalion of infantry, regiment of armour, battery of artillery, HQ formation etc. the numbers of each trade and rank who will comprise the strength of the unit. Just to confuse things though there are conventionally two establishment figures. The number allocated for peace time and duties and the larger number that makes up the 'war establishment' .

- Substantive rank once achieved cannot be revoked by arbitrary action, only a court martial has the power to reduce substantive rank.

- Acting rank can be assumed if a serving member of the army is posted to an appointment that is established as the responsibility of a higher rank. For example a newly graduated officer from Staff Collage (psc) could be a substantive captain and not yet have completed the minimum service to be promoted to the rank of major. His first appointment after Staff College could be as staff officer of a brigade, brigade major (GSOIII). He could well be granted acting rank in this situation.

The difficulty during the war emergency was twofold, the rapid expansion and early casualties of the conflict reduced the number of all ranks of the old regular army and its reserves and there was an influx of a large number of recruits for which NCOs, warrant officers and commissioned officers were needed. Promotion inflation was inevitable which on conclusion of the war had to be resolved with numerous regular soldiers of all ranks reverting to more a humble rank, very uncomfortable for many.

Officers and NCOs who enlisted, served and were promoted for the emergency left the service and returned to civilian status.

British Army officer rank insignia.

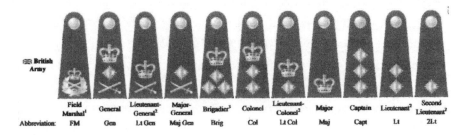

British Army formations.

Britain's Army because like 'Topsy' it just grew, has not only customs but nomenclature that is short on logic. The base unit of the infantry is the regiment, prior to the Cardwell reforms of the 1880s they were numbered in order of seniority (date first raised), following the reforms the numbering became secondary and the regiments took names, e.g. Royal Warwickshire Regiment, frequently but not always, that of their recruitment area. This is the basis for the army that went to war in 1914. The infantry regiments then formed battalions and following the Victorian reforms there were two regular battalions per regiment numbered 1st and 2nd; one on posted service and one at home for training and depot duties. As the army expanded in 1914 the regiments expanded by forming new service battalions, these were additional to the reserve battalions numbered 3 and 4. There were additionally the battalions of the Territorial Forces also listed under the regimental title that came into being following the Haldane reforms of the militia in 1908. These battalions usually numbered 5, 6 and so on also had recruitment localities, hence Albert Lucas was a member of 7th, City of Coventry, battalion. In all cases though with the infantry, battalions do the fighting, regiments do the organisation. In 1914 when the BEF went to France a battalion at full establishment had a strength of 1007 all ranks.

The cavalry though were different, there are, as with infantry, regiments, but no battalions. If additional cavalry units were needed a new regiment was raised. In the same way the artillery and engineers raised new units as expansion was thrust upon them.

It is not the intention to provide a full account of the units and organisation of the British Army, the subject is material enough for another volume at least. The rank descriptions above are indicative of the basis on which the units are organised, although the other arms and the service corps have to arrange their formations to meet the technical demands of their purpose and task the base structure is comparable unit by unit.

To put the organisation into context the units of an infantry division in the BEF in 1915 consisted of the following:

- Divisional HQ, major general commanding plus staff.
- 1 signal company.
- HQ, divisional artillery with 12 batteries of 18pdr guns (48 total), 4 batteries of 4.5" howitzers (16 total), 1 heavy battery 4x 60 pdrs. Divisional ammunition column.
- HQ divisional engineers plus 3 field companies Royal Engineers.
- 3 infantry brigades a total of 12 battalions, each battalion included 4x Vickers MMGs
- 1 squadron of cavalry, one cyclist company.
- 1 pioneer battalion
- 3 field ambulances.
- 1 motor ambulance workshop.
- 1 sanitary section.
- 1 mobile veterinary section.
- Divisional train.

Total all ranks: 19614.

The next level of the command structure was the corps command of lieutenant general, this was a minimum of two divisions and contained additional 'corps' troops such as heavy artillery. The final step was to combine two or more corps into an army of which in 1918 there were five each commanded by a full general, each of whom was subordinate to the Commander in Chief, Field Marshal Haig.

Looking back to the span of control and responsibilities of the component units and the higher formations it is not difficult to recognise the enormous scope of the responsibility that had to be the daily concern of the High Command.

ACKNOWLEDGEMENTS

C. K. Brampton. MA (Oxon): Senior History Master and subsequently Deputy Head Master, Moseley Grammar School, Birmingham. It was his encouragement that established an interest and affection for historical matters and taught the essential lessons of the subject. In particular that the subject is the sum of many parts that cannot be treated in isolation and importantly that any retrospective analysis must be measured with regard to the circumstances of the time as a fragment of the continuum of history. The precept he taught was that the substitution of opinion derived with the benefit of hindsight is not scholarship; decisions and events have to be judged in the context of the times in which they occur.

I stand rebuked by him for my failures to meet the quality of his teaching and the poverty of my scholarship throughout this expedition into the past.

Lt. Col. D. J. Jones, R. Sigs. C.O. 9th Signal Regt, B.F.P.O. 53. 1961/62.
Capt. J.R. Burrows, R. Sigs. Adjutant, 9th Signal Regt.
My own military experience was limited to a two year stint of National Service, 1960 to '62. There were two significant pieces of good fortune during this service. First, I crept under the wire of the selection procedure, then the training at Mons OCS and consequently was commissioned into the Royal Signals. The second ingredient of good fortune was my eventual posting in Cyprus to the unit commanded by Lt. Col. Jones, in which I undertook the duties of assistant adjutant, under the ever watchful scrutiny of Capt. Burrows. It is appropriate at the end of this exercise for me to acknowledge the opportunities presented by them and the other members of the regiment to experience the British Army at work and play. I count myself fortunate in the extreme that I served in this regiment. I was

expected to and allowed to play a role in the life and work of the unit and was in the company of colleagues who treated me as an equal and without reservation offered me their friendship and hospitality. To them must go the credit for drawing back the corner of the curtain of tradition to reveal the awesome scope of the history and achievements of the British Army. I was privileged to be part of their community. I am delighted to acknowledge my debt to all of them, including their families, for their forbearance and hospitality, in the full knowledge that I can never discharge this obligation.

Mons Officer Cadet School, Aldershot. 'A' Company, July to November 1960.

Gentlemen, my appreciation is offered to you all for your good company, humour, competence and determination under which cover I was able to hide my shortcomings and as a consequence experience the British Army as a junior officer after we had marched off to our duties in the pouring November rain.

There are many others to whom I have obligations for their personal and professional support; my family; Betty my wife, son David and daughter-in-law Anne, their patience and affection has made a significant contribution to the completion of this project. Ellen Hall should receive proper credit for the photograph of her great-grandfather's medals. Friends, Paul Renecle whose example of humour in adversity was a lifestyle lesson in itself, David Downing for the early and vital encouragement he offered me in the preparation of this text for publication. These and others, friends with whom I have worked and played, too many to mention specifically, have each in their own way enabled me to make something of opportunities too good to miss as I encountered them and all deserve my gratitude and sincere thanks for the pleasure of their company.

The team at Troubador led by Jeremy Thompson who have steered a novice author through the processes of publication have enabled me to convert a pipe dream to reality and they should know that their patience and professional contribution has been valued for maintaining my confidence that there was a worthwhile project to bring to a conclusion.

BIBLIOGRAPHY AND READING LIST

The numerous authors quoted in the main text of this book have led me through the complicated issues that contributed to the events of the Great War. Each of them can help a reader new to this subject to gain a more detailed understanding of the issues involved. I recommend all of the authors and their books to those who wish to extend their knowledge and appreciation of the subject, each account is more worthy of attention than my contribution could hope to be.

Arthur, Max.   *Last Post.*

Beevor, Anthony   *Inside the British Army.*

Bruhns, Wibke. (Frau)   *My Father's Country.*

Cornish, Paul.   *Machine Guns in the Great War.*

Corrigan, Gordon.   *Mud, Blood and Poppycock.*

Davidson, John. (Tavish) (Maj. Gen. Sir)   *Haig, Master of the Field.*

Duffy, Christopher.   *Through German Eyes: The British and the Somme.*

Dunn, J. C. (Capt)   *The War the Infantry Knew.*

Farrar-Hocklay, A. (Gen. Sir)   *The Somme.*

Graves, Robert.   *Good Bye to All That.*

Hitchock, F. C. (Capt)   *'Stand to', a diary of the Trenches.*

Holmes, Richard.

(i) *Tommy.*
(ii) *Riding the Retreat.*
(iii) *The Western Front.*
(iv) *Shots from the Front.*

Kipling, Rudyard.

The Irish Guards in the Great War.

Keegan, John.

The First World War.

Junger, Ernst. (Lt. later Capt)

Storm of Steel.

Lewis-Stempel John.

Six Weeks.

Liddell Hart, B. H.(Capt)

History of the First World War.

Mallinson, Alan.

The Making of the British Army.

Massie, Robert.

Dreadnought

Neillands, Robin.

The Old Contemptibles.

Simkins, Peter.

Kitchener's Army.

Stone, Norman.

The First World War.

Terraine, John.

(i) *The Smoke and the Fire,*
(ii) *To Win a War.*

Within the text of *Achievement* I have cited references, statistics and quotations from the above authors. Other writers' material has also been influential in the development of the opinions that eventually lead to the conclusions reached in my review of the Great War. I am indebted to all the above, named and anonymous for the stimulation provided by their ideas, whether or not we are in agreement.

REFERENCES

	Author.	**Title.**

Chap. 1.

| Pg 2 | Dunn J. C. (Capt) | *The War the Infantry Knew.* |
| Pg 2 | Sassoon, S. | *Memoirs of an Infantry Officer.* |

Chap. 2.

| Pg 46 | Dunn J. C. (Capt) | *The War the Infantry Knew.* |

Chap. 3.

Pg 56	Kipling R.	*The Irish Guards in the Great War.*
Pg 59	Musson Jeremy.	*In Pursuit of the Best Gun.*
		Westley Richards, Birmingham, England.
Pg 60	Bird Anthony.	Loss of artillery pieces, opening weeks.
Pg 61	McDermott E. T.	*History of the Great Western Railway*,
		revised Clinker C. R. Vol. 2.

Chap. 6.

Pg 95	Hitchcock F. C. (Capt)	*A Diary of the Trenches, 1915-1918.*
Pg 96/7	Junger Ernst (Lieut)	*Storm of Steel.*
Pg 101	Peaty John per Bond	
	Brian and Cave Nigel	*Haig: A reappraisal 80 years on.*
Pg 101	Corrigan Gordon	*Mud, Blood and Poppycock*

Chap. 7.

Pg 123	Corrigan Gordon.	*Mud, Blood and Poppycock.*
Pg 125	Wavell, Archibald*.	*other men's FLOWERS',* an anthology.
	(Field Marshal, Earl)	
Pg 134	Smith Anthony.	Production figures, machine guns.
Pg 137	Bond B and Cave N.	*Haig; A reappraisal 80 years on.*

* The extract from '*other men's FLOWERS*' by A.P. Wavell, published by Jonathon Cape. Reprinted by permission of the estate of Earl Wavell.

	Author.	**Title.**
Pg. 134	Smith Anthony.	Production figures, machine guns.
Pg 137	Bond B and Cave N.	*Haig; A reappraisal 80 years on.*

Chap. 8.

Pg 146	Junger Ernst (Lieut)	*Storm of Steel.*
Pg 148	Holmes Richard.	General officer casualties.
Pg 161	Clarke Alan.	*The Donkeys.*
Pg 161	Clarke J.C.	Newspaper letter, *Daily Telegraph.*

Chap. 9.

Pg 166	Terraine J. C.	*The Smoke and the Fire.*
Pg 166	Crutwell C. R. M. F.	Casualties.
Pg 167	Cox Robin	Casualties
Pg 171	Corrigan Gordon.	*Mud, Blood and Poppycock.*
Pg 176	Mee Arthur.	*King's England.*
Pg 183	Dunn J. C.	*The War the Infantry Knew.*

Chap. 12.

| Pg 216 | Cornish Paul. | The American Expeditionary Force. 'Tactical Mind Set' |

Chap. 13.

Pg 219	Duffy Christopher.	*Through German Eyes.*
Pg 222	Kuhl v. General d. Inf.	*Der Weltkreig 1914-1918,* Band II, Berlin.
Pg 223/4/5	Bruhns Wibke.	*My Father's Family,*
Pg 228	Holmes Richard	*Western Front.*

Chap. 14.

| Pg 235. | Davidson (Tavish) John | *Haig, Master of the Field.* |
| Pg238/9/40 | Maj. Gen. KCMG, CB, DSO | |

Acknowledgement.

Illustrations.

The photographs icluded in the book are from the archive of, and reproduced by arrangement withl the Imperial War Museum, London.

Copyright Material

INDEX:

A.

Albermarle, Duke of, see also Monck, George, Colonel, 24.

Albert, King of the Belgians, 227.

Albert of Saxe Coberg Gotha, (Prince Consort) 19.

Albion,

    perfidious, 15.

    profitable, 190.

Alsace, ceding of, see also Lorraine, 11, 15.

Aldington Frank, ASC and Rifle Corps, 127, 163.

Allied armies, all arms offensive, August 1918, 158.

America, Civil war, 139, 213.

Armour, ancient and modern, 63.

Armada, Spanish, (1588), 245.

Armageddon, 18, 189

Artillery, Royal Regiment:

    ammunition, 71

    ammunition shortages, 79.

    aerial observation/photography, 144, 221.

    branches, Horse, Field & Garrison, 67

    breech loading, recoil system 50, 51, 66.

    comparison with naval gunnery, 42, 66.

    deployment 1918, 157.

    indirect fire and reverse slopes, 68, 144.

    Nery, 'L' battery, 68.

    territorial forces, artillery 144

    weapon of choice, 144..

Armaments, infantry, see infantry

Armaments, Manufacturers, 50,

    artillery production, Aug-Dec. 1914, 60.

Army Medical Corps (Royal) 133, 168.

Army Service Corps (ASC) 54, 126.

Armoured Fighting Vehicles (Tanks) 65, 73, 74.

Army of the United States of America, 214, 216.

Asquith H. H. Prime Minister, 55, 152.

    death of son, 76.

Atkins, Thomas (Tommy) 26, 30, 32, 33, 47, 50, 52, 54, 75, 85, 95, 117, 168, 220, 240.

    cook house comments, 56.

    German evaluation, 220.

    orders for extra duties for general's visit, 95.

    specimen charge, 99.

Austria, Hungary, dual Monarchy, 5, 12.

    the blank Cheque, 76.

Awards and medals, 109.

B.

Baghout Walter, 8.

Balkans, 5.

Barbed wire,135.

Bastille (1789) 15.

Battles Great War.

    Amiens, (1918) 238.

    Arras, (1917) 171.

    Aubers Ridge, (1915) 154.

    Cambrai, (1917). 123, 221.

    Broodseinde Ridge, (1917), 239.

    Festubert, (1915) 154.

    Loos, 148 (1914), 154, 233.

    Le Cateau, (1914). 18, 105, 218, 226, 236.

    Messines Ridge, (1917) 135, 144, 154, 172, 248.

    Marne (1914), 145, 153.

    Mons (1914), 105, 153, 236.

    Neuve Chapelle (1914), 154.

    Somme, (1916). 63, 72, 155, 166, 174.

    Ypres (1st) battle, (1914). 153

    (2nd battle), (1915). 69, 136, 233.

    (3rd battle) Passchendale (1917), 66, 69, 88. 106, 127, 156, 174.

Battles, other:

    Agincourt, (1415) 16.

    Blenheim, (1704) 16.

    Bosworth, (1485), 32.

    Crecy, (1346), 16.

    Dettingen (1743) 24.

    Waterloo (1815), 4.

Bavaria, 7, 217.

Belgium, 81, 159.

    atrocities, 228.

    independence, 4, 5,

    occupation 26, 84, 138 226/7, 228.

Bellingham John, 151.

Binding, CPO, Archie, (RNAS). 202.

Binyon, Lawrence, poet, 249.

Bismarck, Count Otto, 7, 10, 12, 15, 82, 112.

'Blighty', 107.

    'Blighty wound' 168.

Bletchley Park, 203.

Britain, 3, 5, 9, 19 25, 32, 37, 41, 56, 63, 89, 91, 107, 129, 140, 155, 166, 221, 225, 230, 244.

British Sovereigns:

    Charles II, 24

    Edward VII, 18.

    Elizabeth I, 33.

    George II, 24.

    George V, 90.

    Henry VI, 16.

    Henry VII 33.

    Henry VIII, 33, 101.

    James I, 33.

    James II, 19.

    Mary I, 146

    Richard II. 33.

    Richard III, 33

    Victoria, 9, 10, 11, 18, 190.

    William III (of Orange) and Mary II, 18.

Boar War, 68.

Boulton, Matthew, 40.

British Army:

    contemptible little, 87.

    divisional establishment, 257.

    Expeditionary force (BEF) 81.

    1913 plan, 81, 122.

    numbers mobilised, 129.

    staff organisation, 125.

    strength, 1914, 35.

    training priorities/culture change, 118.

British/ French Alliance, 246/7.

Bradford, brothers, Thomas, George, James, Roland, 112/13.

C.

Cadiz, (1587) 199.

Calais, 12, 146.

Casualties, treatment, 168

Casualties,

    artillery, long reach, 183.

    battle comparisons, 174.

    daily rates, 174,

    generals, 148.

    'pals' battalions, 175

    prior experience, 164.

    total war, effect, 165.

    technology, 164.

Casualties, national, 87.

    Britain, France, Germany, 184/5.

examples, specific battles, 174.

Casualties, reporting procedure,

    British, 166.

    French, 166.

    German, 167, 169.

    wounds, effect of multiple incidence on counting, 169.

Casualties, Statistics;

    anomalies, 179.

    average, 180

    causation (artillery/small arms) 169.

    comparisons, caution,164,171, 179.

    death of a generation, 80, 175, 183.

    median. 180.

    perspectives, 105.

    percentage, 180.

    tables of statistics, combatant nations, 170, 174, 177/78,

    wounded, principle combatant nations, 171.

casualties, quality of command, 187.

casualties, prisoners and missing, 187.

Caeser, Julius, Gallic wars, 94

Cambrai, use of mechanised vehicles, 221

Cardwell, Edward, 22, 48.

Cavell, Edith, Nurse, 229.

Central Powers, strategy, 149.

Cenotaph, Whitehall, London, 52.

Chetham's Library, Manchester, 6.

Churchill, Winston, 13, 143, 168, 189,

 First Lord of the Admiralty, 77.

 'Tank' development, 74

C.I.G.S.(Chief of the Imperial General Staff) 25.

Cobbett William, Sgt Maj. and M.P. 47

Cody (Cowdrey) Col. 'Bill', 205,

Coldstream Guards, (Monck's Regiment), 24.

Cordite, 50, 71.

Corfu, 245,

Commanders and Generals, British Army and RFC.

    Allenby, Maj. Gen. Edmund, 238.

    Boyd Maj. Gen. G. F. 111.

    Byng, Gen. Sir Julian, 238.

    Currie Gen. Sir A. (Canada), 238.

    French, Field Marshal, Sir John, 105, 232/3, 247

    Haig, Field Marshal, Sir Douglas, 29, 42, 102, 105, 117, 142, 152, 158, 167, 232/3.

    Grierson, Lt. Gen James. 105, 234.

    Horne, Gen. Sir Henry, 238.

    Maxse, Gen Sir, Frederick, 42, 238

    Monash, Lt. Gen. Sir John (Australia) 238.

    Plummer, Gen. Sir Herbert, 42, 238.

    Rawlinson, Gen. Sir Henry, 238

    Robertson, Field Marshal Sir William, 42, 57, 119, 221, 231/2.

    Smith Dorrian, Horace, Lt. Gen. 102, 105, 218, 234.

    Smuts, Gen. Jan (South Africa) 238.

    Snow, Maj. Gen. T. d'O. 236

    Wilson, , Lt. Gen Sir Henry, 85, 231.

Commander, Royal Artillery, (CRA), 60.

Common Law, 46.

Communicators, Cecil Day Lewis, Robert Graves, Siegfried Sassoon, 241.

Conscription in Britain, 129.

Cox and Danks, scrap merchants, Wolverhampton, 204.

Curzon, Viscount (Foreign Secretary) 232.

Crimean War, 16, 19, 20, 47, 81, 98, 130, 191

Cromwell, Oliver, (Model army) 23, 115.

Cumberland, Duke of, 9

Cyprus, 245.

D.

Davidson, Maj. Gen. Sir John (Tavish) 238

Dardanelles (Churchill, Winston) 243.

Derby Scheme, pre conscription, 129.

Disraeli Benjamin, Prime Minister, 44.

Dedications.

    Aldington F. 163.

    Jones F. E. B. 211.

    Lucas A. M. 162.

    Robinson E. H. 113.

    Snell E. Miss. 187.

Drake, Sir Francis, 199.

Dunn J. C. Capt., RAMC. 2, 46, 111, 183.

E.

Edmonds, James, Brig. Gen, Sir. (Official historian) 240.

Elizabeth of Austria, Empress, 6.

Engels Frederich, 6

Edward VI, Schools foundation, 42.

Encounter battles, (1914), 143.

Emden, commerce raider, German, 195.

Establishment, (unit strength) 117

F.

Farrar Hockley, Gen. Sir A. 1.

Fisher, Sir John, Admiral, First Sea Lord, 189, 193.

Ford, Henry, 58.

Forlorn hope, siege assault, 152.

Forrest, Nathan Brig, Gen (US) 1865, 139.

Force multiplier, 133.

Fog of war, 148.

France, 4, 5, 10, 18, 26, 28, 37, 41, 56, 67 81, 96, 171, 185, 238, 246.

Franz Ferdinand, Archduke of Austria, Heir, 6.

Franz Joseph, Emperor, 6, 29.

Frederick II, (the Great) of Prussia, 7.

Franco Prussian War, 1870/71, 78.

French Army 1914, 83.

    ethos of the offensive, 147.

    plan XVII, 17, 82.

    campaign (1917) (the Aisne) 156.

    mutinies, effect on British strategy, 156

French Army Commanders,

    D'Esperey, Franchet, 240.

    Gallieni, Joseph, 82.

    Neville, 106, 156, 239.

    Petain, 106.

Freyberg B.(multiple wound scars inspection by Winston Churchill), 168.

G.

Garibaldi, 5.

Generals, WW II,

    Montgomery B. 22, 141.

    Slim W. 22, 142

    Wavell, A, see also Viceroy of India, 125.

Geneva convention (conduct of warfare) 120.

German population 1914, 36.

Germany 3, 4, 5, 10, 11, 12, 17, 19, 28, 36, 56, 65, 73, 81, 135, 138, 167, 171, 189, 203, 212, 217 *et seq*, 248..

Germany, under siege, 146, 159.

German Army, 17, 18, 83.

    Prussian influence, 89, 217/8.

    spring offensive, *(Kaiserschlacht)* (1918), 157.

    advantage, (1914), 145

    war experience, 218.

German Army, artillery,

    Bruchmuller, Lt. Col. 144

German Army, commanders and generals;

    Rupprecht, Crown Prince, 221.

    von Falkenheyn, 138, 159, 223

    von Hindenberg, 138, 159, 225.

    von Kluck, 138, 241.

von Kluge, 82.

von Kuhl, 221.

von Ludendorff, 138, 159, 221, 225, 239.

von Moltke, 82, 138, 159.

Gibralter, 245.

Gladstone W. E. Prime Minister, 44.

Grande Armee (France) 14.

Great Western Railway, (GWR) 61.

GWR, General Managers, Potter, Aldington, Pole, 90

Grenades, see weapons.

Greece 4.

Grey, Sir Edward, Foreign secretary, (1914), 32.

Gurkha regiments, 22.

H.

Habsburg, House of, (Austria/ Hungary), 6.

Haig, see Commanders and Generals.

Haldane, Sir Richard. Secretary of State for War, 23, 48.

Hall, Reginald, Capt.(RN) see also, Room 40, 203.

Halifax, Nova Scotia, explosion (1917), 62.

Hanover, 8, 15, 217.

Heligoland, 245.

High Seas Fleet, (German)

Jutland, Battle of, (1916), 195.

surrender, (1918), 203.

scuttling, (1919), 203.

salvage, 203.

ships, Breslau, Emden, Goeben, 194/5.

Hindenberg line, 135.

Hitchcock F. C. Capt. (diarist) 95.

Hitler, Adolf, Corporal, 138.

Hitler Adolf, Chancellor, Declaration of War on USA, December 1941, 216, 225.

Hohenzollern, House of, (Germany/Prussia) 10.

Holstein. annexation, see also Schleswig, 8.

Honourable East India Company (HEIC), 21.

Hurley, Frank, photographer, 249.

Hydrophones, 199.

I.

India, 21.

Indian Army,

reinforcements, (1914), 36.

regiments, Hodson's, Probyn's, Skinner's 22.

Industrial Revolution, 4, 34, 40, 50, 57, 90.

'Indirect approach' (Stone Prof. N), 143.

Italy, 4.

J.

Japan, war against Russia, 13.
Junkers of Prussia, 9.
Junger, Ernst, Lt, 97, 146, 218, 220.

K.

Kaiser (Emperor) of Germany, 10,
'Keflar', 64.
King's German Legion (KGL) 20.
Killing ground, 158.
Kipling, Rudyard, 47, 249.
Klamroth, family, diaries, 223 *et seq*.
Kitchener, Field Marshal, Earl, 29, 72, 73, 127, 231.
    new armies, 56, 86, 118, 128, 156, 231.
    pals' battalions, 128,
    opinion of 'Territorial force', 84, 129.
Korean war (1950- 52) 139
Krupp (German) arms manufacturer 190.

L.

Lawrence, Col T. E. 3.
L'Affaire Dreyfus, 89.
Leadership, 91, 101.
Lewis, light machine gun, 72, 219.
    practical problems,123.
    production statistics, 134.
    Royal Flying Corps, 206.
Limoges, 17.
Liddell Capt. B. H. 241.
Lions, lead by donkeys, explanation,161.
Liverpool and Manchester Railway, 90.
Lloyd George, David, Prime Minister, 29, 53, 57, 142, 152, 157, 231.
Logistics (supplies) 80.
London Transport, 52.
London, City of 41.
Lorraine, ceding of, see also Alsace, 15.
Louise XIV, King of France, 16.
Louisiana Purchase (USA) 213.
Louvain, sacking and destruction of library, 228.
Lucas, Albert, Corporal, MM. 108, 127, 162.
Ludwig II, King of Bavaria, 12.
Lusitania, RMS, sinking of 1915, 227.

M.

Maccabaeus, Judas, 32.

Machine Gun Corps (MGC). 123, 219.

    heavy branch (tanks) 123.

Malta, 245.

Manchester, 6.

Marlborough, Duke of, 245.

Marsden, George (RNVR) 110.

Marx, Karl, 6.

Mauser, rifle, 11, 17.

Maxim Hiram, 131.

Maximilliam of Mexico, 214

May Island, 'battle' of, 195.

Medium machine gun, (MMG)

    Maxim, 17.

    Vickers, 79, 122, 219.

    operational use 132/3

    production statistics, 134

Mechanics' Institutes 45

Messines ridge, tunnels, 135.

    attack in snow, April 1917, 248

Mersey ferries, Iris, Daffodil, active service, 200.

Mexico, 213, 226.

Military concepts,

    doctrine, 86.

    imperative, 93.

    maxims, Napoleon, 80.

    Von Clausewitz, 77.

    Wellington, Duke of, 77.

Military historians, (army) Liddell Hart B. H. (Capt), Fuller J. F. C. (Lt. Col.) 241.

Military historians (academic) Barnett Correlli, Bryant Arthur, Taylor A. J. P. Keegan John. 242

Military historians (contemporary), Corrigan Gordon, Mallinson Alan, Terraine John. 242

Military law, 46.

    Adjutant, 100.

    Army Act, 97.

    courts martial, 100.

    death sentence, 101.

    discipline and orders,92.

    manual of military law, 98.

    orders, military offence, 92.

Minorca, 245.

Mobilised army totals, 129.

Monck, George Colonel see also Albermarle, Duke of, 24.

Monroe Doctrine (USA), 213.

Moscow, retreat from (1812), 14, 141.

N.

NAAFI. 99.

Napoleon I, Emperor, 4, 16, 22, 27, 44, 77, 141, 151.

Napoleon III, Emperor, 11, 214.

National Socialist Party (Germany) 225.

Naval arms race, 12, 189.

Navy, Royal see R.

Naval battles/engagements, Great War see R

Naval Intelligence (Room 40) 203.

Netherlands, 5.

O.

Officers,

    commissions, 20.

    leadership, 101,104.

    original authority, 99.

Opinion, acid test, 149

Ottoman Empire, 4, 191.

P.

Parliament, 24,25.

Parsons, Charles, 190

'Pax Brittanica' 180.

Pearl Harbour, 215.

Peel, Sir Robert, Prime Minister, 40

Pershing, Gen. John (US), 216, 238.

Photo reconnaissance (RFC), 207

'Poliu' ('Private' French army), 156.

Poland, Grand Duchy, 4.

Population statistics, Britain, 1801 & 1851, 34/5.

Portugal, 5.

Princip, Gavrilo, 27, 245.

Prussia, 7, 9, 10, 11, 89, 217.

Q.

Quartermaster General (QMG), 25.

R.

Radio (wireless), 65, 72.

    use of 'Morse' code, 70.

Radar, 199.

Railways, 50, 52.

    engineers, Brunel *et al* 90.

Ranks and promotion, (army) 107,108.

Ranks and unit organisation, 117, 119, 122.

Royal Army Medical Corps (RAMC), 168.

Recruits, (army) quality, 46, 94.

Reichstag, 10, 89,

Regiments (British army) concept, 48.

    Durham Light Infantry, 103.

    Green Howards, 91.

    Irish Guards, 106.

    King's Royal Rifle Corps, 209

    King's Shropshire Light Infantry, 113

    Leinster Regiment, 95.

    North Staffordshire Regiment, 113

    Northumberland Fusiliers, 78, 95,155.

    Queen's Regiment, 128

    Royal Fusiliers, 143.

    Royal Warwickshire Regiment, 128, 162.

    Royal Welch Fusiliers, 2, 46, 111, 183.

Renaissance, Florentine, 39.

Reppington, Charles (Times correspondent) 234.

Richtoffen von, 'Red Baron' 71, 207.

Riqueval bridge, 111.

Rome and Army of, 52, 60, 116, 228, 244.

Rommel Gen. Erwin (German WWII) 102.

Royal Flying Corps (RFC). 117, 205 *et seq.*

    aerial combat, 206

    aerial photography, 70, 207.

    armament, Lewis gun, 206.

    artillery observation, spotting, 70, 96, 144, 208, 221.

    bombing, 208.

    casualties, aircrew, 209.

    Trenchard, Maj Gen. Hugh (RFC) 71, 96, 210.

Royal Military Academy, (Sandhurst) 43, 94

Royal Navy. 4, 28, 50, 88,142.

Armament development, Ship design, 188.

Anti submarine provisions, 199.

Battles and Engagements;

    Coronel and the Falkland Islands 194.

    Dogger Bank, 195.

    Jutland, 112, 195

    Zeebrugger, 199.

Battle Squadrons,(2nd & 5th) 196

Battleships & Battlecruisers, 190.

Commanders and Admirals.

    Craddock Admiral, Christopher, 194.

    Beatty, Admiral Sir David, 197, 203.

    Doveton Sturdee, Vice Admiral, Frederick, 194

Evan Thomas, Rear Admiral Sir Hugh, 197.

Fisher, Admiral, Sir John (Jackie) 189, 193, 201.

Hood, Rear Admiral, Sir Horace, 197

Jellico, Admiral Sir John.197, 200,

Jeram, Vice Admiral, Sir Martyn, 197.

Keyes, Vice Admiral Sir Roger, 199

Scott, Admiral Sir Percy, 193.

Tyrwhitt, Commodore Reginald, 201

Grand strategy (naval contribution) 86.

gunnery, general, 66.

signalling procedure, 198.

Ships (RN), by name.

Aboukir, 194

Audacious, 194.

Camperdown, 191.

Canopus, 194.

Crecy 194.

Dreadnought, 189.

Engadine, 202.

Glasgow, 194.

Good Hope, 194.

Hampshire, 231

Houge 194.

Inflexible. 194.

Invincible 194

Monmouth, 194

Victoria, 191.

Vindictive, 199.

Warwick, 199.

submarines, C 1, C3, 200.

K14, K22, 196.

submarine Flotillas, (12ᵗʰ & 13ᵗʰ) 196.

Harwich, light forces, (RN) 201.

Queen Elizabeth Class, (Dreadnought), 190.

Room 40, (see also Hall, Capt. Reginald) 203, 215.

Rosyth, naval base, (RN) 196.

Royal Naval Air Service (RNAS) 117, 201.

Rudolph, Crown Prince of Austria, 6.

Russo Japanese War, 191, 246.

Russia, 4, 12, 13, 36, 212, 222, 245.

S.

Salford, Lancashire, 6.

Sarajevo, 4, 27.

Sassoon Siegfried, 2.

Saxony, 7, 217.

Scapa Flow

    War station, Grand Fleet, 77, 196.

Schlieffen, Field Marshal Alfred von Plan (Germany) 12, 81.

Schleswig, see also Holstein, 8.

Scotland, 33.

Scientific managers, (F.W. Taylor) 58.

Scientists, Einstein, Faraday, Newton, 64

Ship, design, 188.

    steam turbines, 188.

Siege, effect of deployment in Europe 145.

    breaking, 150

    Ancient, Jericho, Troy, 145, 150

    Historical, Badajoz, Delhi, 145, 151.

    Great War, Germany, 146, 150.

Silvertown, (explosion) 59,

Soho Foundry, Aston, 40.

South Africa, Boer war, 47.

Spencer Perceval, Prime Minister, (1812), assassination, 151.

St. Quentin Canal, 111.

Strategy, domination of enemy thinking, 141.

    Naval responsibility (1914-1918), 142.

Suez campaign 1957, Britain, France and Isreal. 139.

T.

Tanks, see armoured fighting vehicles.

Tank Corps, 123.

Territorial Force, 48.

Terraine John, 1,166

Thankful Villages, 176.

Tirpitz, Admiral Alfred von, 12.

Togo, Admiral Heihachiro (Japan) 192.

Torpedos (Whitehead) 67, 189.

Torres Vedras, Lines of, 151.

Treaty of:

    Amiens, (1802), 35.

    Brest Litovisk, (1918), 212.

    Gaudalope Hildago, (1849), (US), 213

    London, (1835), 5.

    Versailles, (1871), 9

    Versailles, (1919), 165, 224, 248,

    war guilt clause, 248.

    Westphalia, (1648), 4.

Trenchard, Maj Gen. Hugh see RFC 205.

Tripartite reinsurance provisions, 11.

Tsar Nicholas II of Russia, 13, 28.

Tsushima, Battle of (1905), 193,

'Turbina' at Diamond Jubilee review, 190.

Turbines, replacement of reciprocating engines, 188.

Tyron, Adml. Sir George, C in C, Mediterranean Fleet 191.

U.

United States (America) 5, 24, 55, 158, 179, 181, 212, 222.
 civil war, 213.
 declaration of war 1917, 215.
 war against Germany. 1941, 216

United Kingdom, 32.

V.

Vatican, 5.

Verdun, Battle of, 155, 220, 235.
 allied alternatives if assault successful, 159
 duration and casualties, 159.
 German attack, 153.
 von Falkenheim 155

Vickers, 25, 80, 123, 190

Viceroy of India, Wavell, Field Marshal, Earl, 125.

Vienna, Congress of, 1815. 5, 8.

Victoria Cross awards, army.
 Bradbury Edward, Capt. 68.
 Bradford, Roland, Lt. Col. 112
 Coltman William L/Cpl, 113
 Dorrell Thomas, BSM, 68.
 Foster E. Cpl, 110
 Freyberg, Bernard, Lt. Col. 110, 168.
 Garforth, Charles, Cpl. 110
 Nelson David, Sgt. 68.
 Smyth, J. Lt. 110.
 Tandy. H. 110.

Victoria Cross awards, navy,
 Bradford George, Lt. Cmd. RN. 112.

Vladivostock, 192.

W.

Wars, European historical
 Austrian Succession, 7.
 Spanish Succession, 7.
 Seven Years War, 7.
 Thirty Years War, 4.
 Austro, Prussian. (1866). 8, 10.

Franco, Prussian, (1871), 8, 10.

Watt, James, 40.

Wavell, Archibald, Field Marshal, Earl, 38.

Weitzmann, Chiam, Dr., 71.

Wellington, Duke of, (Wellesley, Hon Arthur), 21, 27, 43, 46, 77, 141, 151, 161, 235.

    sepoy General, 27,

    siege of Badajoz, 151.

Wesley, Charles, 40.

Westley Richards, gun makers, 59.

Western Front, consider as a whole,153.

Weapons,

    Development, 8, 130/1.

    Gas, 136.

    Grenades (Hand) 97, 219.

    Mortars, 96, 219.

    Rifles, (British) Lee Enfield, mk. 3, 119.

Wilde Oscar, 17, 193.

Wilhelm II, (Willie) Kaiser, (Emperor) of Germany, 10, 11, 12, 27, 49, 51, 77, 89, 91, 112 138, 149, 189, 215, 217.

Weitzmann, Chiam, Dr, 45.

Winterhalter, see Elizabeth, Empress of Austria. 6.

Whitehead (torpedo) 189

Wright, (brothers) Orville and Wilbur, 64, 165, 205.

Wilson, Woodrow, President of USA, 215.

    Peace Plan, 227.

Y.

Ypres. third battle of (Passchendale), 66, 69, 88, 106, 127, 141, 156, 174.

Z.

Zeebrugge raid (1918), 112, 199

Zeiss, of Jena, optical equipment, 207.

Zimmerman telegram, 203, 215, 226.

Zollverein, 8.